IMAGES
of America

BONNEVILLE SALT FLATS

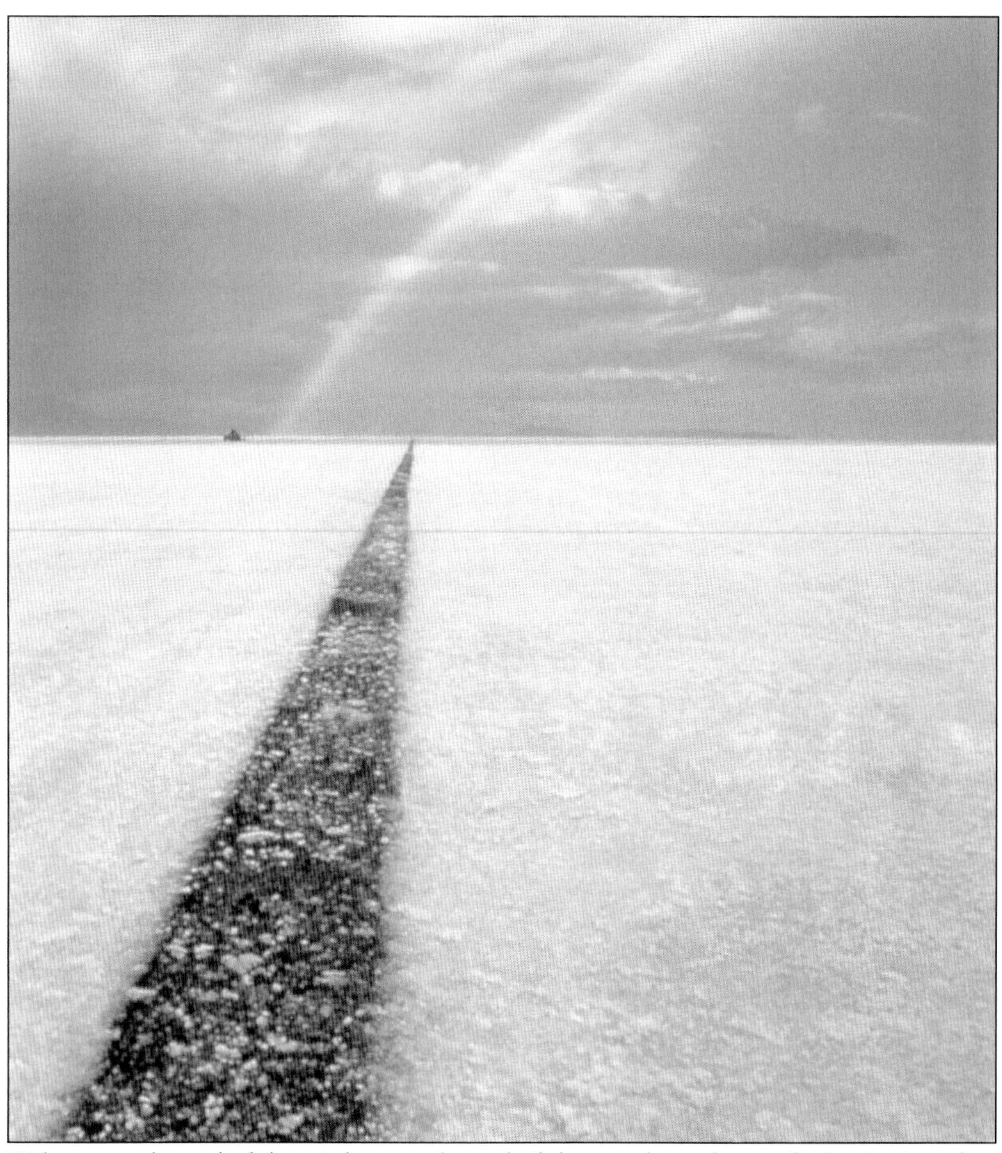

Welcome to the end of the rainbow, to the end of the speed run, but to the beginning of an armchair adventure with the fastest people on earth. Most all are overwhelmingly ordinary folk who accomplish extraordinary deeds of speed. Just one visit to this Utah wonder when the speed machines are present is a thrilling experience of the all-inclusive American amateur motorsport spirit that has been so vibrant for more than 100 years. It has been said that even without the speed machines, just being there has made atheists think about God. (Courtesy of LandSpeed Louise.)

On the Cover: It is the 1952 Maremont trophy presentation taking place on the starting line at the Bonneville Nationals. Just behind the "City of Burbank" streamliner No. 61 are, from left to right, winners George Hill; Howard E. Wolfson, president of Maremont Automotive Products, Chicago, Illinois; and Willie Davis. At the nose of the No. 6 "Belond Special" belly tank are owners "Frankie" and Tom Beatty with sons Mark, in the silver pith helmet, and Jim. In front is the completely hand-built, Pontiac-powered lakester pictured with owner and builder Eddie Miller Jr. and Ray Brown (arms folded). (Courtesy of Rick Hill/Ed Elliot photograph.)

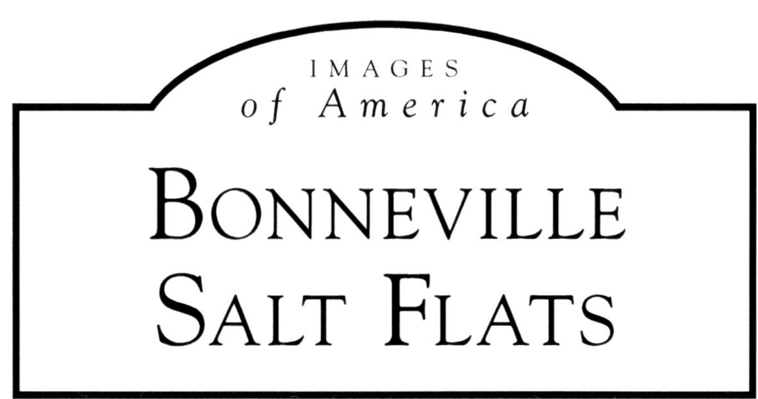

Bonneville Salt Flats

"Landspeed" Louise Ann Noeth
Foreword by Alex Xydias

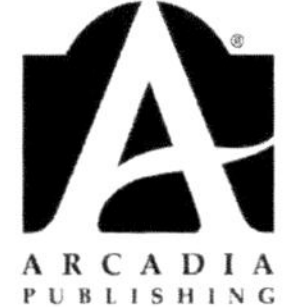

ISBN 978-1-4671-0595-8

Published by Arcadia Publishing
Charleston, South Carolina

Printed in the United States of America

Library of Congress Control Number: 2020941011

For all general information, please contact Arcadia Publishing:
Telephone 843-853-2070
Fax 843-853-0044
E-mail sales@arcadiapublishing.com
For customer service and orders:
Toll-Free 1-888-313-2665

Visit us on the Internet at www.arcadiapublishing.com

Without my loving husband, Mick Lanigan, his enormous patience, fabulous feasts, and decades-long support, this, or any other book I have written, would be only a dream.

Contents

Foreword

What had been a long, impossible dream had suddenly become a reality! The Southern California Timing Association had been granted a one-time week of competition at the iconic Bonneville Salt Flats in Utah.

This was a great opportunity! The SoCal Speed Shop Racing Team gathered together to decide what we should do. Our goal became "world's fastest hot rod."

But first, we had to build it. We chose a smooth, streamlined design, but could we form aluminum like that? What size? We only had a few months. Night and day, day and night we worked on it. Finally, it was finished, and it was beautiful! White with gold-leaf lettering on the side read "So-Cal Speed Shop Special."

Bonneville was 700 miles away, and we were pulling trailers over narrow, two-lane roads through some of the most remote areas in the country. We drove for hours, too tired to count, finally cresting a hill and unexpectedly, still 30 miles away, there it was, a huge, gleaming, white area in the middle of a desert brown landscape.

Now we were hell-bent for our destination and getting answers to so many of our questions. We were standing on salt—yes salt—as far as the eye could see. So bright you have to shield your eyes, so big, it was impossible to grasp. It was hard to say anything.

Where were we? Shangri-La? Mars? In the distance, at the end of the black line, a mountain was floating in the air. Was it a mirage? Do they have mirages on Mars?

We came to race against the clock, against time, and to prove a concept new to hot rodding but famous in Europe—wheels enclosed inside the body that eliminate problem-causing air turbulence. But would our version work? Would it create lift and suddenly fly?

There were 60 entries, and everyone was curious about our streamliner. We made a few practice runs on the 10-mile course to slowly find out what we really had.

The hot rod record was 160 miles per hour. We went 193 miles per hour! And then the front treads flew off the tires, but driver Dean Batchelor brought it to a safe stop. We had built the world's fastest hot rod, and it appeared on the cover of *Hot Rod Magazine* three times!

It was an odyssey I will never forget. When we returned in 1950, we upped our record to 210 miles per hour!

—Alex Xydias

Acknowledgments

No one sets a land speed record by herself or himself. It is the same for books. I need the help and support of many land speed racers to bring into being a personal and resonating glimpse into the ever-challenging world of time trials and record setting. The heavy historical lifting goes to the archivists at the Utah State Historical Society and the University of Utah's Marriott Library Special Collections that kept so many precious pictures safe until I needed them.

I will forget someone, but for now know these incredibly helpful names: Josh Ackerman, the Art Arfons family, John Baechtel, Dean Batchelor, Glynne Bowsher, Lee (Breedlove) Frank, Craig Breedlove, Tom Beatty, Bill Burke, Burly Burlilie, Betty Burkland, Gigi Carlson, Eric Dahlquist, Wilford Day, Jim and Marian Deist, Tammy and Sean Donohoe, Ed Elliot, Bruce Geisler, Pete Farnsworth, the Ferguson family, Firestone Tire and Rubber Company, Norm Gernhardt, Zeldine Graham, Scooter Grubb, Just Hallen, Cody Hanson, Gary Hartsock, Bob Higbee, Rick Hill, the Ab and Marvin Jenkins family, Ed Justice Jr., Kay Kimes, Tim Kraushaar, Delvene Manning, Milton McCard, Paula Murphy, Zane McNary, Tom Medley, Jim Miller, Wally Parks, Robert "Pete" Petersen, Dave Petrali, Gail Phillips, Robert Rampton, Jim Richards, Robin Richardson, Tim Rochlitzer, Doug Rose, Bud Schmitt, John Sprenger, Dwianna and Bill Taylor, Al and Jane Teague, Danny and Judy Thompson, Gregory Thompson, Will Scott, Ritchie Valen, John Veenstra, the Vesco family, Tony and Darrell Waters, Lee Wendelboe, Alex Xydias, and Lynn Yakel.

Please note LandSpeed Productions Research Library (LPRL) is an archive of prints, negatives, transparencies, and physical mementos assembled by donations from the original work and property of land speed racers, professional photographers, and enthusiasts who asked me to keep their collections safe and useful to promote the sport. When you see "LPRL/", it means the original material is on file with me, but it was created by or came from the person noted after the forward slash. If only LPRL is listed, it means the creator of the material is still unidentified and the search continues.

Introduction

First-timers at the Bonneville Salt Flats are affectionately called "salt virgins," because walking out onto the panoramic, sodium-soaked pancake always has a startling effect. Awash with the pure joy of being immersed there, it does not matter what anyone might have read, heard, been told, or watched, the real deal is a gargantuan knockout.

Forget the speed machines for a moment and simply consider the location. So vast, astronauts use the salt's splendid, shimmering whiteness as a landmark as they orbit the earth.

Smart people get out of bed before the sun to watch the fiery orb awakening from the salt. It is they who are treated to unexpected grandeur, a brain-stretching vista that invokes a dose of humility wrapped up in a personal outpouring of thankfulness.

There is something inviting about being reduced, put in your place, and made to understand how stinking small and insignificant a person can be in relationship to the planet. It is an honor just to be standing there.

Still as dangerous as it was to the pioneers' Conestoga wagons, vehicles get righteously stuck—especially when trying to peel off the highway hoping to enjoy a quick salt cruise.

Spinning the wheels only drives the vehicle deeper into the plastic-like mud that has been trapping things since the 1800s. The salt flats are thick in the middle but thin out to practically nothing on the edges.

And yes, it is salt, just like the stuff that comes out of the shaker at home. Taste it. Most everyone does, whether they admit it or not.

Know this: Anyone can earn a time slip driving their own car, truck, or motorcycle, in addition to purpose-built race cars. Just try that at Indy or Daytona. Spectators walking through the pits and staging lanes, marching right up to the starting line, absorb a visual treat of the greatest mechanical menagerie on earth.

This is the realm of amateurs who handcraft all sorts of speed machines for a chance to drive unlimited. Most arrive from all corners of the planet with a precious handcrafted cargo of speed. The few professional teams lured to the place quickly understand they are nothing special, and no one is going to be genuflecting or showering them with adoration. This is a first come, first run process, and respect is earned through a time slip.

A gracious and gregarious tip of the helmet is due all the amateur drivers, riders, builders, mechanics, and volunteers who breathe life into land speed racing. Mostly unknown, they are the fastest people on earth.

Every single one of the race-ready speed machines represents a dearly held dream as each face the truth revealed by passing the timing clocks thousands and thousands of times each season.

And the sound—that traveling, thundering, pulsating sound—reverberates against the mountains and imprints on the brain to repeatedly stir the soul sometimes years after the deed is done. The thrill of witnessing a 300- or 400-mile-per-hour run has been compared to watching a launch at Cape Canaveral.

One

Ice Age to Train Age to Speed Age 1914

Birthing the Fastest Place on Earth

With no roads in 1914, speed had to hitchhike a ride from the Denver & Rio Grande Railroad, which agreed to carry cars, racers, and 150 ticketed spectators 120 miles west from Salt Lake City to the deserted railroad siding at Salduro, 10 miles east of the Nevada state line. This single act launched a 100-year pageant of power on Utah's unknown salt flats.

This vast, ancient, glistening white lake bed is so flat that the actual curvature of the Earth can be observed with the naked eye. Once covered by a trapped inland sea 135 miles wide by nearly 325 miles long, the minerals and salt layers left behind as the water evaporated created the world's largest natural dynamometer, a test track of immense proportions.

Still easily seen today, three distinct shorelines of the ancient inland sea are etched into the hillsides. Temperatures climb above 110 degrees during the day and plunge below 50 degrees at night, all within a 24-hour period.

The sun ferociously beats down on the crystalline surface reflecting the rays back up to burn the skin under noses, ear lobes, armpits, and any unprotected body parts. Without eye protection, "salt blindness" is assured, because "bright" takes on new meaning here.

Racing impresario Ernie Moross brought a fleet of racing machines to Salt Lake City for an auto-racing exhibition on its fairgrounds' half-mile oval dirt track. The jewel of the stable was the mighty 2.5-liter, 300-horsepower, record-setting "Blitzen Benz" No. 2, driven by "Terrible" Teddy Tetzlaff, a renowned lead foot of the day. He was joined by other notable hot shoes who drove a collection of thoroughbred racers. Advertisements in the local papers promised "a hair-raising, thrilling, soul-gripping speed contest. Bring your own watches and check up on the official timers."

On his official speed run, Tetzlaff knocked out a record-beating speed of 142.85 miles per hour and, with it, ushered in an epochal chapter for auto racing.

News of Tetzlaff's remarkable speeds on the salt beds soon spread throughout the racing community, sowing seeds of curiosity about the godforsaken western wasteland that gobbled up wheel spin and spat out speed.

Motor Age Magazine's August 20, 1914, issue proclaimed: "Smooth as the proverbial billiard table and hard as a cement highway, it would not be surprising that soon salt-bed racing will completely displace beach racing."

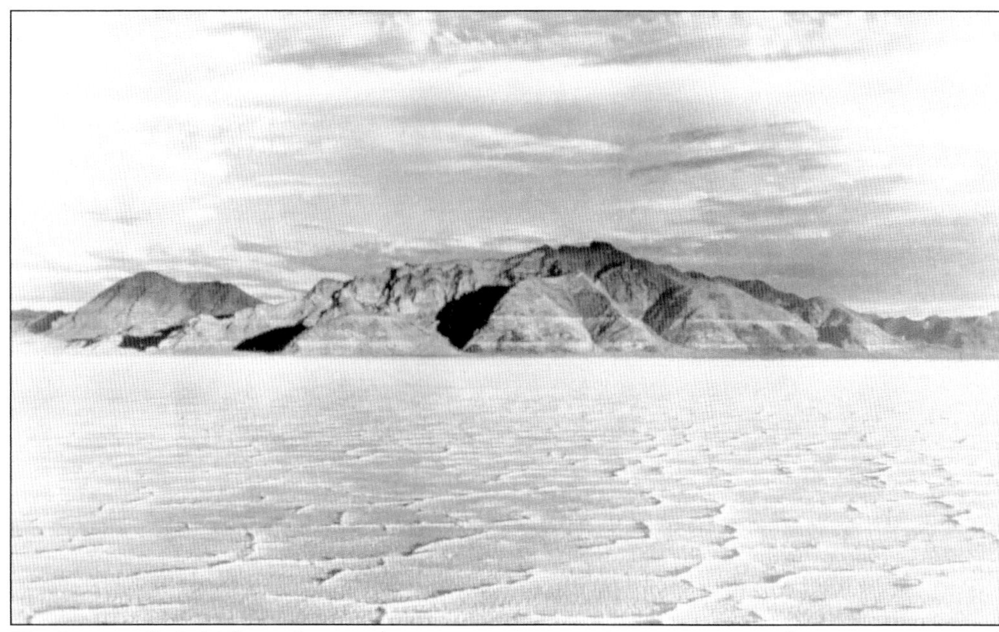

The Bonneville Salt Flats, where nothing grows except one's imagination and mirages, was named after the longest-serving man in the US Army, Benjamin Louis Eulalie Bonneville. Pressure ridges, from less than an inch to more than a foot, form along the salty cracks each year after the water evaporates; they are scraped away to allow safe high-speed runs. The lines scored into the mountainside are ancient seashores. (Courtesy of Will Scott.)

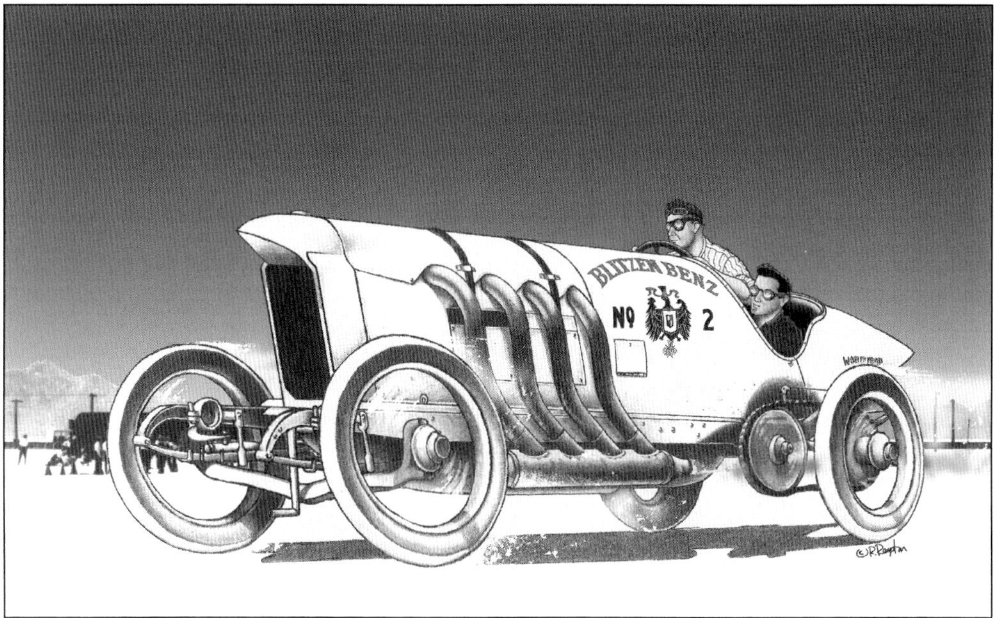

Officials and spectators with stopwatches witnessed the first timed salt race—a record-setting 142.85 miles per hour in a flying half-mile. Tetzlaff drove the "Blitzen Benz," heavily relying on riding mechanic Domenich Basso as they ripped across the flats in an area known at the time as the Salduro Salt Marsh, or Pan. Much of the Salduro racecourse was gone by 1920, having been plowed up and sold as common table salt and livestock salt licks. (Courtesy of Robert Rampton.)

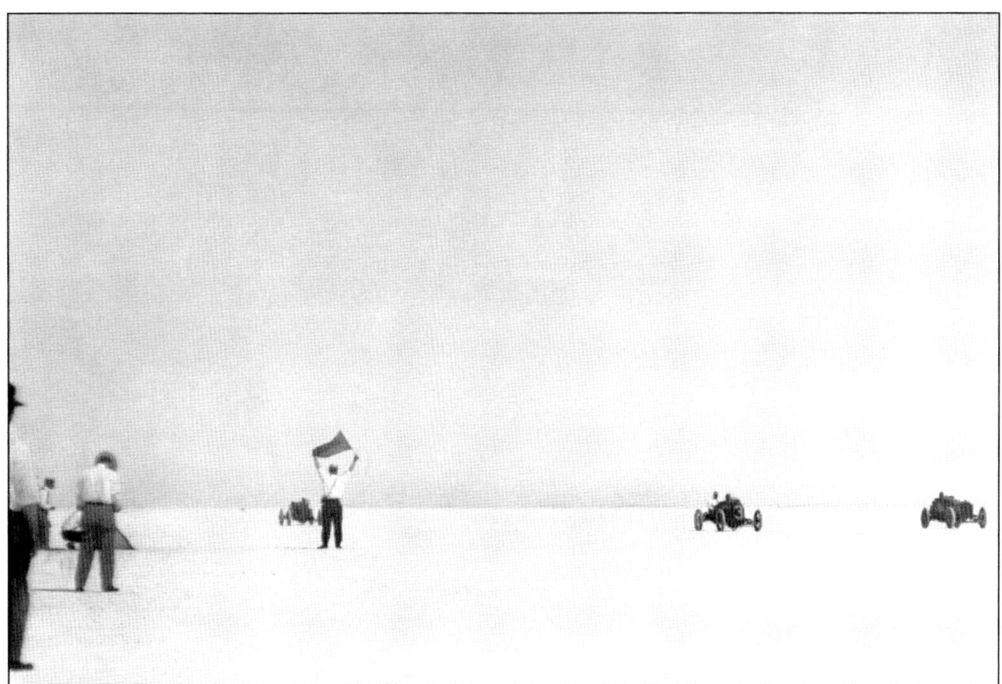

Flagman Ernie Moross waves the finish toward the close of the inaugural speed event on the salt flats. Tetzlaff had instigated a challenge leveled at Billy "Coal Oil" Carlson and Wilbur D'Alene to have an impromptu match race with a passenger. Gov. William Spry, who could barely fit, climbed into Tetzlaff's Maxwell. Odds are there was some "money where your mouth is" wagering involved. Seen on the right side of the frame, Tetzlaff and Spry take the flag followed by the Marmon. (Courtesy of the Utah State Historical Society.)

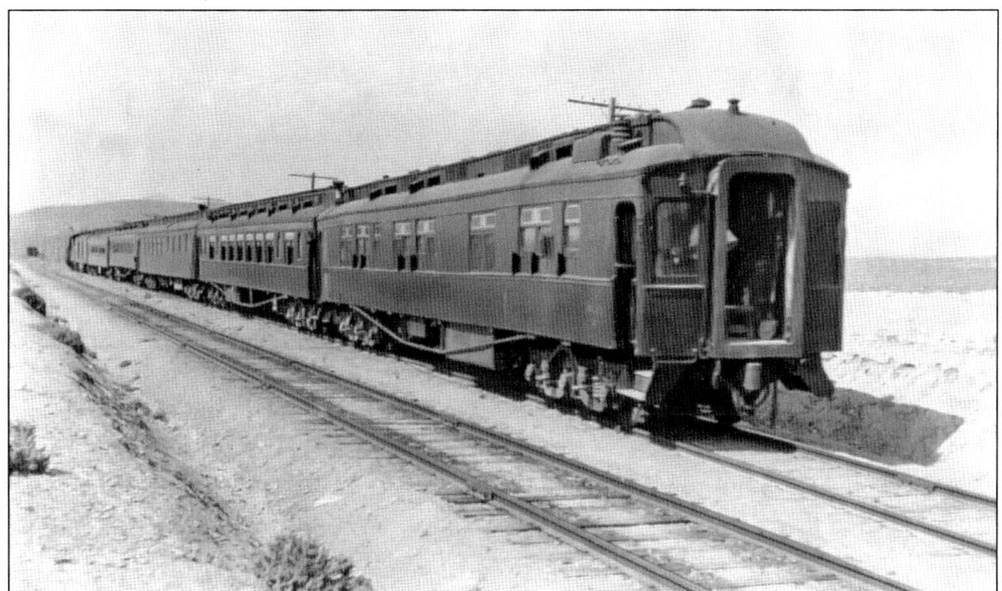

The Western Pacific Railroad was, for many years, the only safe way to cross the salt beds. For the inaugural 1914 event, the rail line transported everything to the Salduro Station, a deserted train stop with a small station house and a telegraph shed. (Courtesy of the Lee Wendelboe family.)

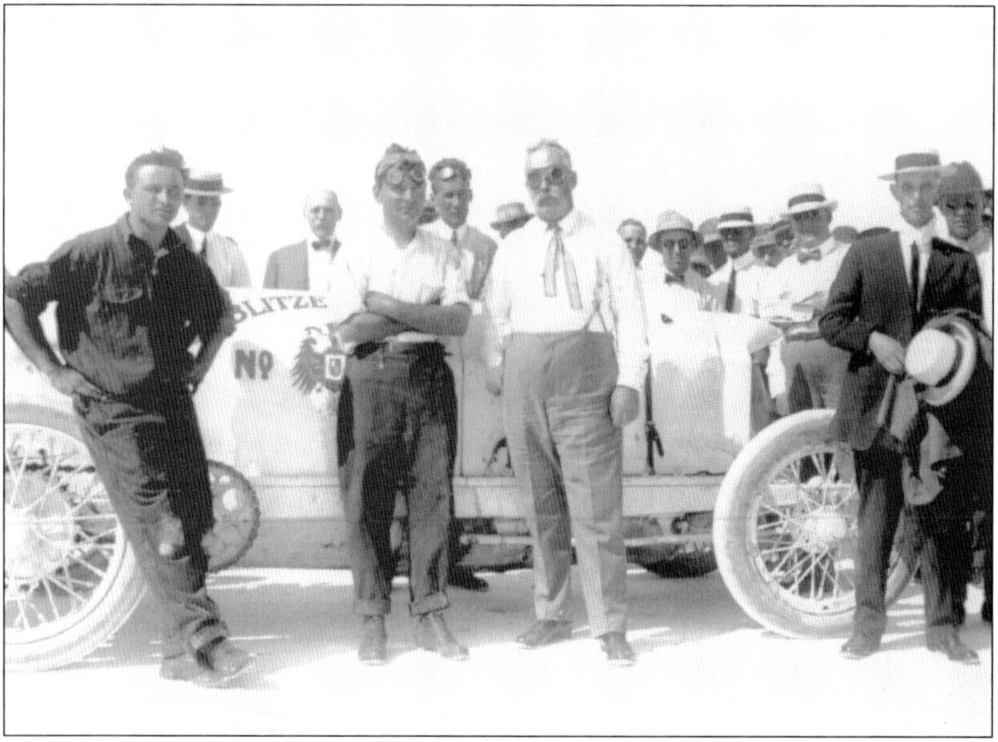

King of the West Coast drivers "Terrible" Teddy Tetzlaff, with arms folded, was already the holder of innumerable course speed records. Here, he stands next to Utah governor William Spry, still living the dream with his goggles on. Leaning on the "Blitzen Benz" tire is riding mechanic Domenich Basso, who probably wishes all the press would go home so he can back to working on the car. (Courtesy of the Utah State Historical Society.)

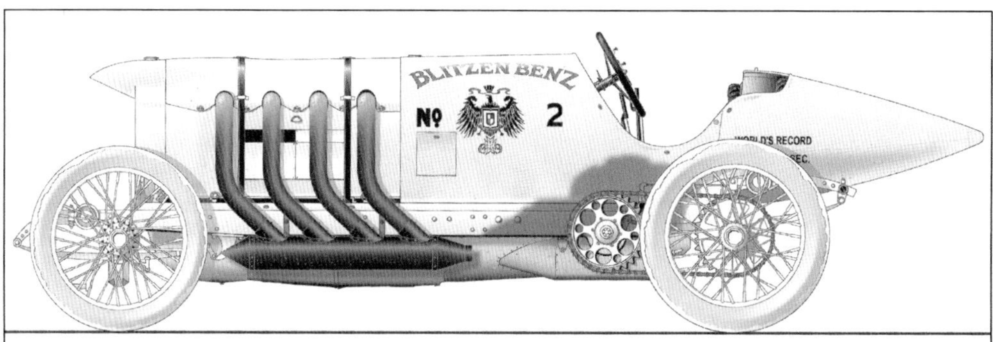

"Terrible" Teddy Tetzlaff drove this 1910 behemoth designed by Victor Hémery and built by Benz & Cie in Mannheim, Germany. The Benz-type RE four-cylinder engine displaced 1,312 cubic inches and gulped a mix of gasoline and ether. The eyeball-shaking, 110.2-inch wheelbase held the narrow 52-inch track with 34.4-by-4-inch-wide front tires and 36.8-by-5-inch white rubber rears. Illustrator Robert Rampton's quest for quality took 22 years of one improved drawing upon another to incorporate every verifiable structural detail. Doubtlessly the most accurate depiction of the chain-driven beast as it appeared on the salt in August 1914. At the time, it was considered the fastest automobile on earth. (Courtesy of Robert Rampton.)

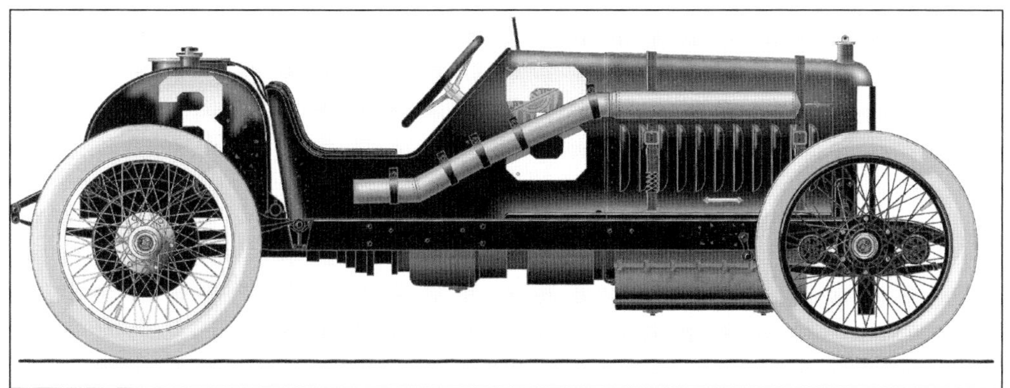

On the salt, star driver Teddy Tetzlaff drove No. 3, one of Detroit's Maxwell Motor Company's three factory team racers designed and built in 1914 by Ray Harroun that used a four-cylinder, 445-cubic-inch Harroun-designed engine. The trio was painted black, with No. 3 running on gasoline and No. 25 (driven by Capt. Harvey Kennedy) and No. 32 (driven by "Coal Oil" Billy Carlson) drinking kerosene go juice. Wheelbase was 106.3 inches on a 55-inch track. Front tires were 33 inches by 4.5 inches, and the rears were 34 inches by 4.5 inches. Although appearing identical, each was constructed slightly different. No. 25 and No. 32 featured a unique carburetor/exhaust manifold that used engine heat to vaporize the kerosene. (Courtesy of Robert Rampton.)

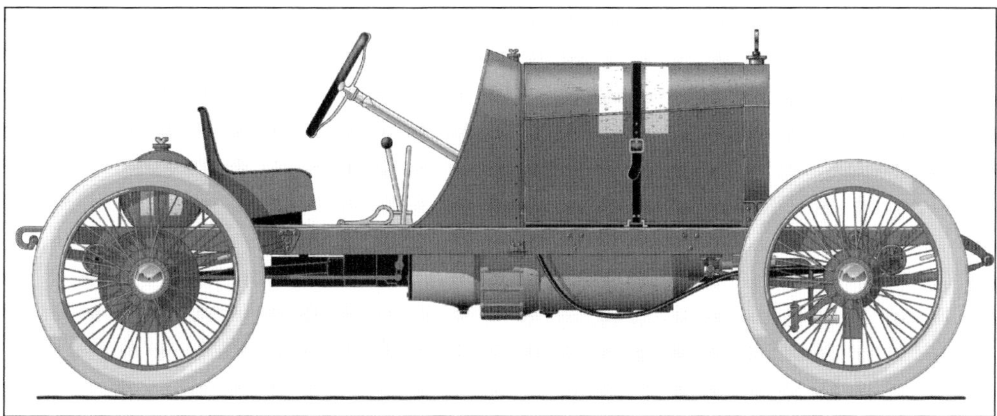

Completed in early 1913 by Nyberg Motor Works in Anderson, Indiana, this racer was designed by Indiana native Harry Endicott, who chose a four-cylinder gasoline Rutenber 230-cubic-inch engine. The 100-inch wheelbase, together with a 55-inch track, is supported by 34-inch-by-4-inch tires front and rear. Named "The Little Red Devil" by Endicott, it was renamed the "Endicott Special" by owner Ernie Moross after Endicott died in an auto race accident. Driven on the salt by Harry Goetz, the car had unusual, yet elegant, Frayer wire wheels. Note the three filling ports: the fuel is behind the driver's seat, oil filler on the cowl in the middle and the water replenished by removing the radiator Motometer in front. (Courtesy of Robert Rampton.)

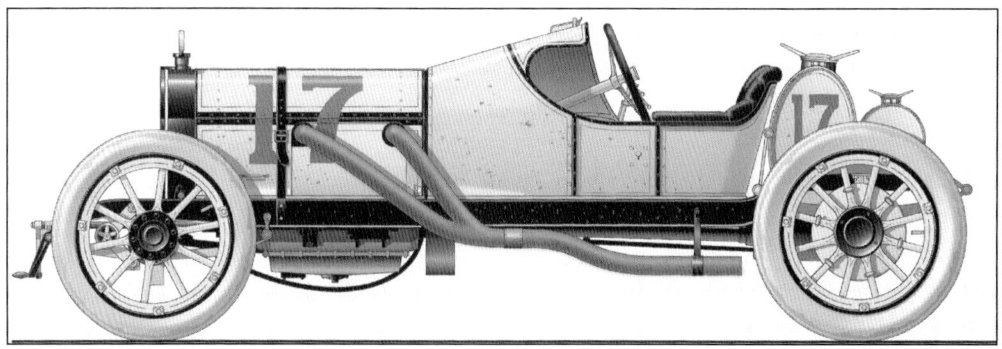

Driven by Wilbur D'Alene, the Marmon was fitted with a four-cylinder, 496-cubic-inch gasoline engine. The yellow and black racer's 116-inch wheelbase has a 56-inch track with 34-inch-by-4-inch tires in the front and 35-inch-by-5-inch tires on the rear. D'Alene became the first professional American Automobile Association (AAA)–licensed driver to pilot a purpose-built race car over a measured and timed course on the flats. Introduced in 1909, the Marmon model 32 chassis was wildly popular. Marmon's chief engineer, Ray Harroun, also made the versatile chassis the cornerstone of the company's successful racing program, building a fleet of capable racing machines on the platform. Fortunately, the most famous model 32, the 1911 Indianapolis 500 winning "Wasp," still exists. (Courtesy of Robert Rampton.)

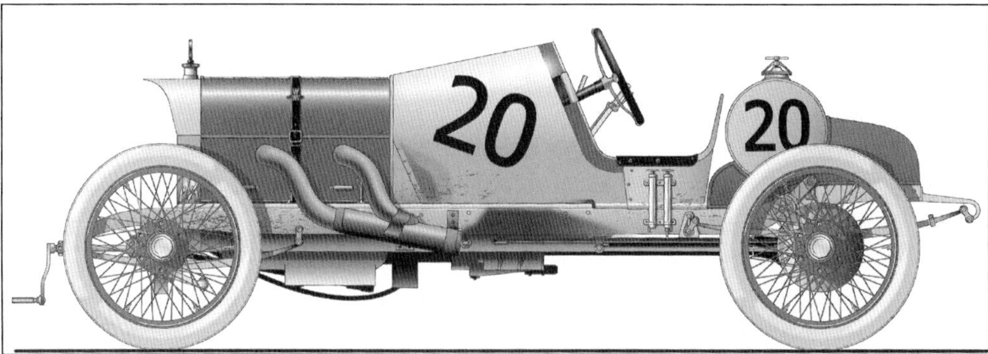

Promoter Ernie Moross, at the Salduro speed trials, mistakenly told reporters this gray and red car was a Stutz, but it was a well-worn Mercer chassis formerly known as "The Monk." S. Frank Brock and Fred Ray had rebuilt the car with a new Wisconsin engine, rumored to be a marine variant taken from a speedboat. It became generally known as the Brock-Ray. On the last day of trials on the salt, during a warm-up run, novice driver Brock blew the engine, bringing to an end his short career as a racer. The wheelbase was 108 inches, with a track of 56 inches, running 33-inch-by-4.5-inch Silvertown Cord tires front and rear. (Courtesy of Robert Rampton.)

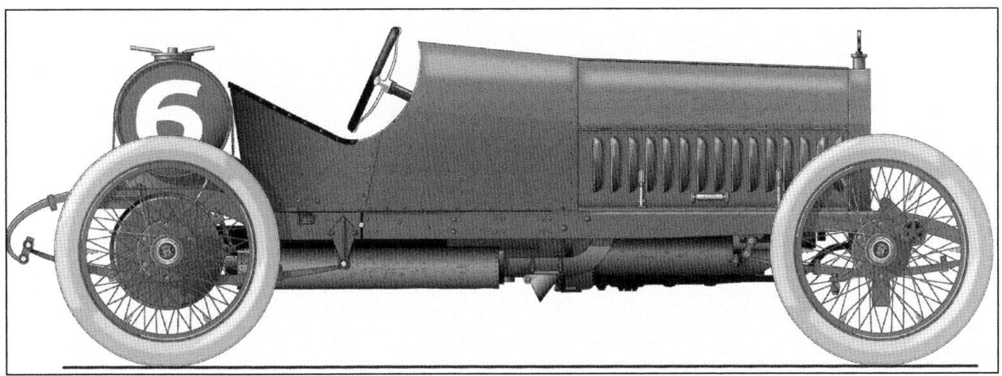

In August 1914, Ernie Moross rolled into Salt Lake City with his own baggage car full of racing machines to stage a day of auto races; a Chalmers 24, a six-cylinder car converted into a racer by shortening the frame, was among them. Driven by Harvey Kennedy, also known as Captain Kennedy, the car was called "The Blue Bird," by reporters, a nickname left over from the marque's race-winning days, even though it was painted red. The car was on the salt for the Salduro trials, but no speeds or photographs of it have ever turned up. (Courtesy of Robert Rampton.)

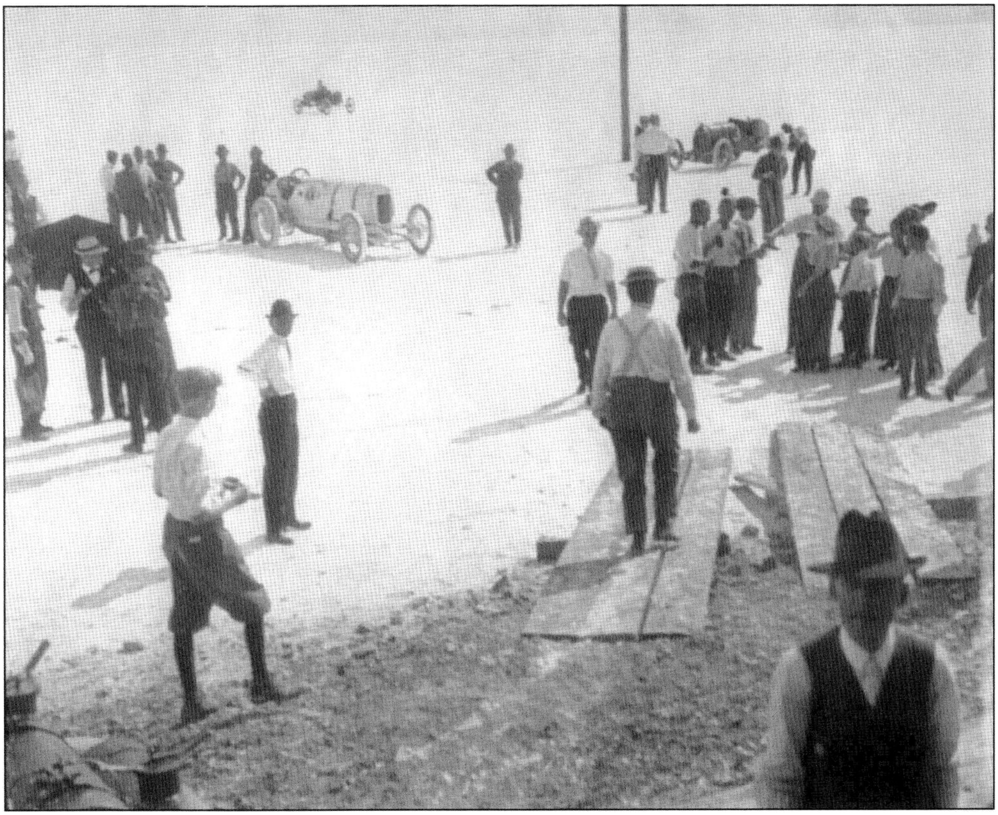

Ernie Moross, in the group to the right, is pouring something in someone's glass. Teddy Tetzlaff is holding a tumbler, and next to him is possibly Wilbur D'Alene. One of the women could be Moross's new wife, as he was on his honeymoon at the time. The girls taking swigs from bottles might be drinking the new big thing: Coca-Cola! (Courtesy of Robert Rampton.)

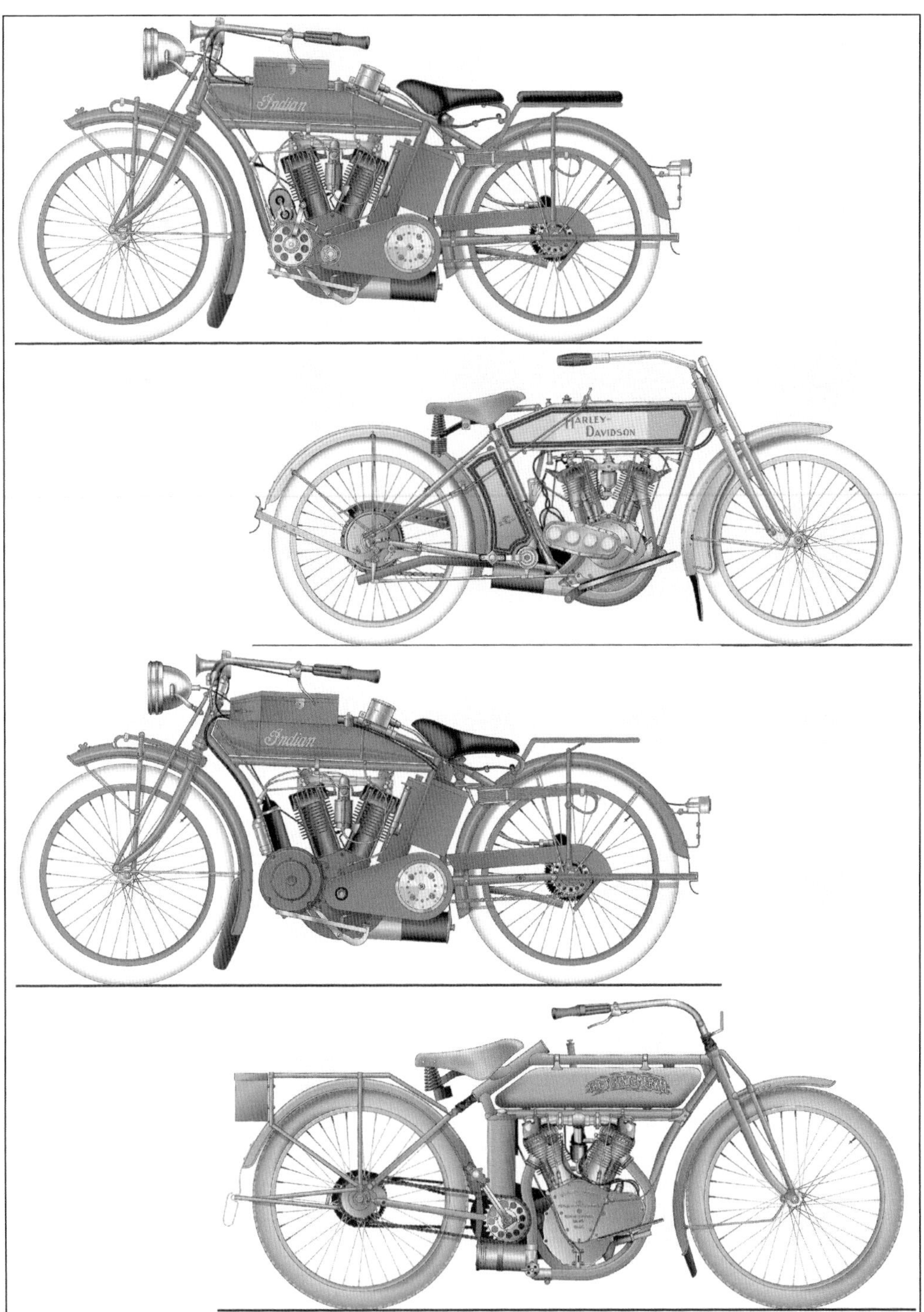

Pictured here are, from top to bottom, an Indian Standard V-twin motorcycle, a Harley-Davidson motorcycle with full-floating seat, an Indian Hendee Special touring motorbike, and the Flying Merkel, a seven-horsepower chain-drive "Yellow Jacket" Model 473. All competed at Salduro on the flats. (Courtesy of Robert Rampton.)

Two

Monster Cars of the Gentlemen Racer 1915–1948

The British Invade . . . Again!

An ego-driven squabble between racers and the AAA Contest Board made the salt flats a racing pariah after the 1914 inaugural event. Everything changed in 1925. Utah locals convinced the federal government that the New York–to–San Francisco transcontinental Victory Highway should be built on the Wendover Cutoff to tame the wild, 40-mile stretch over the salt beds.

To commemorate its completion, Ab Jenkins bet the Salt Lake Rotary $250 that he could beat the special excursion train from Salt Lake City to Wendover—125 miles and five hours away.

Driving a black Studebaker roadster shod with newly developed balloon tires, Jenkins took off with the auto dealer's secretary, Alta McCaffery, and Salt Lake City policeman Tommy Dee.

After passing 15 railroad crossings, the trio rattled into Wendover sounding like an untuned brass band 2 hours and 40 minutes later—five minutes before the train puffed into town.

That deed began a remarkable 30-year career of record breaking for the soft-spoken Mormon, who also became the "Father of Bonneville" by shepherding the world's racing elite onto the vast saline speedway.

In the 1930s, Britain's John Rhodes Cobb, Capt. George E.T. Eyston, Reed Railton, and Sir Malcolm Campbell often grabbed headlines with hand-built racing machines. These were gentlemen racers who "dressed" for breaking records by wearing white shirts, ties, and polished shoes in addition to helmets and overalls.

Once called "preposterous," Jenkins's 24-hour and 48-hour endurance records became anticipated. In 1956, the multiple record-setting marks he set driving the Series 860 prompted GM's Pontiac Motor Division to honor the feat by renaming the car "Bonneville." To date, it is the only automobile to earn its name, not be given its moniker by marketing staff. The Jenkins velocity bloodline extended to son Marvin, who also scribed indelible hard marks in motorsports record books.

Not a passing fad, national champion Harry Hartz said of Bonneville: "It's freedom from dust, hard, solid and smooth; the salt base which retains moisture and thereby exercises a cooling influence on the tires; its outstanding safety factor in having so much room, make this the greatest racing track in the world."

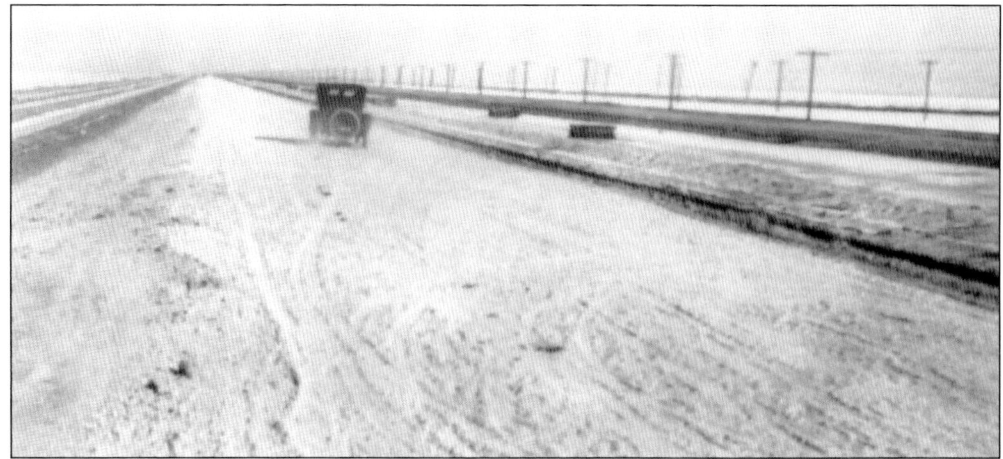

It is salt, not dust, being kicked up by the tin lizzie on the only road, if it can be called that, out of Wendover to Salt Lake City. It was more an access trail next to the railroad tracks seen at right. Steam trains needed water as they chugged over the desolate landscape, so a station was established at a sheepherder's stop by tapping into the pioneer water source at nearby Pilot's Peak. Water was gravity fed through a 26-mile pipeline, and thus, the tiny village of Wendover winked into life. (Courtesy of LPRL/Lee Wendelboe.)

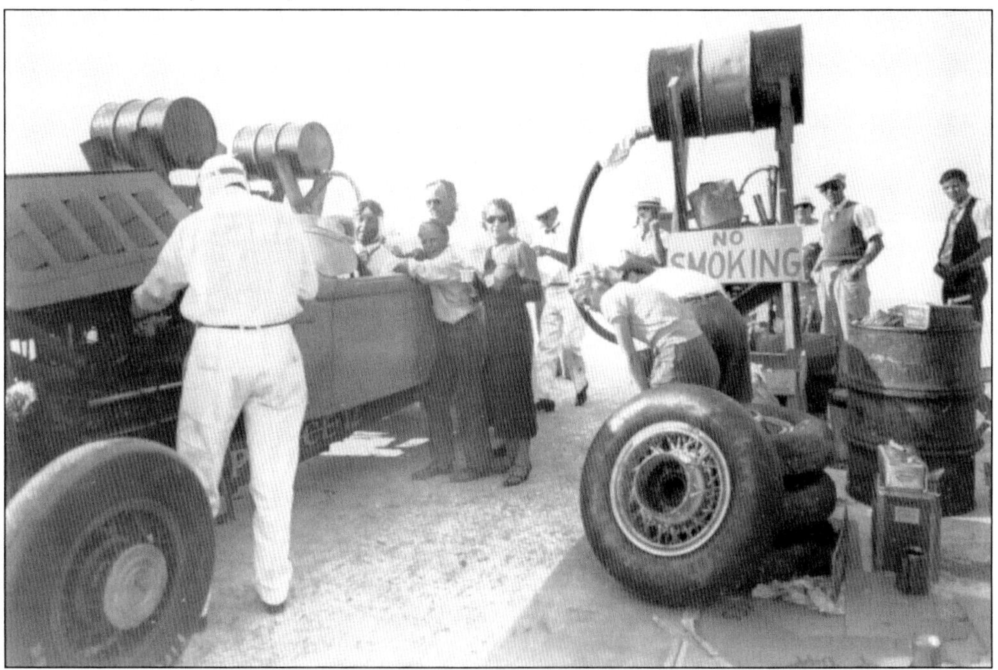

Burt Updike tends to the engine while driver Ab Jenkins visits with his son Marv and wife Evelyn. Pierce Arrow advertising manager Bill Baldwin looks on as racing history unfolds on the Bonneville Salt Flats in 1932 as Jenkins inks the first official endurance record. The Utah State Road Commission surveyed and scraped smooth the salt to mark a 10-mile circular track. Jenkins only stopped for gas and rarely changed a tire or got up from behind the wheel the entire time. Temperatures soared above 100 degrees, and timers took turns resting in an old sheepherder's wagon, while Jenkins's only protection was a thick coating of goose grease slathered over his hands and face. (Courtesy of LPRL/Marv and Noma Jenkins.)

Ab Jenkins, now 50, went back to the salt in 1933 with AAA sanctioning. He snapped up 56 new records in one attempt on the 10-mile circle track. In the early-morning hours of August 7, more than halfway through the run, the car's right rear tire blew out at 123 miles per hour. It exploded with such force that the black and silver roadster was jerked into a wicked swerve, cannonballing a reverberating echo through the mountain slopes. (Courtesy of LPRL/ Marv and Noma Jenkins.)

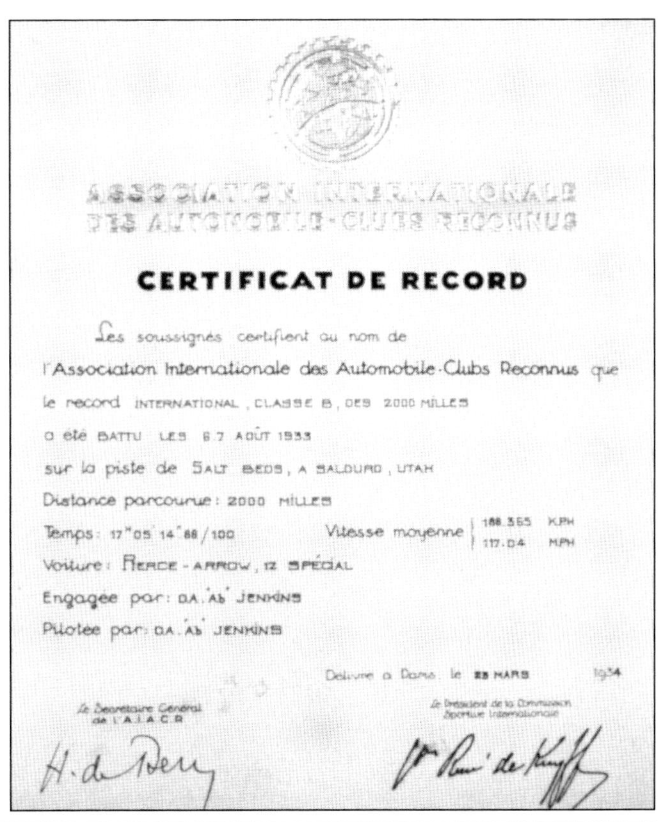

ASSOCIATION INTERNATIONALE
DES AUTOMOBILE-CLUBS RECONNUS

CERTIFICAT DE RECORD

Les soussignés certifient au nom de
l'Association Internationale des Automobile-Clubs Reconnus que
le record INTERNATIONAL, CLASSE B, DES 2000 MILLES
a été BATTU LES 6.7 AOÛT 1933
sur la piste de SALT BEDS, A SALDURO, UTAH
Distance parcourue: 2000 MILLES
Temps: 17h05'14"88/100 Vitesse moyenne 188.365 KPH / 117.04 MPH
Voiture: PIERCE-ARROW, 12 SPÉCIAL
Engagée par: D.A. "Ab" JENKINS
Pilotée par: D.A. "Ab" JENKINS

Délivré à Paris, le 23 MARS 1934

Le Secrétaire Général de l'A.I.A.C.R. — H. de Perry

Le Président de la Commission Sportive Internationale — Vte René de Knyff

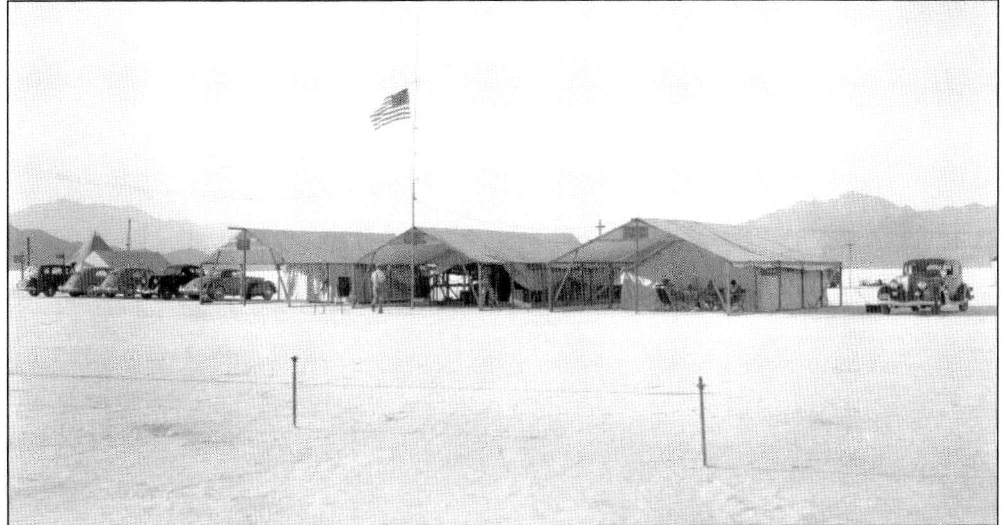

Out on the salt, wood-framed, canvas-covered tents made great sleeping quarters and refuges from the sun. Huge iceboxes held an array of fresh food to rival fine restaurants. "It sure was luxury camping back then," chuckled Marvin Jenkins about the racers' camp. Trying to collect any world hour record at Bonneville was considered the toughest because car and driver could never relax. Still, in all of Jenkins's 24- and 48-hour runs, there was never a bobble. "We asked the timers for all kinds of information, the last lap completed, the average for the time, and it was never a problem," recalled Marvin Jenkins. (Courtesy of Firestone Tire and Rubber Company.)

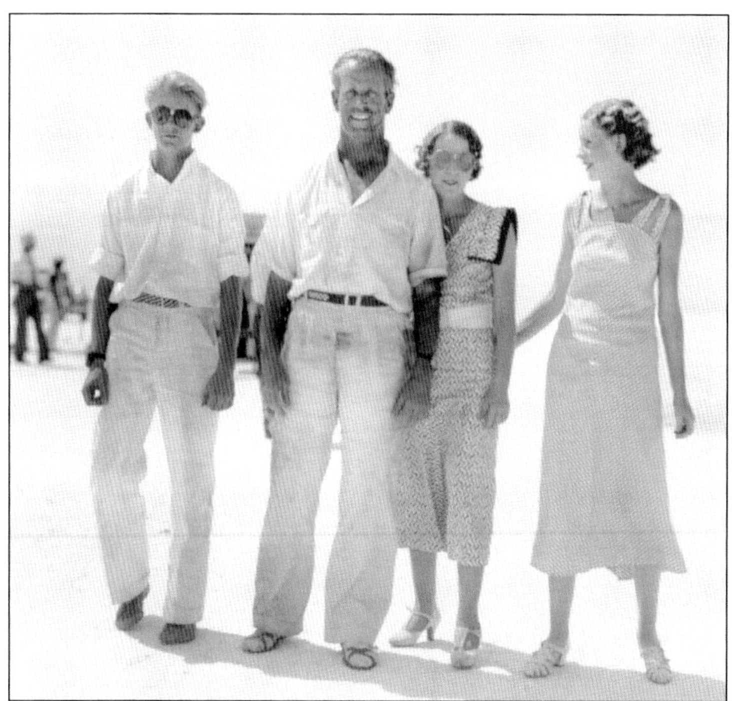

The Jenkins family is pictured here. From left to right are Marvin, Ab, Evelyn, and Ruth enjoying some family time in 1934 moments after dad had finished another astonishing endurance run on the salt flats. Jenkins was renowned for nonstop driving, ingesting only orange juice, milk, and an occasional pint of ice cream handed to him directly from a family member during his multi-day marathon record runs. (Courtesy of LPRL/Marv and Noma Jenkins.)

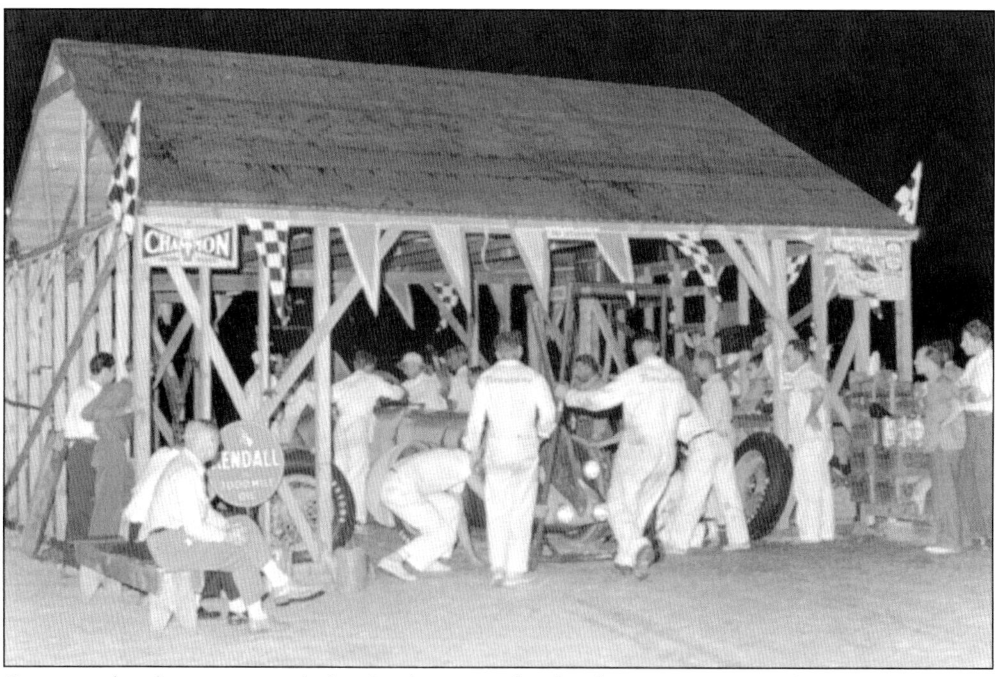

Gone are the observing crowds, but for those people who thrive on grease and iron with numbers and nerve, setting records is rarely an easy victory. As the cars drive on through the night, the crew stays ever vigilant, ready to respond to any hiccup. The harder the mark sought, the sweeter its etching is savored. Fortune can frown one moment and then smile the next on racing hopefuls. Preparedness, moxie, and, many times, a prayer temper this ever-revolving wheel of fate. (Courtesy of Firestone Tire and Rubber Company.)

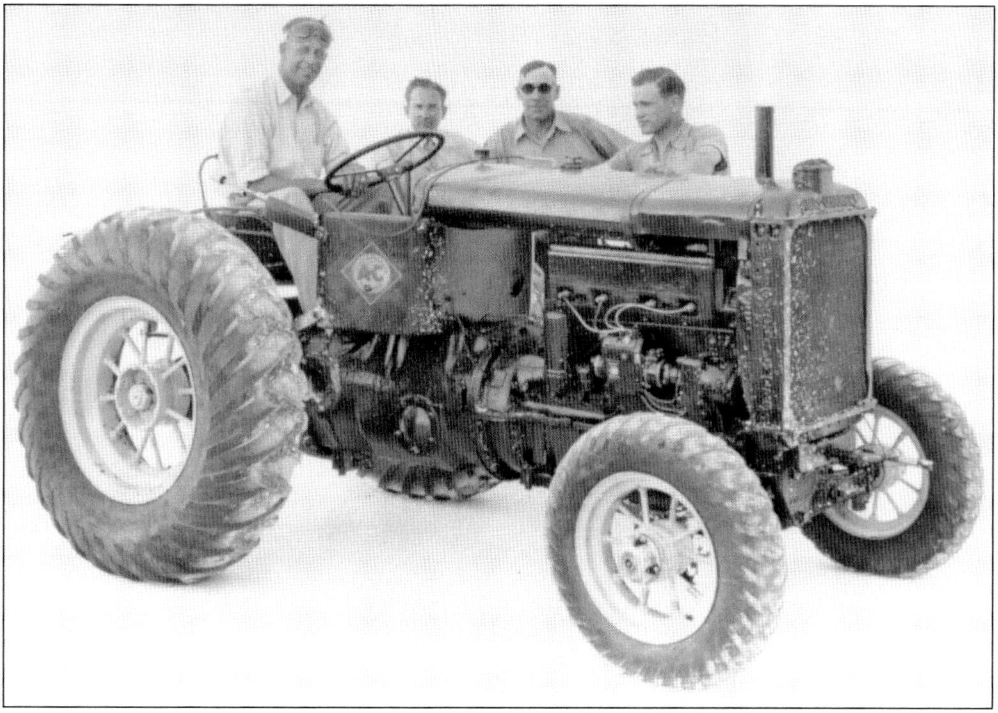

Ab Jenkins, seated, set the first farm implement speed records by driving the bumping bejeebers out of Allis-Chalmers tractors on the salt beds. There was something wacky about trying to race a machine that was designed to perform at its best at a crawl, but manufacturers needed a speed record to capture the attention of the fickle buying public. Of his new world mark of 68 miles per hour, the mild-mannered Mormon remarked, "Driving those tractors were the hairiest ride I ever took on the salt. It was like riding on a frightening bison." (Courtesy of LPRL/Marv and Noma Jenkins.)

The local Wendover kids emulated Utah hero Ab Jenkins by riding 295.6 miles in a bicycle endurance race on the salt flats near Jenkins's camp. Some of the people pictured here are Ab Jenkins, in the back row wearing the striped shirt; Brownie Carslake, head of the Firestone Tire and Rubber Company Racing Division, in the white shirt; and Glenda Lyman Green, the girl standing at right. (Courtesy of LPRL/Green and Lamus family.)

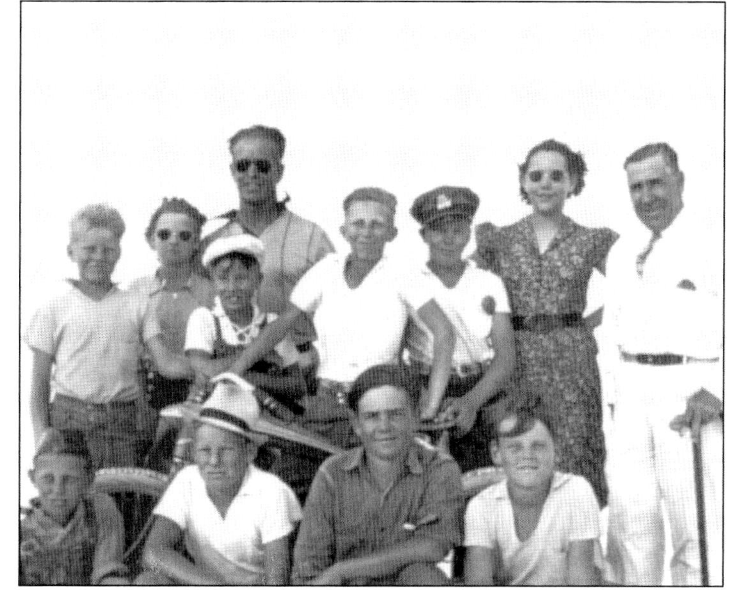

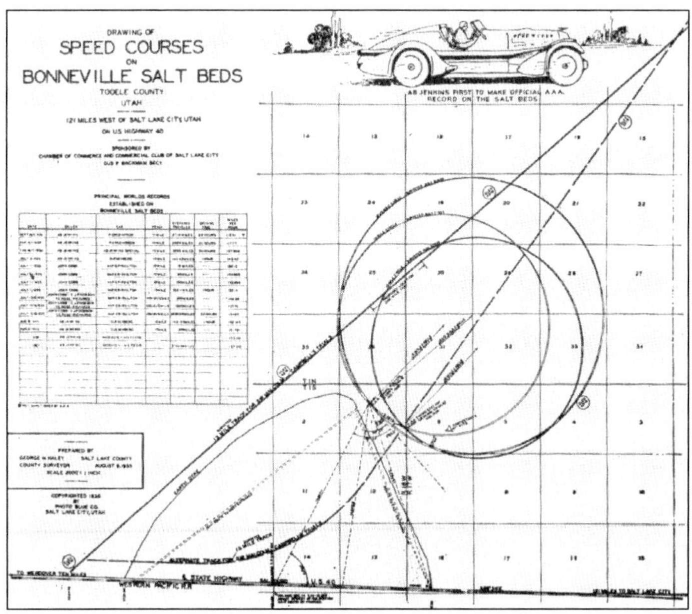

This 1935 chart shows how the 10- and 12-mile endurance circle tracks were laid out on the flats as well as the 13-mile straightaway surveyed specifically for Malcolm Campbell's first, and only, "Bluebird" runs. From the notation, it is also clear not only that Ab Jenkins (with help from Augie Duesenberg) set the first certified world record at Bonneville but also that the deed demonstrated that the flats were only getting started as a speed laboratory. (Courtesy of LPRL.)

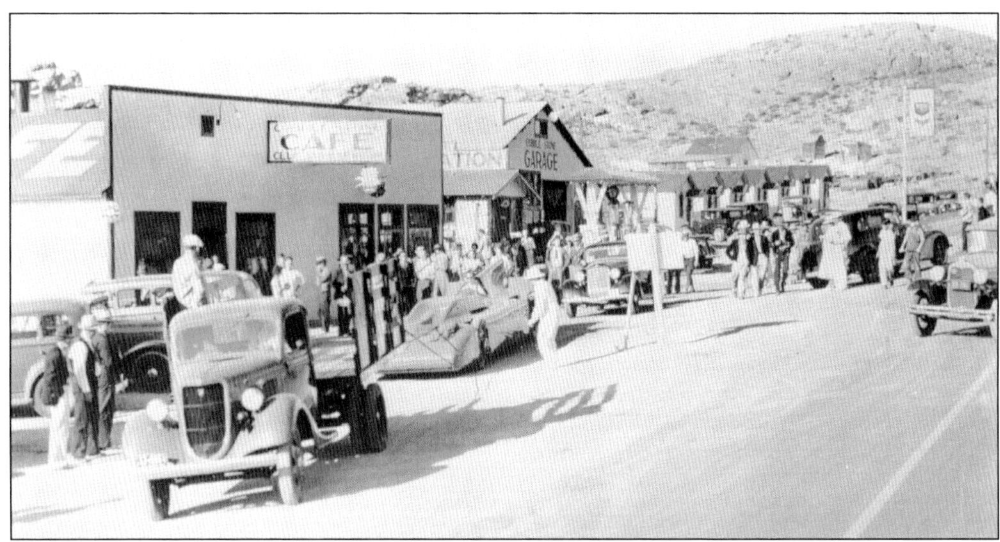

Malcolm Campbell caused a stir on Wendover Boulevard when he arrived in front of W.F. Smith's Cobble Stone Café for lunch towing his world famous "Bluebird" world land speed record car. Campbell was the first person to set a straight-line world land speed record on the salt flats. The town of Wendover, population 400, with its white line painted across Wendover Boulevard marking the state line, was besieged. Though no official tally was made, several reports estimated 2,000 people watched Campbell's first runs. (Courtesy of the Utah State Historical Society.)

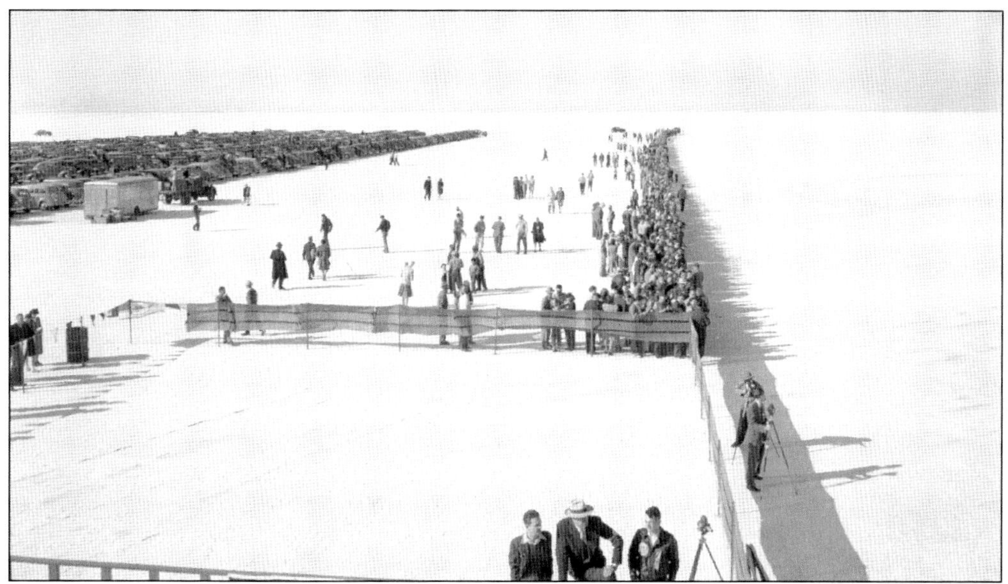

Once the racing world discovered the rock-hard salt flats pancake, it fled Daytona's soft, undulating sand that robbed cars of precious speed by inducing gobs of wheel spin. It was like a tiger trying to catch a rabbit on a highly polished surface. Spectators came from all over Nevada and Utah—some even farther—to witness the pageant of power. Endurance records could last up to 48 hours nonstop. Ab Jenkins once set 60 new world speed records in one go. When he stopped and stepped out, the crowd was dumbfounded because he was sporting a clean-shaven grin! Thank Ab's son Marvin for passing him a safety razor and can of aerosol shaving cream a few laps from the end! (Courtesy of Firestone Tire and Rubber Company.)

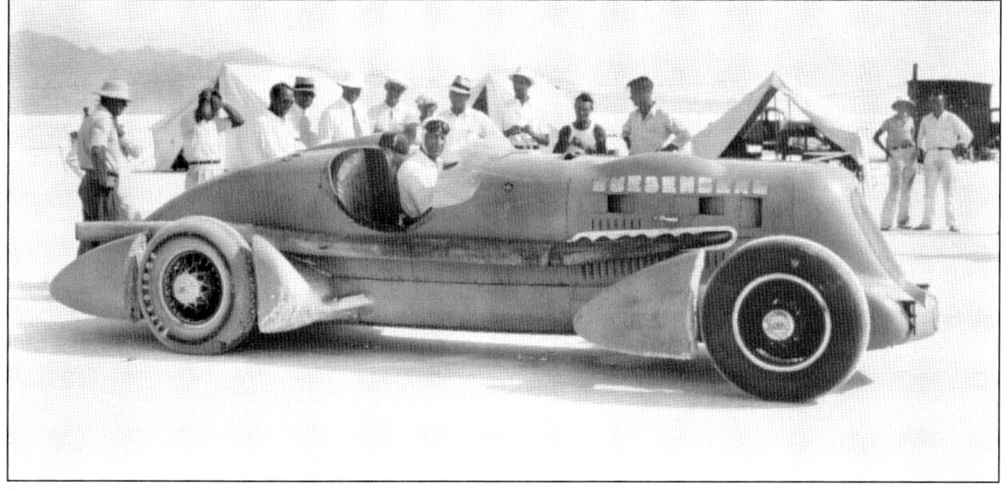

In 1936, screaming along at 159 miles per hour, Ab Jenkins's tires hit a soft spot, and the specially built Duesenberg went into a 400-foot wingding, wahoo, mammoth skid. To avoid tipping over, he deliberately cranked the steering wheel to the left and nailed the accelerator, which sent the car spinning for 2.5 miles, darting past telephone poles and between parked automobiles, tents, and spectators. Indy codriver Babe Stapp was riding shotgun and dove under the cowling. Nothing was damaged, and Jenkins continued until a burned-out front universal joint parked the car. (Courtesy of Firestone Tire and Rubber Company.)

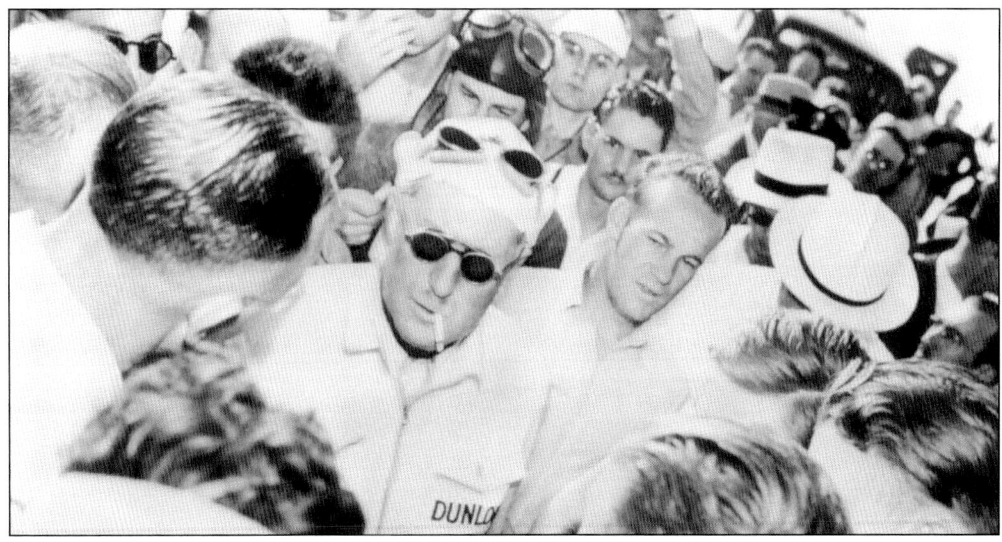

It is August 28, 1938, and Capt. George E.T. Eyston, wearing black sunglasses, is surrounded by well-wishers moments after he eclipsed his own world speed record with a 345-mile-per-hour mark, 34 miles per hour faster than his previous record. Driving "Thunderbolt," the eight-wheel behemoth, Eyston told the crowd he did not open the car's throttle to its fullest extent. (Courtesy of Dan and Jay Haugh.)

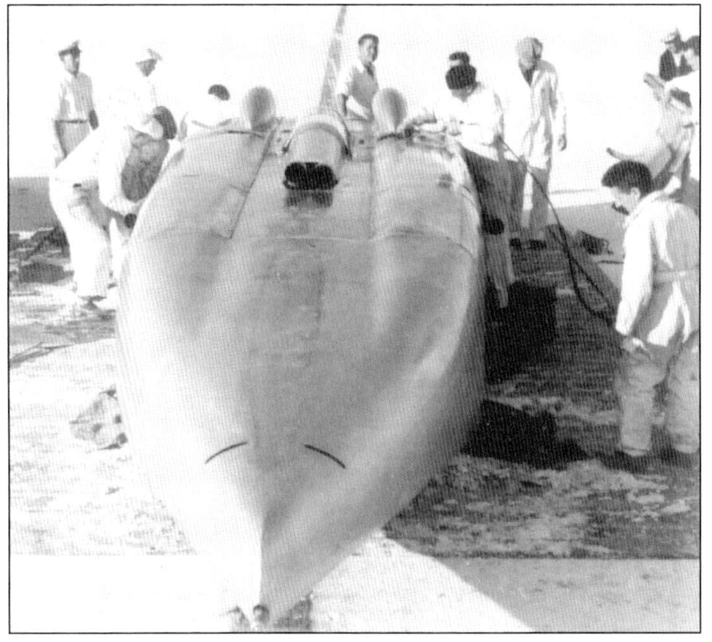

Captain Eyston's crew worked feverishly on the starting line to prepare "Thunderbolt" for a world-record speed attempt. The painted black center line at the top of the pane curves off to the right in the distance where the actual speed course is located . . . a sort of a salty on-ramp to a salty speedway. Of the salt beds Eyston observed, "There is no place in the world offering so many favorable conditions for scientific testing of a car." (Courtesy of the Utah State Historical Society.)

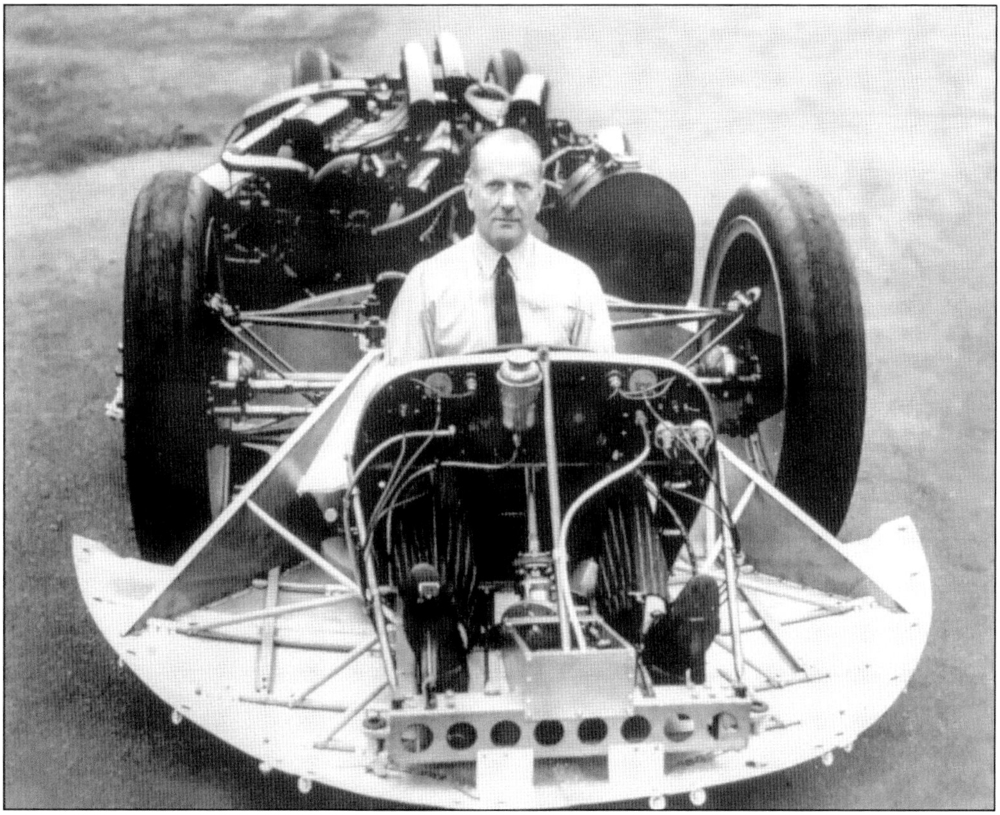

Behind driver John Cobb are two Napier supercharged Lion VIID (WD) W-12 aircraft engines that delivered power to the Dunlop tires. Originally the "Railton Special" in 1938, it was rebuilt as the "Railton Mobil Special" for Cobb's world land speed record attempts in later years. Betty "Joe" Carstairs gifted Cobb the engines out of her powerboat *Estelle V.* Reid Railton solved the problem of distributing such massive horsepower by simply splitting the drive from each engine to a separate axle and stable four-wheel drive. (Courtesy of Robin Richardson.)

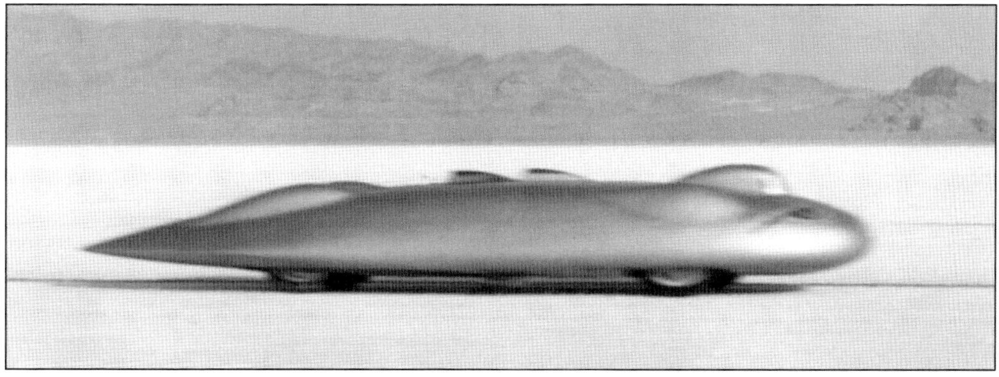

Encapsulated under the elongated jelly bean body is London furrier John Cobb on a final test run, driving his "Railton Red Lion" and averaging 368.85 miles per hour on August 23, 1939. After World War II, Cobb became the fastest man alive—again—when, in September 1947 on the salt, he was the first to exceed 400 miles per hour on one of two record runs, inking the world-record mark of 394.19 miles per hour. The record held until 1963, when American Craig Breedlove brought world honor back the United States. (Courtesy of Dan and Jay Haugh.)

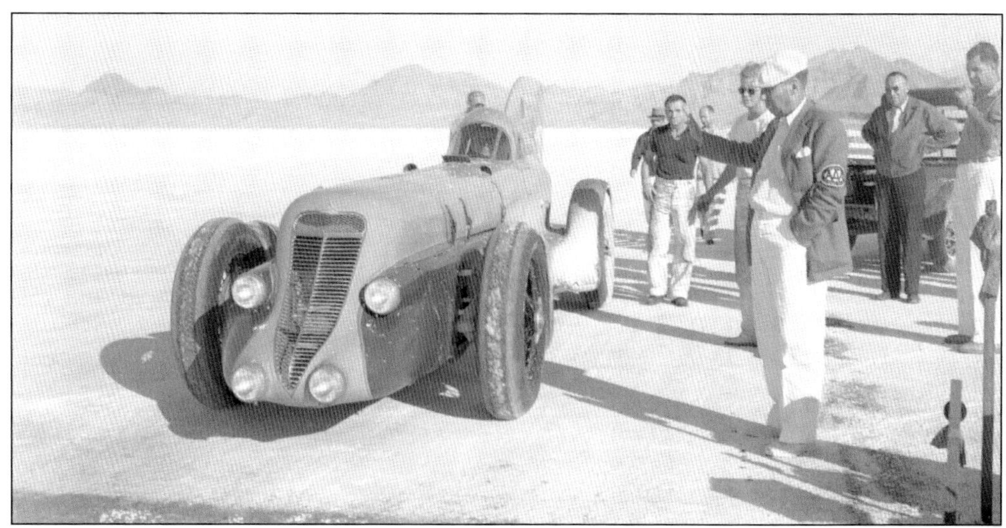

Driver Ab Jenkins is given a "wait" signal from the AAA Contest Board official, causing consternation throughout the team. Among them is son Marvin Jenkins, in the dark glasses, who may very well be wondering how long the car can sit and idle before overheating in the triple-digit desert heat. (Courtesy of Firestone Tire and Rubber Company.)

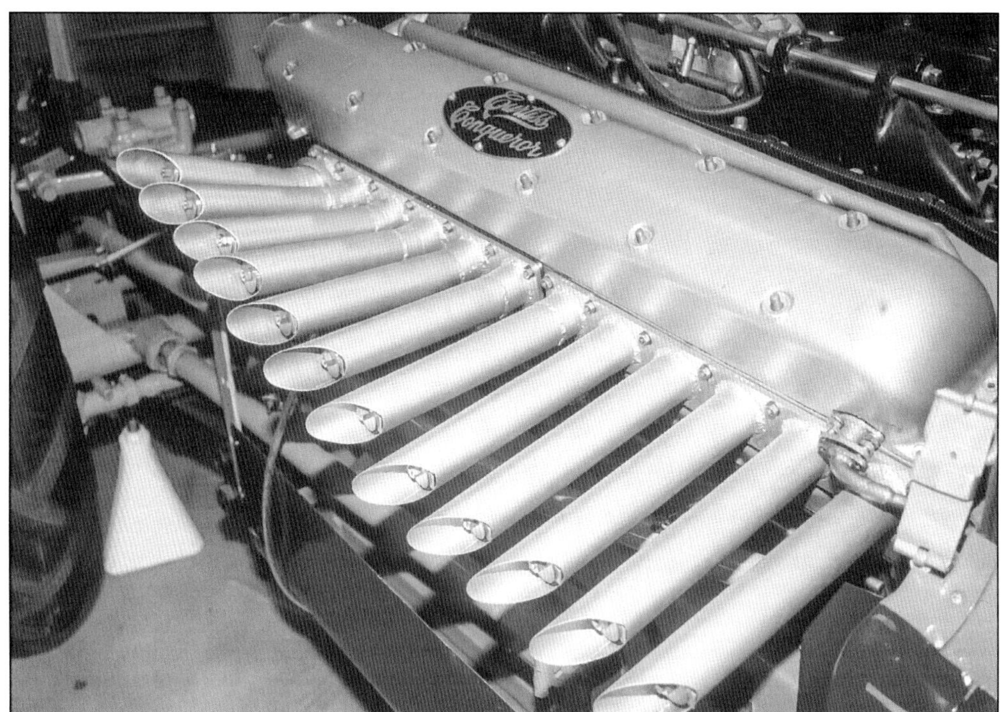

In 1937, Ab Jenkins sent his 16-year-old son Marvin to Indianapolis, Indiana, to help Augie Duesenberg build the "Mormon Meteor III," fitted with a hefty Curtiss Conqueror airplane engine. Ab, driving solo, set a 24-hour record of 161 miles per hour in 1940 that would not be broken until 1990—and required several drivers to eclipse the mark! (Courtesy of LandSpeed Louise.)

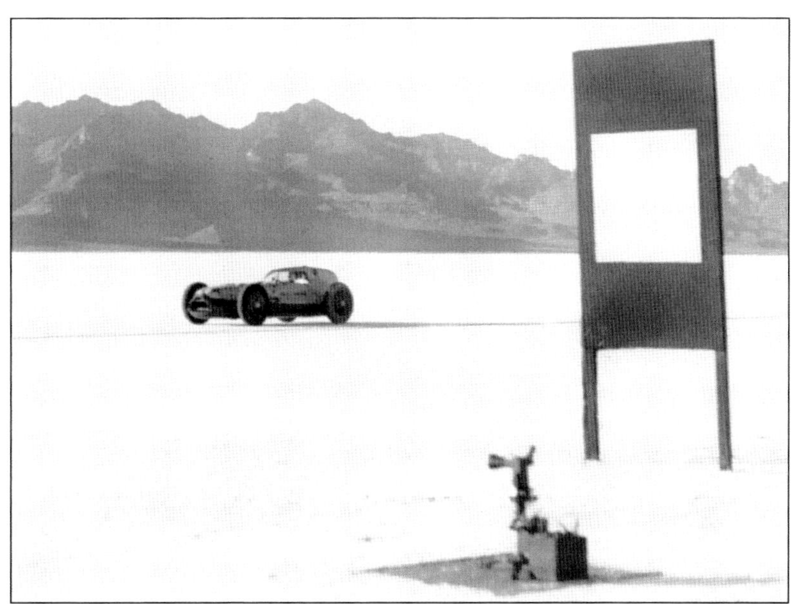

It is 1947, and Marvin Jenkins, driving Lewis Welch's "Novi Special," enters the timed flying mile to several records officiated by the AAA Contest Board. Note a car battery powering the timing light at lower right. (Courtesy of LPRL/Marv and Noma Jenkins.)

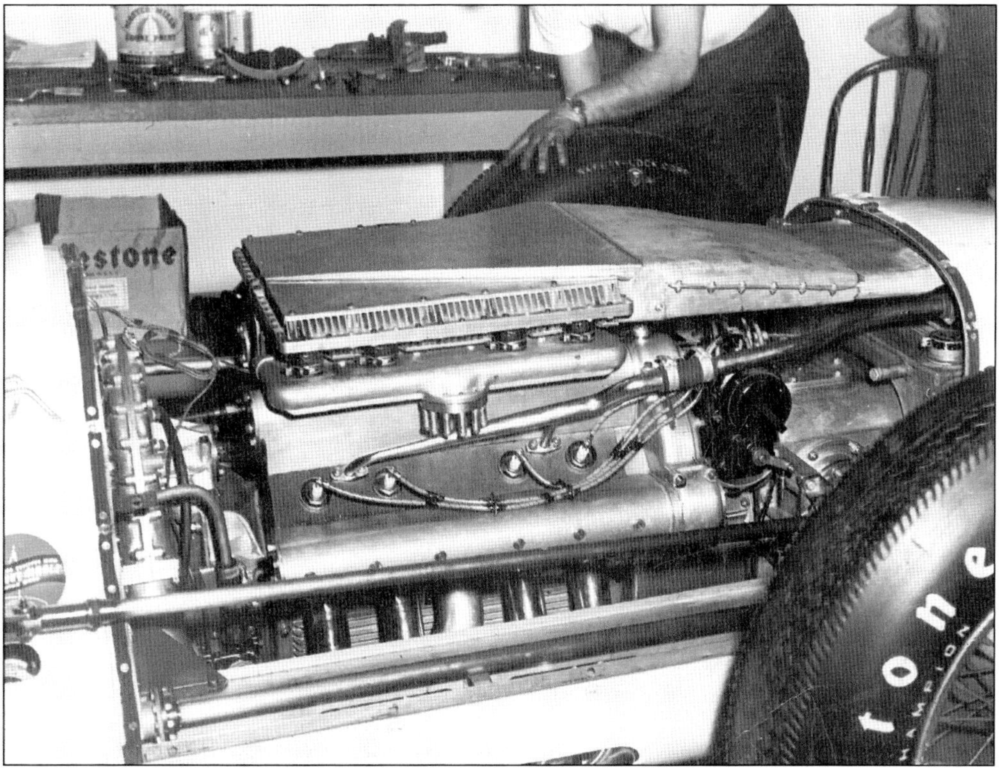

Bud Winfield was in charge of running the "Novi Special" for owner Lewis Welch. Drivers Ab and Marv Jenkins had the job of wresting the Class C record (three-liter engine) away from the Germans. With this engine, at twilight, averaging 179.434 miles per hour, Marvin Jenkins drove the "Novi Special" to eight new national and international records in the 5- and 10-kilometer distances, improving on the existing record set seven years prior at 155 miles per hour. (Courtesy of LPRL/Marv and Noma Jenkins.)

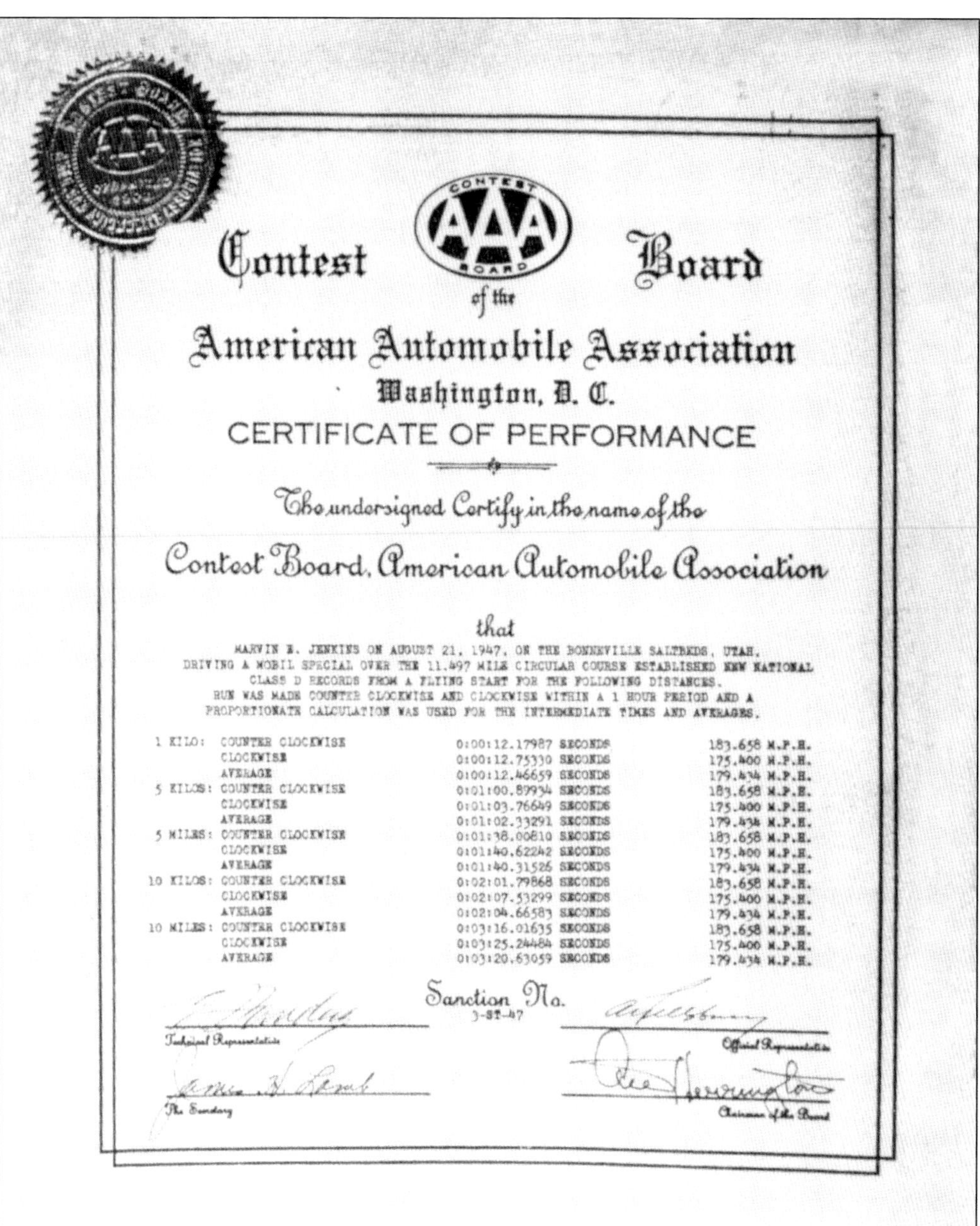

Contest Board
of the
American Automobile Association
Washington, D. C.
CERTIFICATE OF PERFORMANCE

The undersigned Certify in the name of the
Contest Board, American Automobile Association
that

MARVIN E. JENKINS ON AUGUST 21, 1947, ON THE BONNEVILLE SALTBEDS, UTAH, DRIVING A MOBIL SPECIAL OVER THE 11.497 MILE CIRCULAR COURSE ESTABLISHED NEW NATIONAL CLASS D RECORDS FROM A FLYING START FOR THE FOLLOWING DISTANCES. RUN WAS MADE COUNTER CLOCKWISE AND CLOCKWISE WITHIN A 1 HOUR PERIOD AND A PROPORTIONATE CALCULATION WAS USED FOR THE INTERMEDIATE TIMES AND AVERAGES.

1 KILO:	COUNTER CLOCKWISE	0:00:12.17987 SECONDS	183.658 M.P.H.
	CLOCKWISE	0:00:12.75330 SECONDS	175.400 M.P.H.
	AVERAGE	0:00:12.46659 SECONDS	179.434 M.P.H.
5 KILOS:	COUNTER CLOCKWISE	0:01:00.89934 SECONDS	183.658 M.P.H.
	CLOCKWISE	0:01:03.76649 SECONDS	175.400 M.P.H.
	AVERAGE	0:01:02.33291 SECONDS	179.434 M.P.H.
5 MILES:	COUNTER CLOCKWISE	0:01:38.00810 SECONDS	183.658 M.P.H.
	CLOCKWISE	0:01:40.62242 SECONDS	175.400 M.P.H.
	AVERAGE	0:01:40.31526 SECONDS	179.434 M.P.H.
10 KILOS:	COUNTER CLOCKWISE	0:02:01.79868 SECONDS	183.658 M.P.H.
	CLOCKWISE	0:02:07.53299 SECONDS	175.400 M.P.H.
	AVERAGE	0:02:04.66583 SECONDS	179.434 M.P.H.
10 MILES:	COUNTER CLOCKWISE	0:03:16.01635 SECONDS	183.658 M.P.H.
	CLOCKWISE	0:03:25.24484 SECONDS	175.400 M.P.H.
	AVERAGE	0:03:20.63059 SECONDS	179.434 M.P.H.

Sanction No.
3-ST-47

Technical Representative
Official Representative
The Secretary
Chairman of the Board

This photograph was taken at Marv and Noma Jenkins's St. George, Utah, home when Marvin, age 70, was restoring his father's "Mormon Meteor III" back to running condition after more than 50 years. Jenkins was quick to note all his records were due to his father's careful tutelage and faith in his son. Considering his many record certificates, it is clear young Jenkins never squandered anything his dad shared. (Courtesy of LPRL/Marv and Noma Jenkins.)

Three

Boys, Toys, and Noise 1949–1960

Amateur Motorsports Rise to Worldwide Distinction

Before the 1940s closed out, straight-line salt racing would arrive, and it would stay for decades, energized by racers of all ages possessed with adventurous spirits. They would be strong, heaving with intestinal fortitude, and exploding with enthusiasm and impatient creativity.

The racing conditions on Southern California dry lake beds had deteriorated from overuse. Poor course surfaces combined with faster racing vehicles led to increasingly more crashes, injuries, and deaths on the loosening dirt surfaces.

Driving on the granite-like salt meant the speed machine could still spinout but with less chance of flipping over and only making the hapless driver dizzy. Those embarrassed few earned an unofficial Spin Out Club fraternity pin.

Before the Department of Interior's Bureau of Land Management took over in 1946, the Salt Lake City Chamber of Commerce was in charge of scheduling. Anyone wanting to use the salt flats for racing purposes had to gain permission from the Bonneville Speedway Association, a chamber committee. The State of Utah graciously prepared the racetrack annually until 1976.

Kong Jackson paved the way for Wally Parks, who, with Petersen Publishing manager Lee Ryan and *Hot Rod* publisher Bob Petersen, drove up to Salt Lake seeking permission to use the flats. Fortune favors the brave, and soon after the trio returned to Southern California, a decision was rendered by the powerful, influential chamber secretary Robert D. "Gus" Backman.

His April 4, 1949, letter announced, "We will be pleased to allocate the salt beds to your organization at some time during the month of August, for the purpose of conducting time trials."

The people with a need for speed deeds rejoiced! The first annual Bonneville Speed Trials were set for August 22–27, 1949. This decision percolated months of controlled chaos to hook sponsors, work out logistics, and plan a publicity strategy.

Entries arrived from Texas, Colorado, Nevada, Tennessee, Florida, Iowa, Utah, Arizona, Minnesota, Illinois, and Nebraska, but only 60 roadsters, lakesters, streamliners, coupes, and sport and racing cars paid the $7.50 per car entry fee and showed up.

In the years that followed, the competitors increased nearly tenfold, but this began the amateur march to becoming the fastest people on earth, still true today and still organized and operated by volunteers.

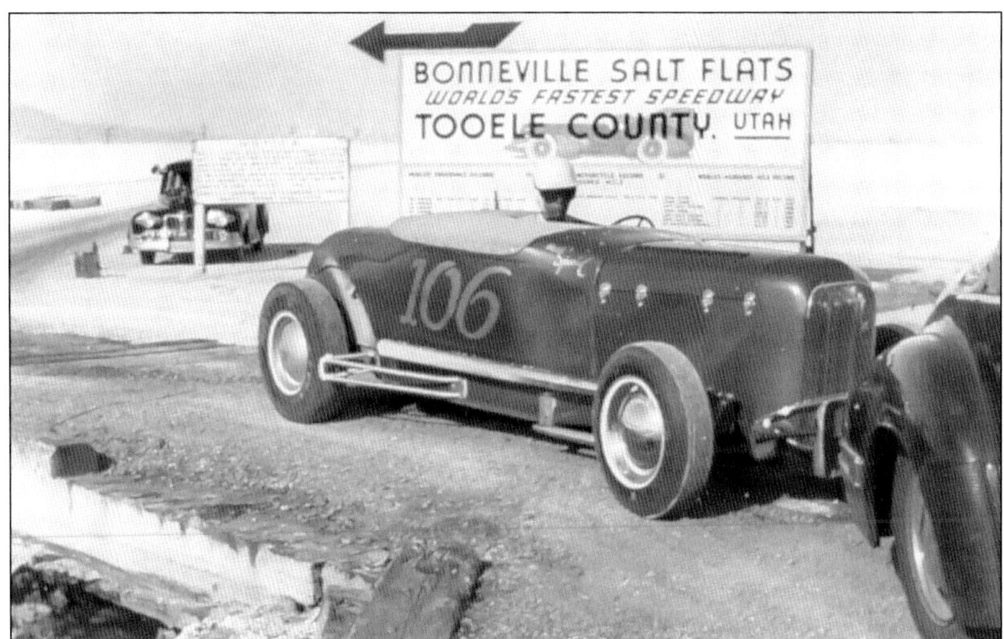

Race officials sent off a car every minute at the inaugural Speed Week, so it is no surprise a dejected-looking Marvin Webb leaves the flats after his first, and only, 119 mile-per-hour run in his No. 106 "Webb Special" roadster competing in Class C. (Courtesy of Marvin Webb.)

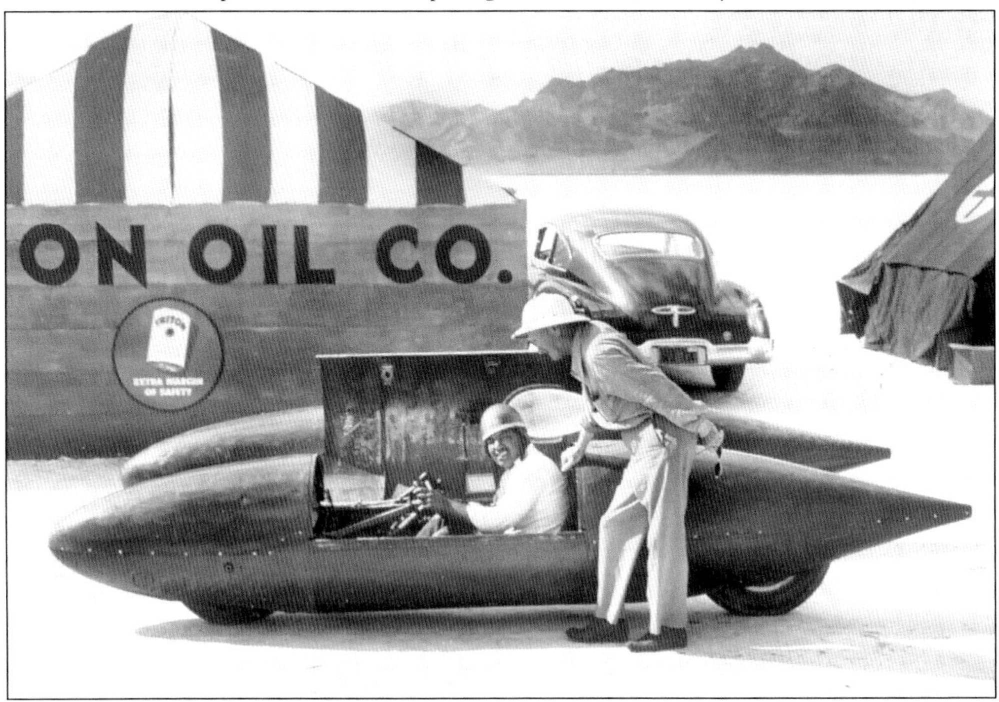

Howard Johansen, of Howard's Cams, shows off his twin-belly tank to Union Oil's Earl Cooper. Fitted into the other pod is a Mercury engine. Sadly, the unique speed machine was an evil devil to control and scared more onlookers than it thrilled, especially when it spun out at 147 miles per hour! (Courtesy of LPRL/SCTA Archives.)

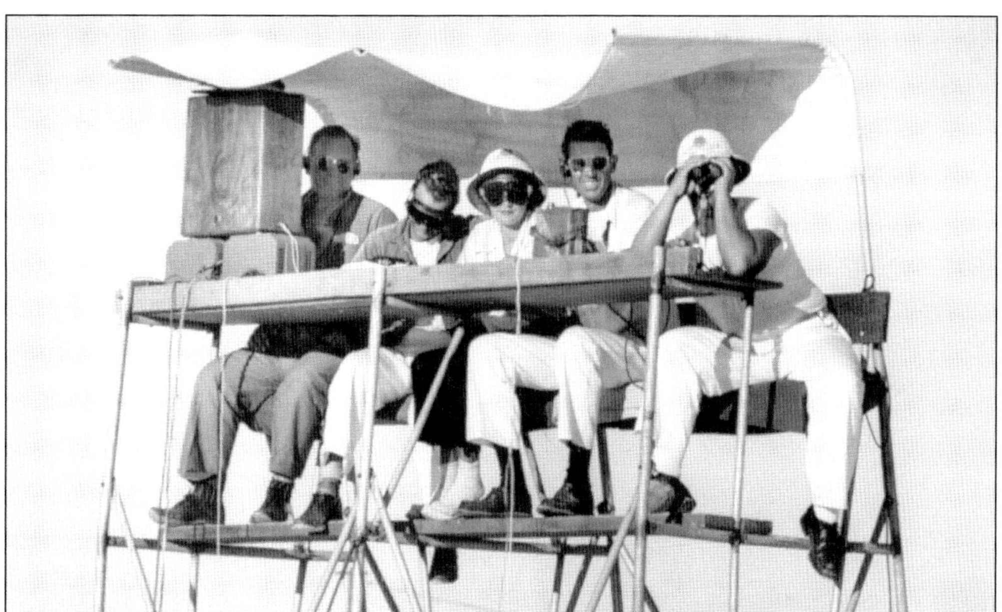

Was this tubular, steel, shaded timing stand built by Southern California Timing Association (SCTA) volunteers the best seat in the salt house? Chief timer Otto Crocker, far left, has a commanding view of the course as Bob Higbee records the time and Phyllis Lindsley and Wally Parks check out the starting line action. The man with his eye glued to the binoculars is possibly Jim Lindsley. (Courtesy of LPRL/SCTA Archives.)

CERTIFICATE OF SPEED

Clocked By J. Otto Crocker *Electronic Timer*

THIS Certifies that Wally Parks & Racer Brown

with PETE PETERSEN'S CADILLAC

has attained a speed of 103.122 *miles per hour. Date* SEPT. 1 1952

at BONNEVILLE SALT FLATS, UTAH

Timed by J Otto Crocker

Witness: [illegible]

J. O. CROCKER OFFICIAL TIMER FOR AMERICAN POWER BOAT ASSOCIATION SOUTHERN CALIFORNIA TIMING ASSN., INC.

OFFICE AT 4749 REDLAND DRIVE • SAN DIEGO 15, CALIFORNIA

More for bragging rights fun than a record honor, pals Wally Parks and Racer Brown borrowed Robert "Pete" Petersen's car for romp down the speedway, grinning all the way. Yet it was an official document from respected chief timer J. Otto Crocker. (Courtesy of Petersen Publishing Company.)

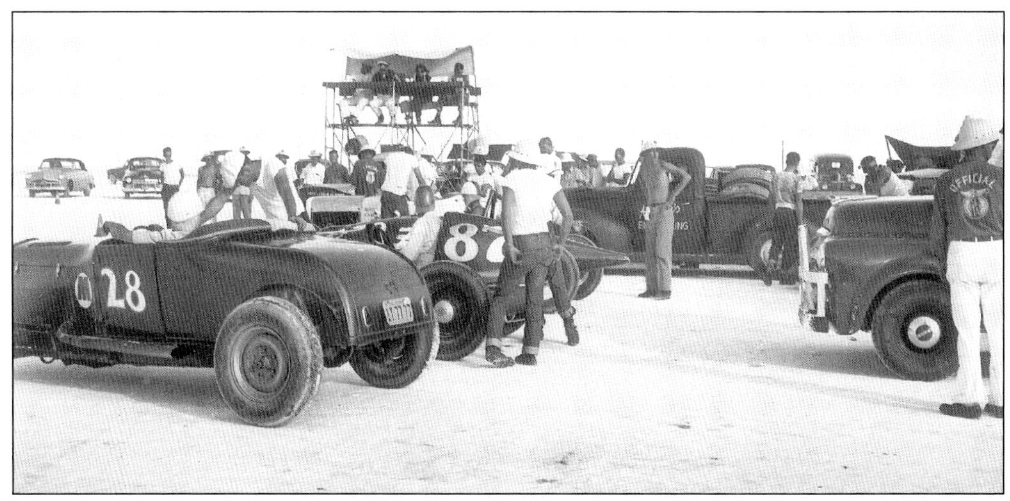

Waiting for their turn on the starting line are Don McLean of San Diego, California, sitting in his No. 28 highboy roadster before his 128-mile-per-hour run and a belly tank lakester entered as the "Dietrich Special" out of Southgate, California, which clocked 141 miles per hour. The elevated timing stand is seen on the right side of the staging lanes. (Courtesy of LPRL/Kay Kimes.)

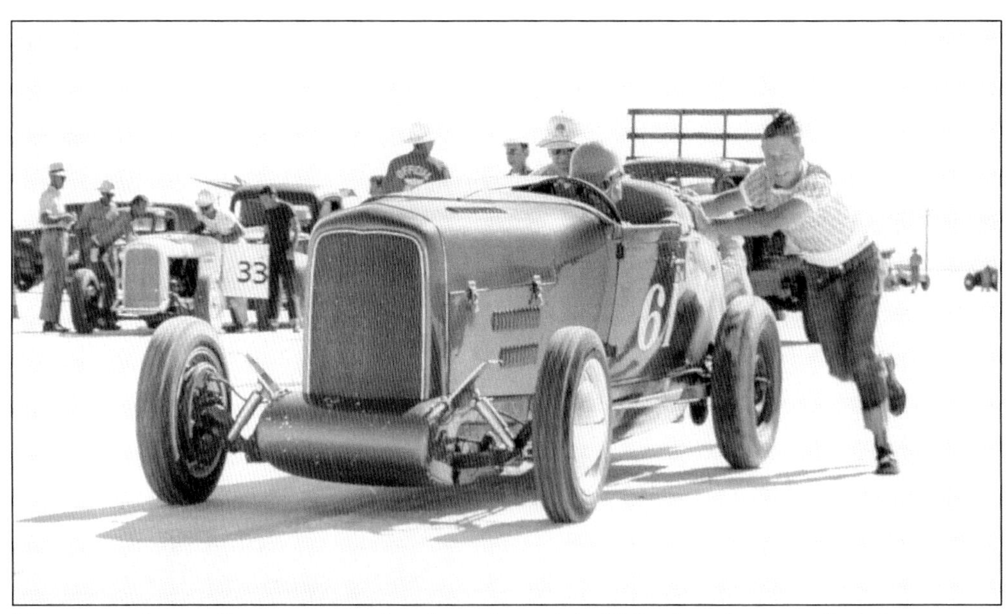

There were plenty of human-powered push-trucks back in 1949, when the upper limit for roadsters was 135 miles per hour. Here, Art Tremaine gets a push to start his 126-mile-per-hour run through the course. During the first five days of competition, there was no limit put on how many runs a car could make. (Courtesy of LPRL/SCTA Archives.)

The puddle of oil under the belly tank's body just aft of the front axle is not a good sign for the crew as they begin disassembling the engine to check for damage. The dirty overalls are a sign that things may not be going too well for the team and that this is not the first time the engine is getting a deep look. (Courtesy of LPRL/ Bruce Geisler.)

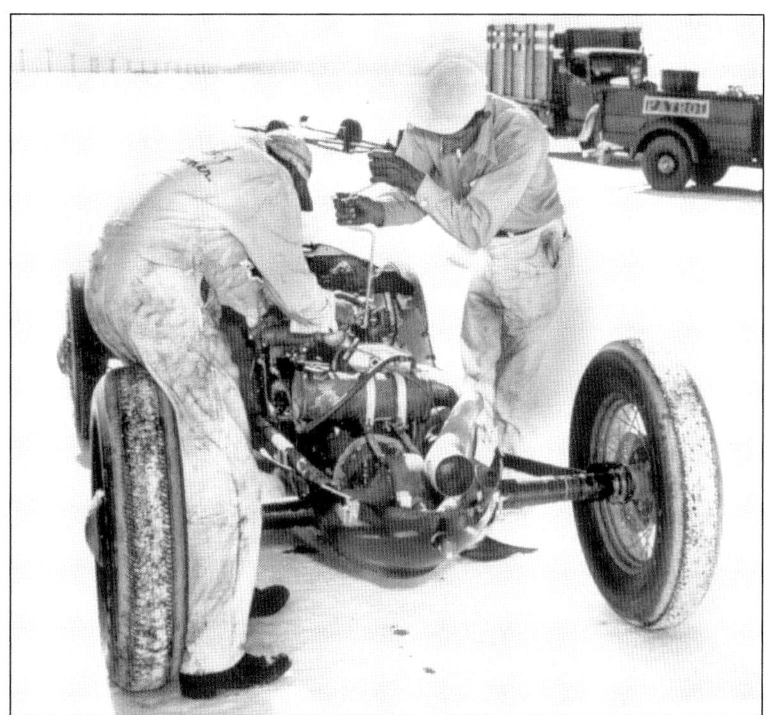

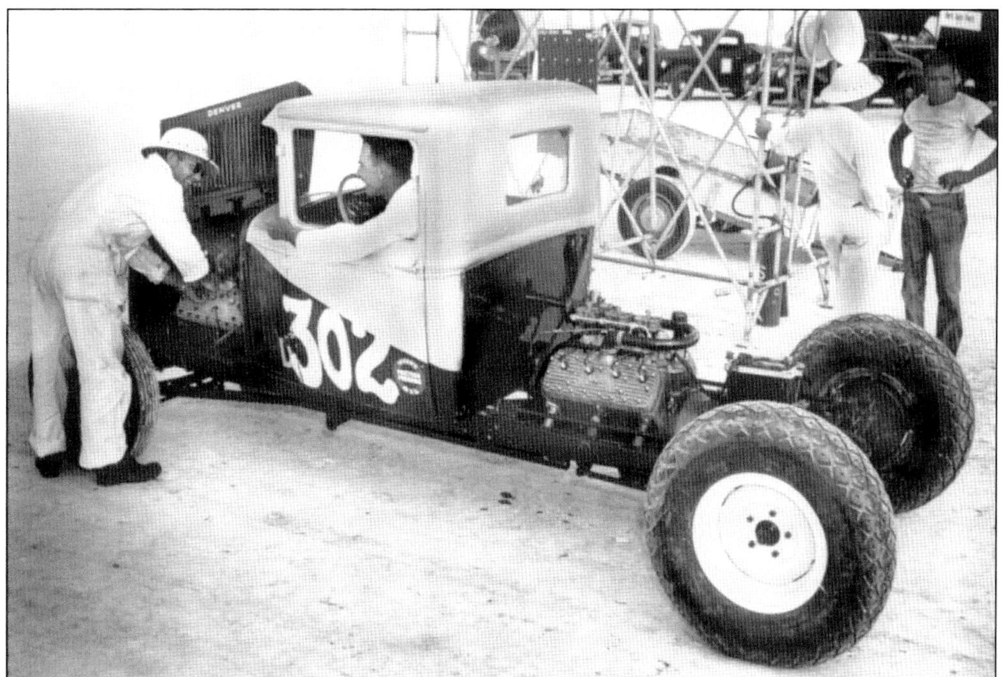

Bill Kenz, in the driver's seat, showed up with a twin-engine flathead-powered pickup dubbed "Odd Rod." Frank Liston made last-minute adjustments on the starting line to one of the two Ford V8s. The truck posted a very respectable 139-mile-per-hour average despite the treaded tires. Racers would soon learn treadless tires ensured more speed through less rolling resistance. (Courtesy of LPRL/SCTA Archives.)

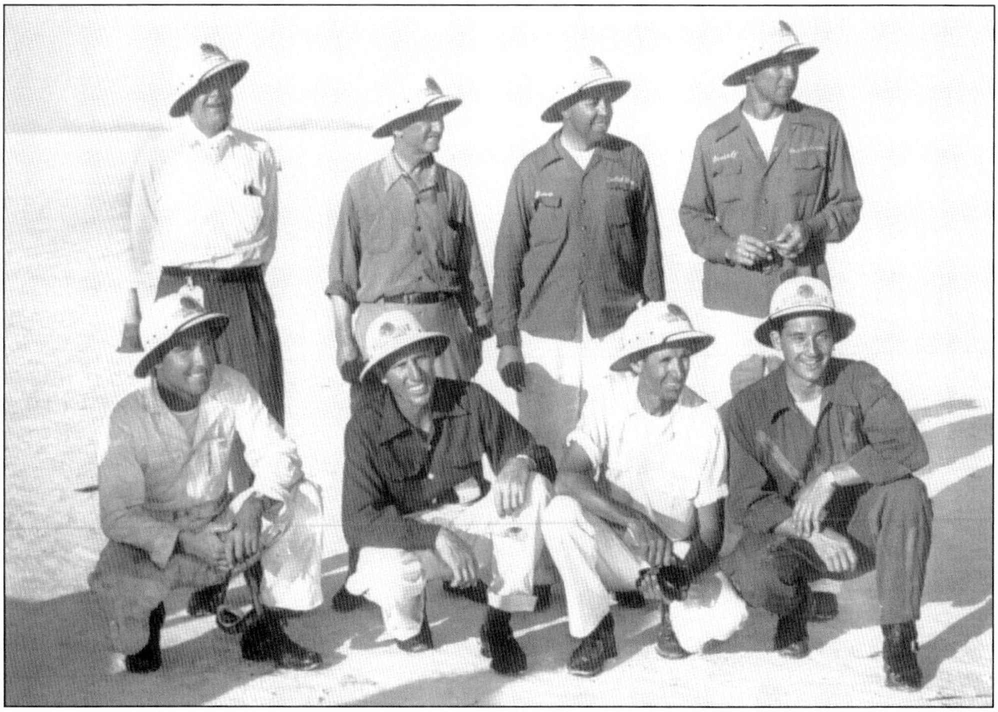

Pictured are, from left to right, (first row) George Radnich; Marvin Lee; Wally Parks; and Robert Petersen, Petersen Publishing; (second row) Lee O. Ryan, publisher of *Hot Rod* and *Motor Trend* magazines, who went to Salt Lake City with Parks to solicit the use of Bonneville Salt Flats for a one-time SCTA trial event; Union Oil's Earl Cooper; Bozy Willis; and race chairman George Prussell. The pith helmets became treasured mementos. (Courtesy of LPRL/SCTA Archives.)

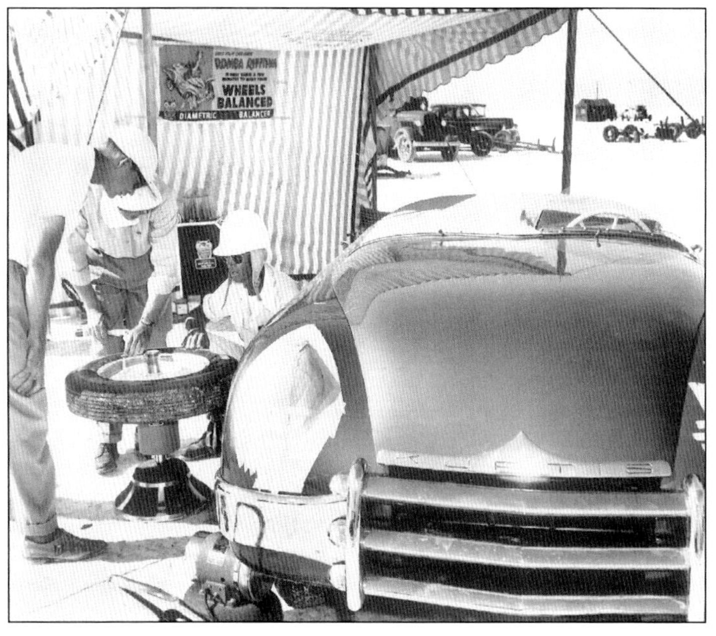

In addition to helping racers in the salt, Service Sales Company of Dallas, Texas, was a manufacturer of the official wheel balancer of speed trials, presenting the "Fastest Two-Way Record Speed Average at the Meet," which included the gift of a complete diametric wheel balancing unit, parts, and tools. The prized wheel weights with spring steel clips that do not loosen at high speed came from Kokomo, Indiana, maker Lucas Mfg. Co. (Courtesy of LPRL/Tim Rochlitzer.)

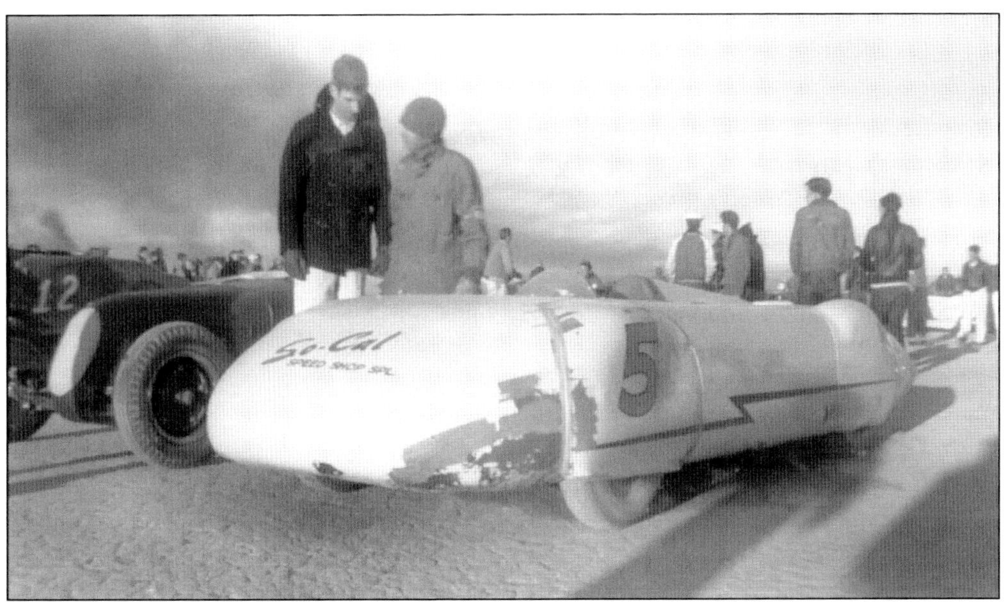

Despite the highway mishap driving up 750 miles from Los Angeles, the Dean Batchelor and Alex Xydias Class C aluminum-body streamliner entry clocked an eyebrow-raising 193.540 miles per hour at Bonneville during the inaugural Bonneville Nationals amateur speed trials. This feat also inspired *Hot Rod Magazine* to bestow national champion honors, presenting the duo with its Top Time trophy for the fastest one-way recorded speed. (Courtesy of LPRL/Norm Gernhardt.)

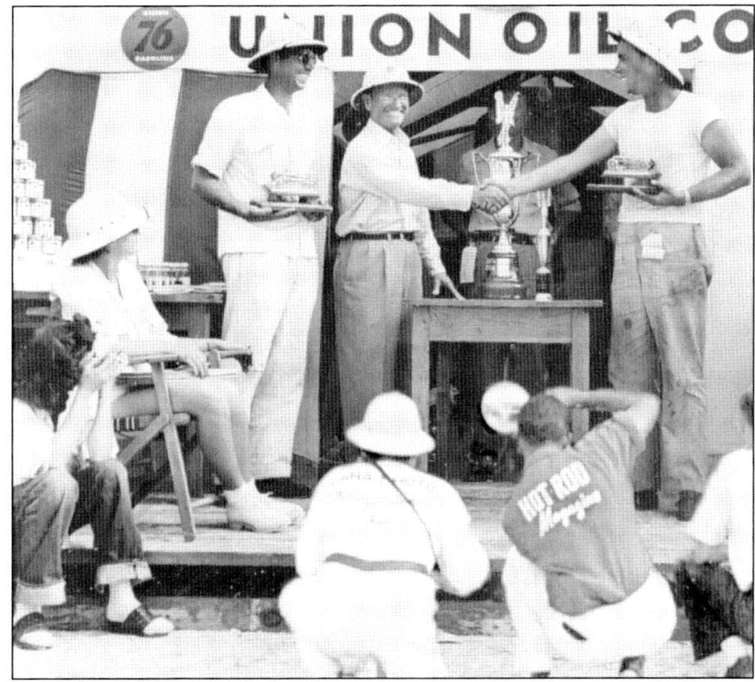

From left to right are Alex Xydias, owner of the SoCal Speed Shop; Union Oil's Earl Cooper; and Dean Batchelor. The seated lady with the white pith helmet is Phyllis Lindsley, who was a tremendous contributor in many ways to the first speed trial event. In the foreground are Eric Rickman, working for Dana Photo, and Robert "Pete" Petersen, in the *Hot Rod Magazine* shirt. (Courtesy of Petersen Publishing Company.)

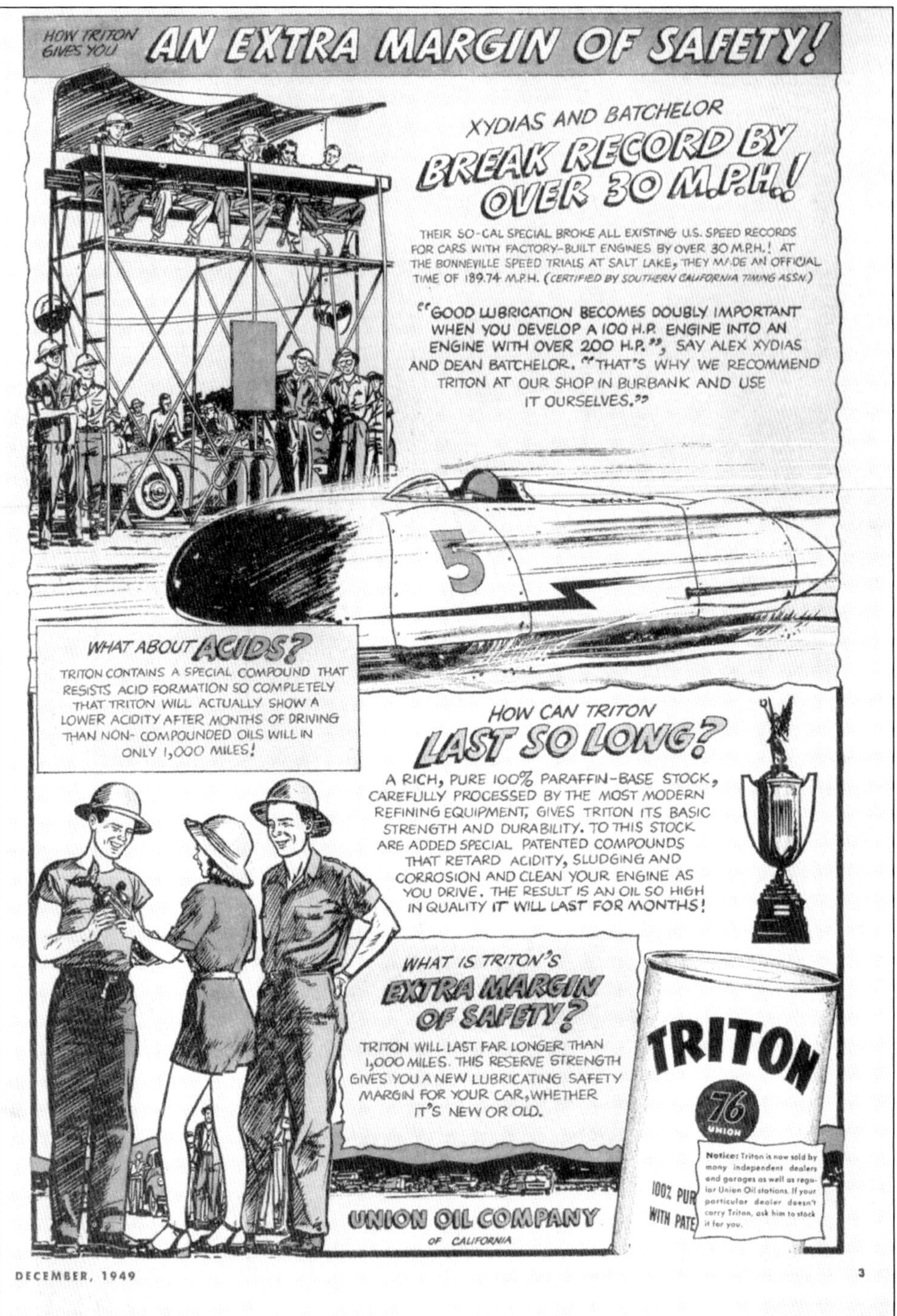

Alex Xydias and Dean Batchelor came to the salt hot rod hopefuls and went home hot rod heroes. None were more surprised (and pleased) than they were at the 189-mile-per-hour record they posted at the first Speedweek in 1949. It was 30 miles per hour higher than any previous amateur land speed record. Union Oil ran this advertisement repeatedly all over the country, making the pair as famous as an Indy 500 winner. (Courtesy of Union Oil.)

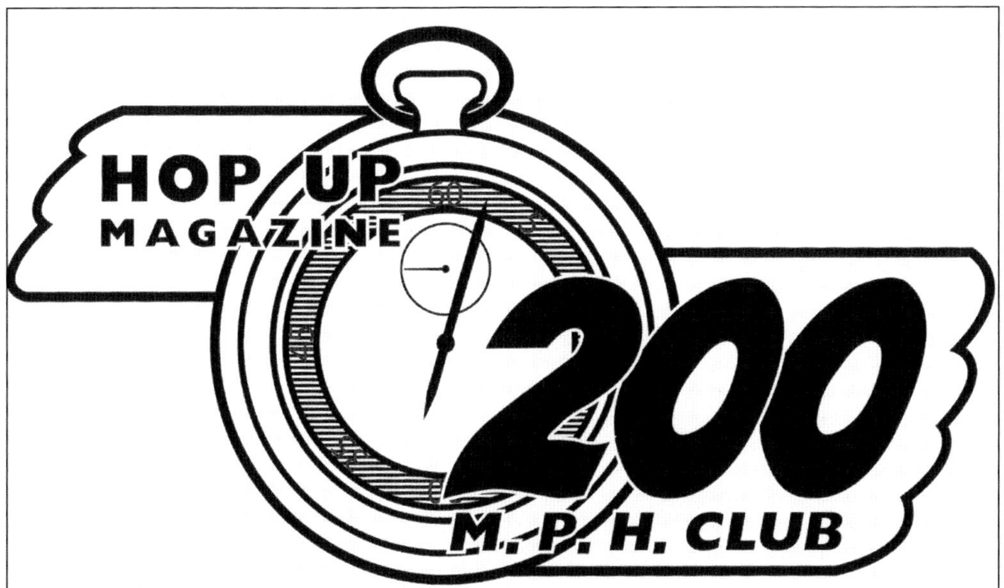

This was the first logo designed to promote the Bonneville 200 MPH Club after its founding in 1953 and was only to be worn by inducted members. The club had five charter members who voted to include three more European members, including Capt. George Eyston, who then served as the club's first president. (Courtesy of LPRL/Bonneville 200 MPH Club.)

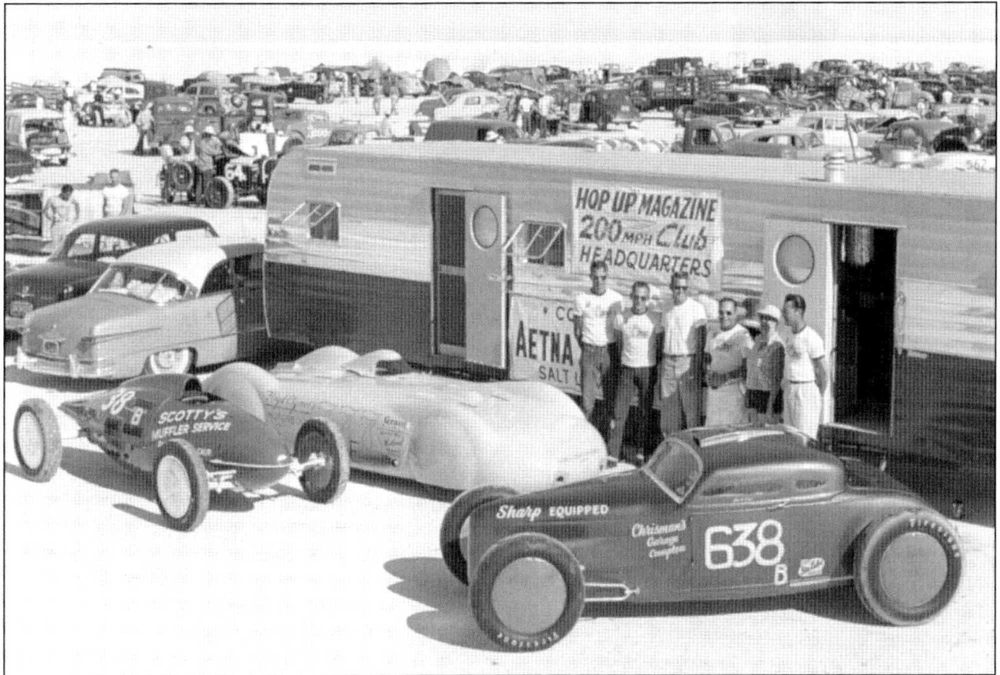

Hop Up Magazine publisher Bill Quinn sponsored not only the Bonneville 200 MPH Club year-round but brought up the headquarters trailer for the 1953 event. Standing behind the race cars are, from left to right, Otto Ryssman, Art Chrisman, Leroy Holmes, Willie Young, unidentified (possibly Young's mother), and George Hill. Note a jam-packed pit area surrounding the group. (Courtesy of Rick Hill/Ed Elliot photograph.)

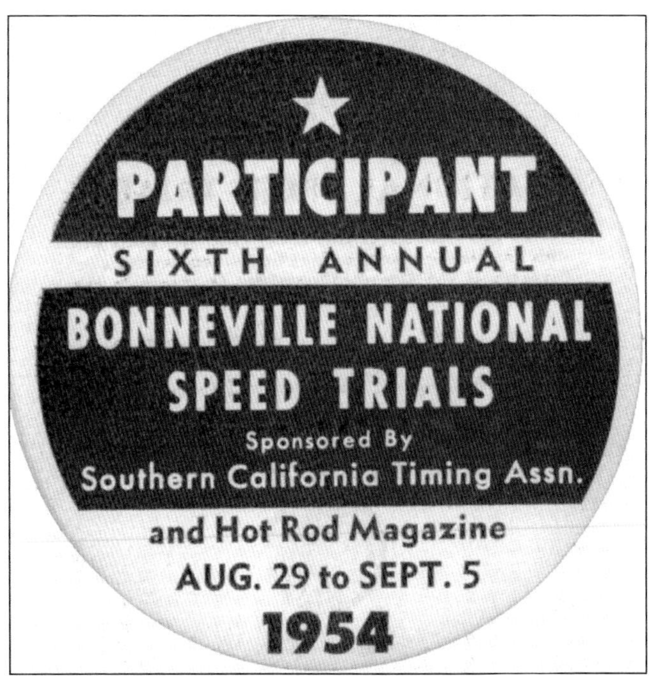

Part of the entry fee included a participant sticker, something that set apart the racers from the spectators. Most stickers were immediately applied to the speed machines as a badge of speed honor to remain for years on end. (Courtesy of LandSpeed Louise.)

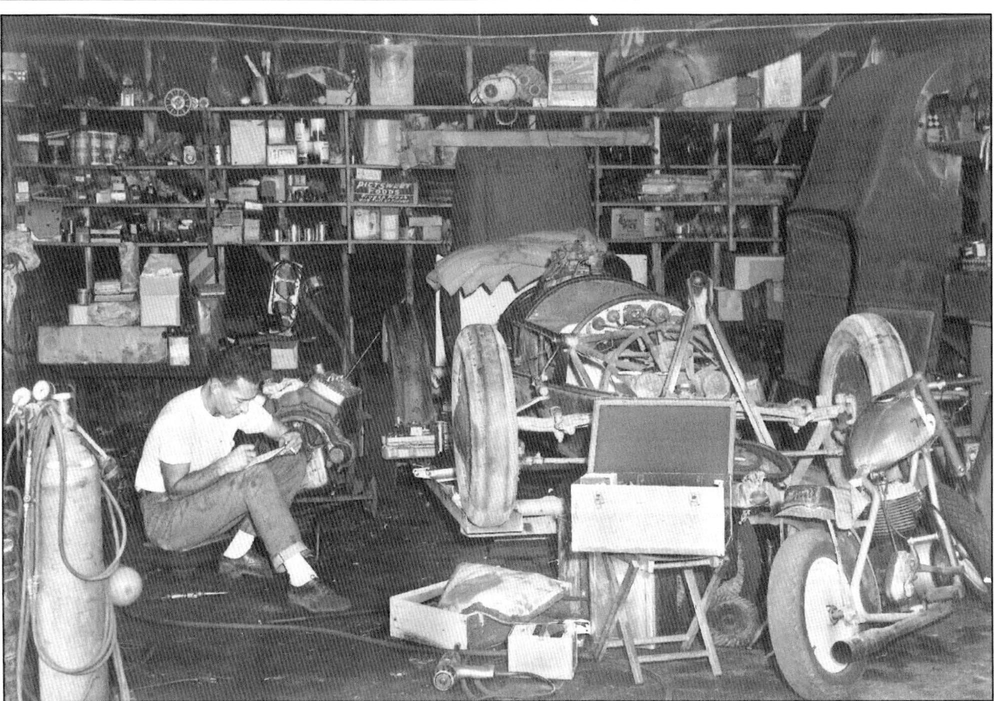

Before a driver can get all the glory from speed records set, the speed machine must be carefully designed and built. Tom "Blow or Go" Beatty works out a detail in his Southern California home garage, where he built everything himself. It is certain the acetylene tank in the lower left got a quite a bit of use. On the top shelf above the belly tank lakester sits one of many roots blowers for which he was famous for extracting speed or explosions—upwards of seven in one Speedweek! Note the Mustang motorcycle at right. (Courtesy of LPRL/ Frances "Frankie" Beatty.)

Coming to Bonneville to watch races meant driving directly on the salt. In wet years, the loose salt is thrown off tires with the vengeance of cottage cheese on an angry fan blade. Every car would look like this not long after visiting the starting line, pits, and high-speed shutdown area. (Courtesy of LPRL/Milton McCard photograph.)

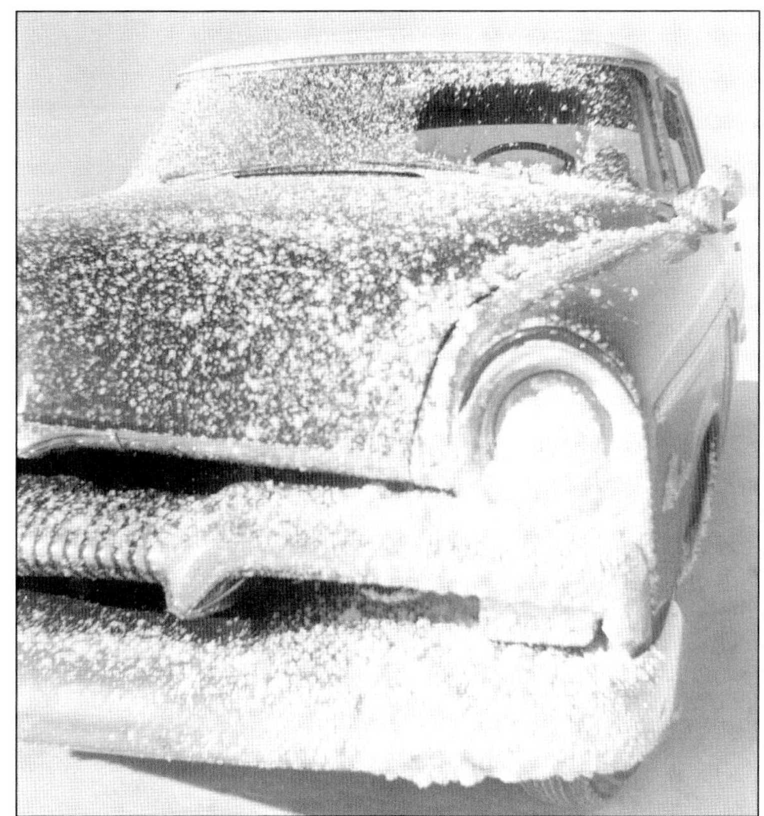

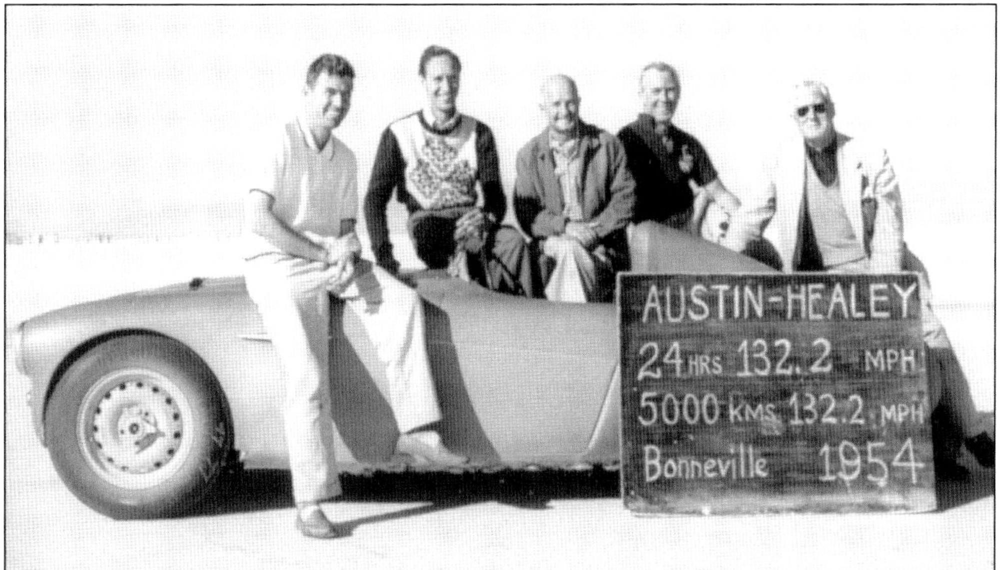

Healey mounted an endurance record run attempt in 1954 to boost confidence among the buying public. The leader board touted two significant records: a 24-hour run performed by alternating drivers and a kilometer distance effort. Pictured are, from left to right, Carroll Shelby (still a hot shot driver at the time), Roy Jackson-Moore, Donald Healy, M. Morris-Goodall, and world-record setter Capt. George E.T. Eyston. (Courtesy of Roy Jackson-Moore.)

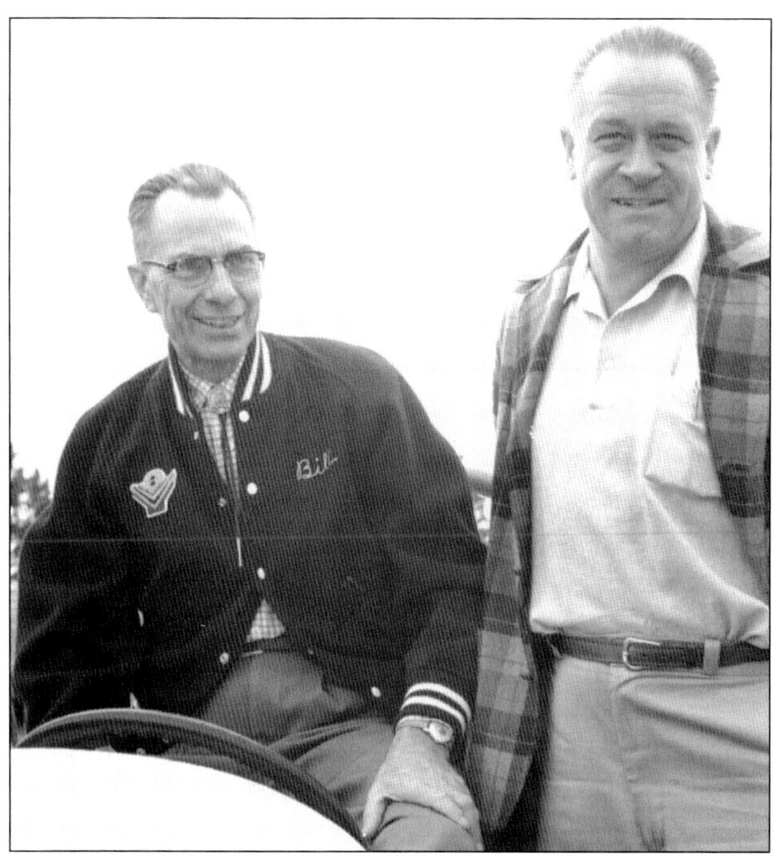

More people remember the names of the innovative, record-setting race cars than they do the names of the men who built and raced them. Fewer still recall what they looked like. Bill Kenz (left) and Roy Leslie (right) were partners responsible for the seriously fast 777 streamliner as well as the 1949 "Odd Rod" truck. (Courtesy of Tim Rochlitzer.)

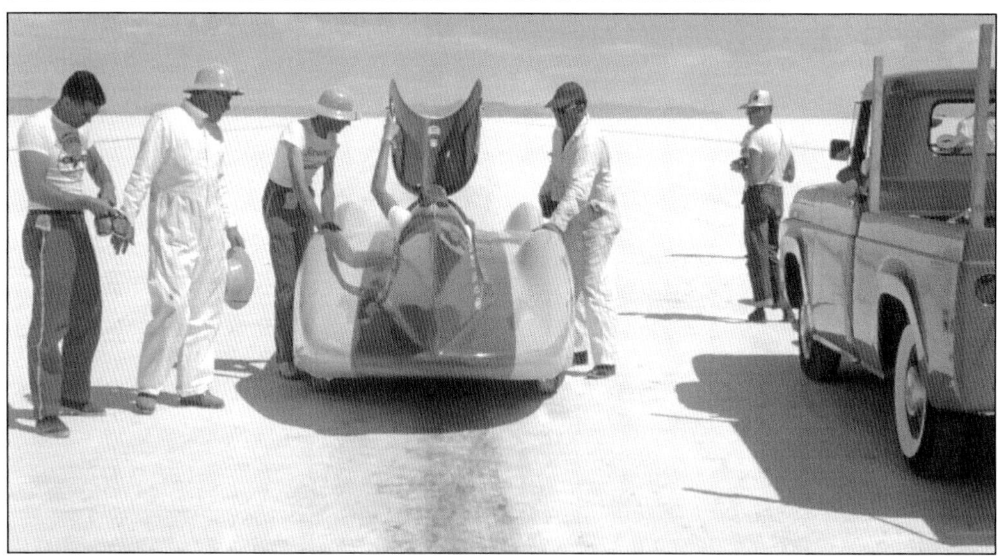

The Denver, Colorado–based "777" streamliner crew on the left of Cal Kennedy, Roy Leslie and Bill Kenz leaning on the car, help driver Willie Young into the driver's seat. Entered as the "Floyd Clymer Motorbook Special," it was painted bright yellow and red. The 200-plus-mile-per-hour car could always be counted on to run at speeds around 250 using a pair of 1946 Ford flathead engines. (Courtesy of LPRL/Lynn Yakel.)

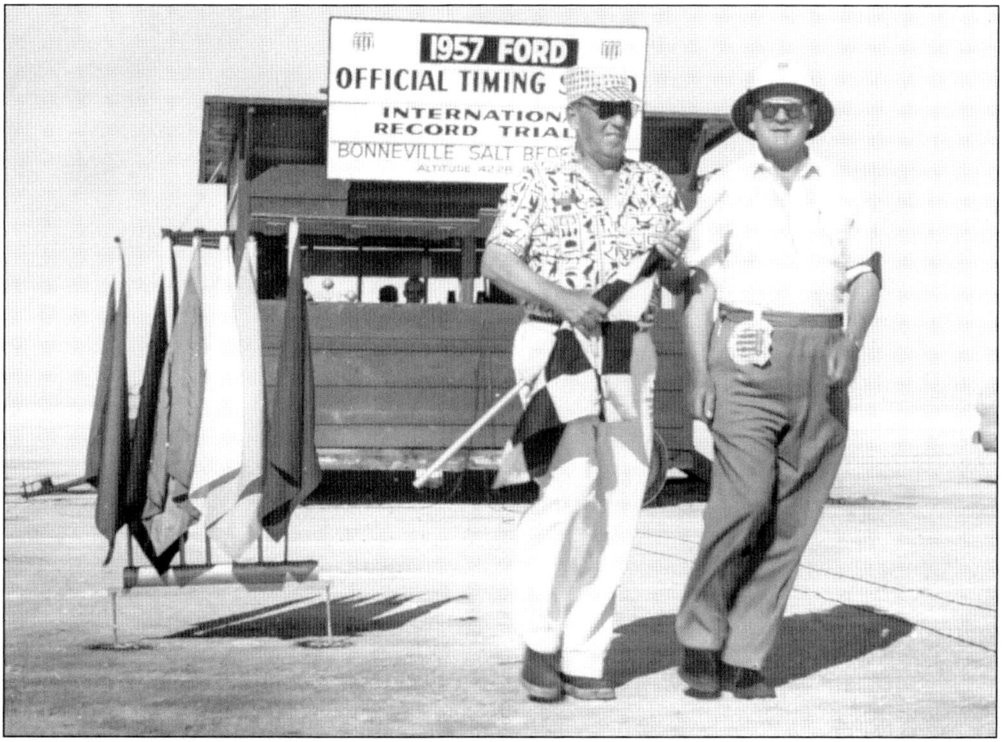

The 1957 endurance runs were officiated by the United States Auto Club (USAC) and Federation Internationale de l'Automobile (FIA). USAC regional director A.C. Pillsbury (left) and Maj. H.D. Parker (right) step from the timing stand to flag a signal to the passing driver. (Courtesy of LPRL/Tim Kraushaar.)

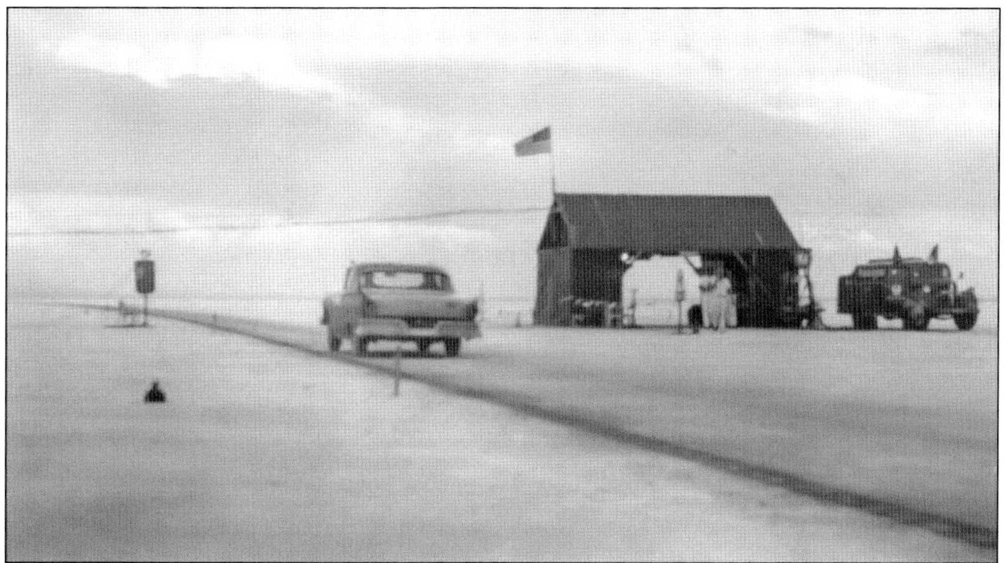

Dawn breaks in the east, and a Ford test car continues its 1957 night-and-day tour of the 10-mile circle at a speed well in excess of 100 miles per hour. Seen to the left of the car is a kerosene smudge pot, one of hundreds that marked the course each night. The structure to the right flying the American flag is the pit stop service building. (Courtesy of LPRL/Tim Kraushaar.)

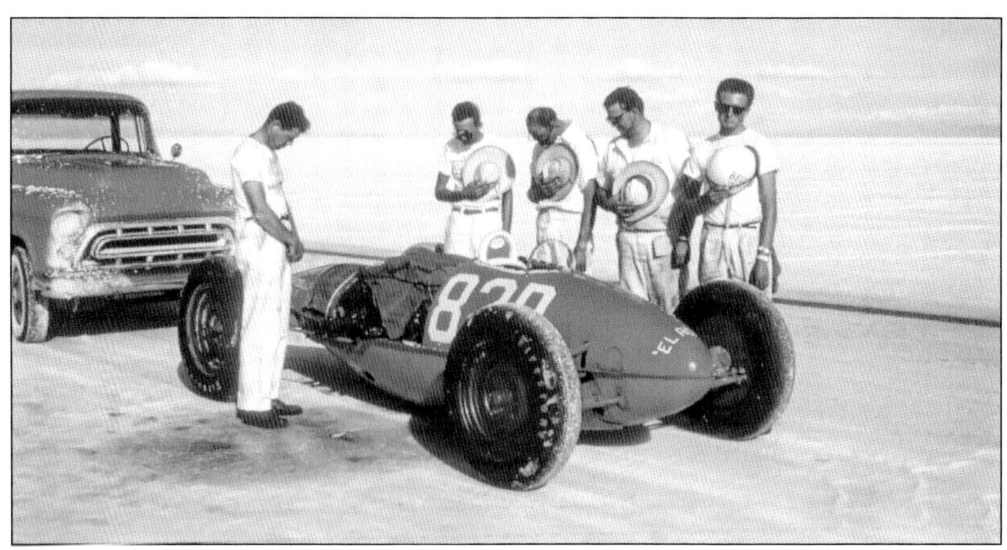

Behind every speed record set is a woefully long trail of broken parts. Here, the 1957 crew of the Specialty Automotive cherry-red belly tank lakester performs a salt-side memorial service honoring the passing of the 342 Nailhead Buick engine. The 193-mile-per-hour run was trouble free until just past the timing traps. Backing off the throttle, the valves sank and destroyed the cylinder heads. Pictured are, from left to right, Kay Kimes, Lynn Yakel, Bill Fowler, Jerry Eisert, and driver Bob Opperman. (Courtesy of LPRL/Lynn Yakel.)

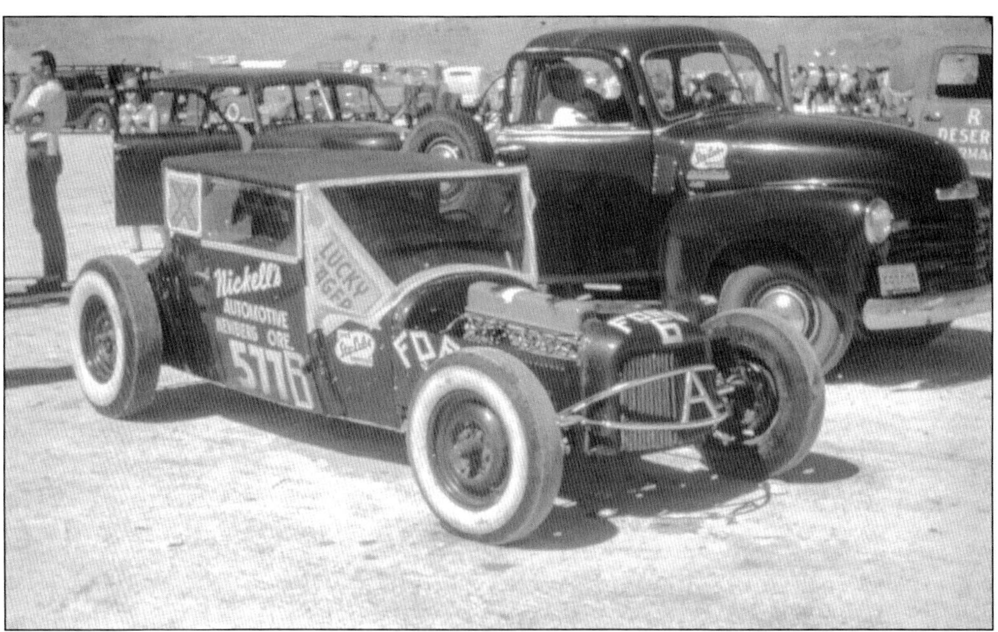

The 1950s were a decade of intense experimentation when it became obvious that slippery body shapes were as essential as horsepower. Here, Kenny Austin's unusual street-driven car has a 1927 Model T body that has been chopped and channeled onto a homemade chassis. Austin taped Plexiglass and cardboard at strategic points to offset the body bluntness and create a more slippery airflow to help the overhead valve Ford V6 engine. Did it work? Only the timing clocks would tell the tale. (Courtesy of LPRL/Tony Waters.)

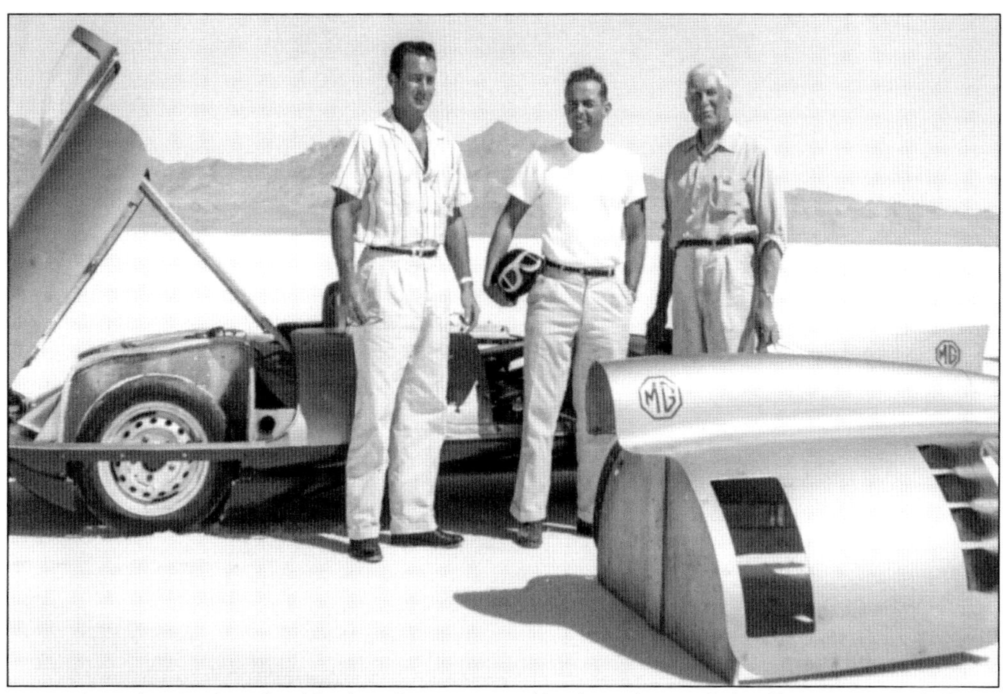

It is 1959, and MG of England had Stirling Moss and back-up driver Phil Hill strapping on helmets to set various speed and endurance records to boost marketing efforts. Wet weather quashed many hopes, though. Later, on October 3, Hill returned to ink a 254-mile-per-hour Class F record. Pictured are, from left to right, George Hill, Phil Hill, and Capt. George Eyston. (Courtesy of Rick Hill.)

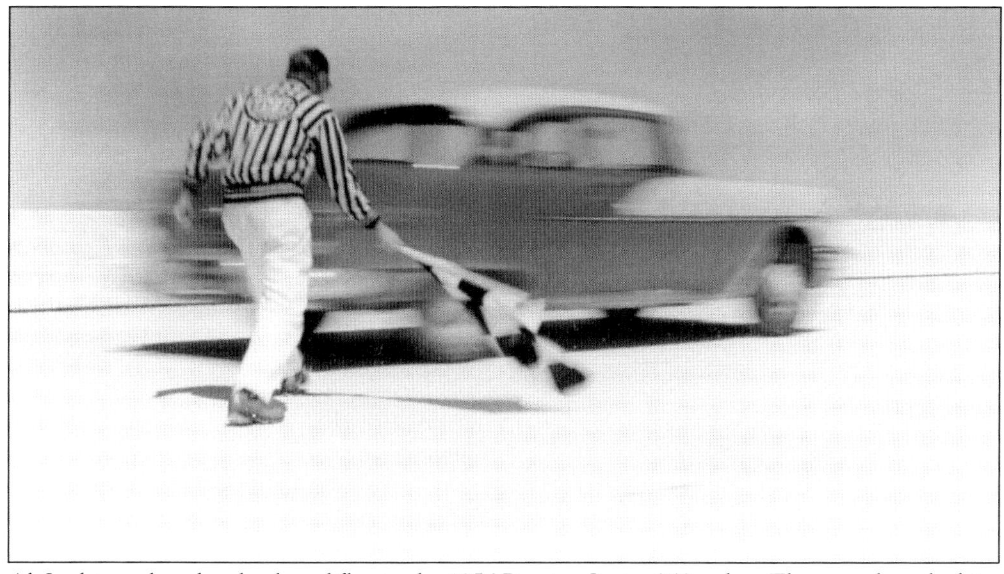

Ab Jenkins takes the checkered flag in the 1956 Pontiac Series 860 sedan. The records set by him and his son Marvin inspired the GM division to rename the model "Bonneville" the following year. This was Ab's last speed record. The racing giant died in Detroit later that year while on a promotional tour for GM at age 73. (Courtesy of Noma and Marvin Jenkins.)

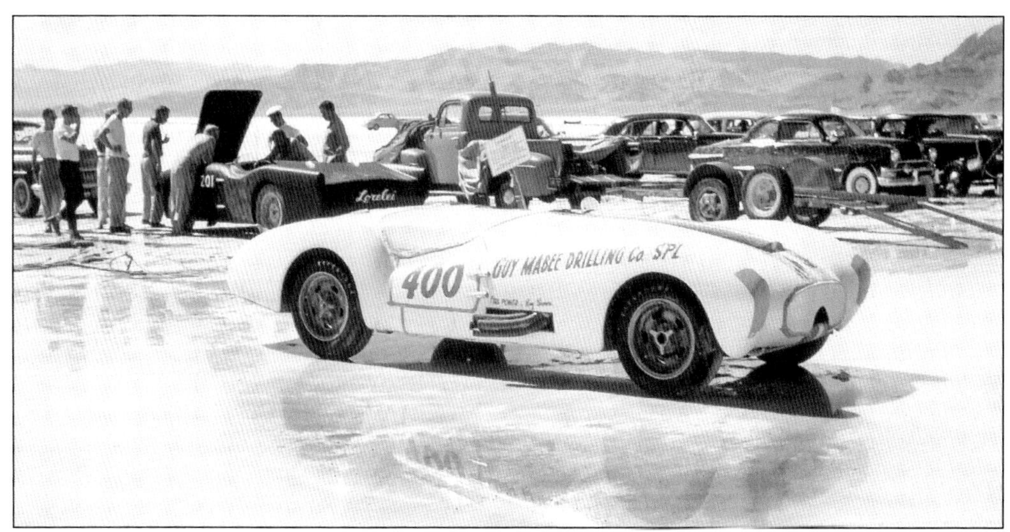

In the 1950s, Texans Guy and Joe Mabee built a sports car hoping for a Bonneville speed record as well as something to blast up Pike's Peak and go road racing. They relied on the help of Denny Larsen and engine builder Ray Brown to create their Victress-bodied "Special," which appeared for the first time in 1953. Running on a volatile mix of alcohol and nitro methane, Joe Mabee drove the car to a 203.105-mile-per-hour two-way average. The press hailed it as "The World's Fastest Sports Car," and the car had many years of racing successes. (Courtesy of LPRL/Tony Waters photograph.)

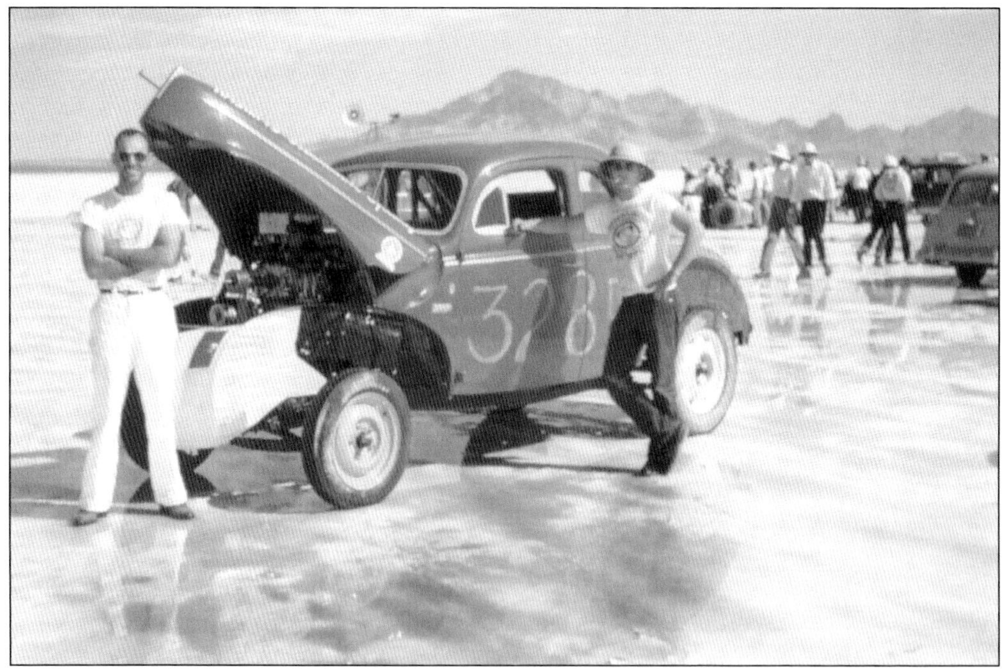

Waiting for the rain shower to evaporate, the No. 328 entered by the Haskim-Aubrey pair from Bakersfield, California, confidently poses for posterity. Running in Class D (coupe and sedan), the team's Mercury engine managed a top speed of 141.06 miles per hour, some 20 miles per hour off the record-setting pace, but they returned for years, improving all the time. (Courtesy of LPRL/Tony Waters.)

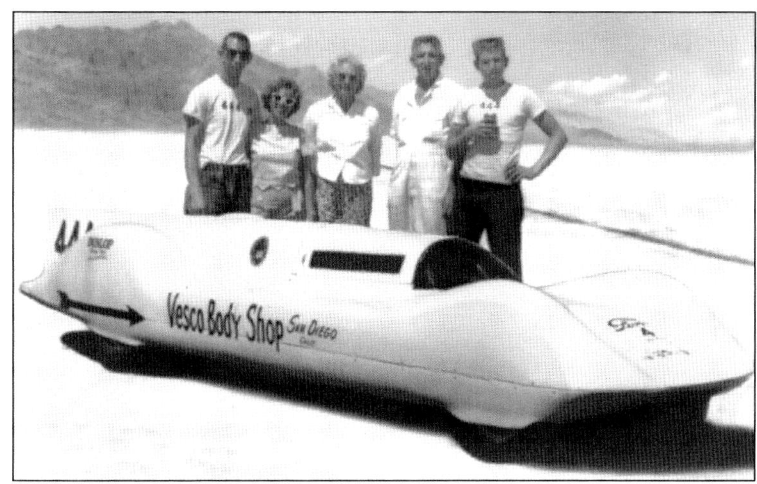

It has always been a family affair on the salt for the Vesco clan. Pictured here in 1961 are, from left to right, Don and Norma Vesco, mom Betty, dad John, and young Rick Vesco in front of the 444 streamliner, a vehicle that continues to race today with the same number. (Courtesy of the Vesco family.)

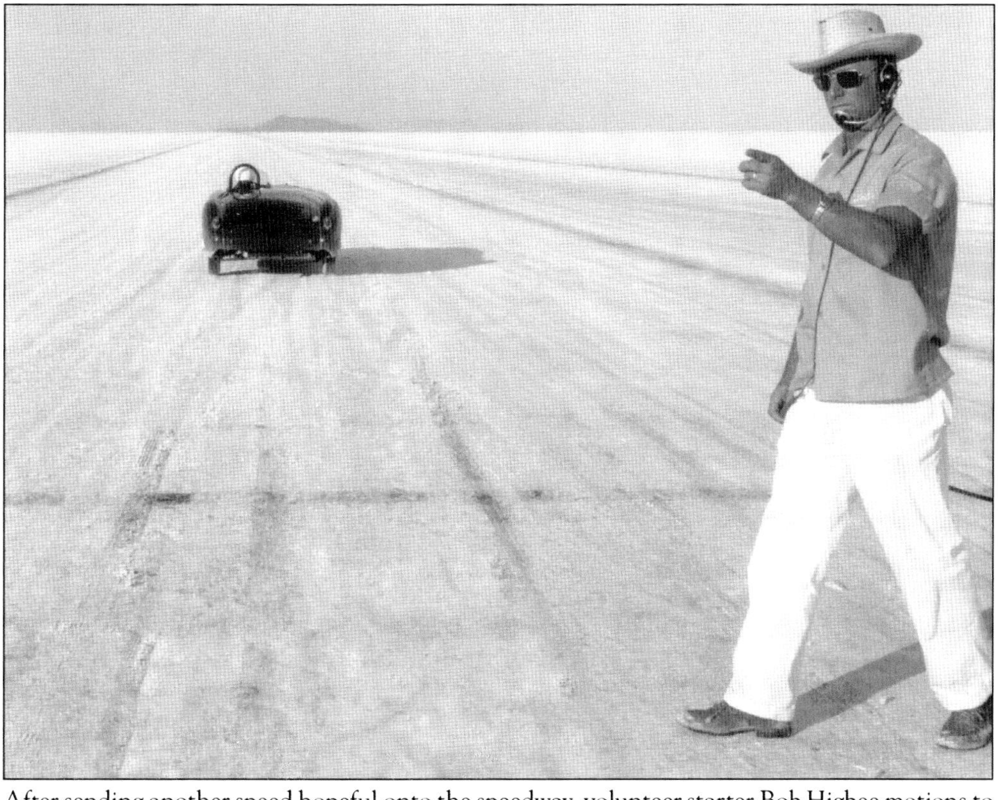

After sending another speed hopeful onto the speedway, volunteer starter Bob Higbee motions to the next 1959 participant to come to race. None of these speed machines come to the salt without plenty of volunteer help. Very few are big operations; most are small gatherings of like-minded speed hopefuls who delight in sharing tales with spectators who have unrestricted access to the pits. (Courtesy of Bob Higbee.)

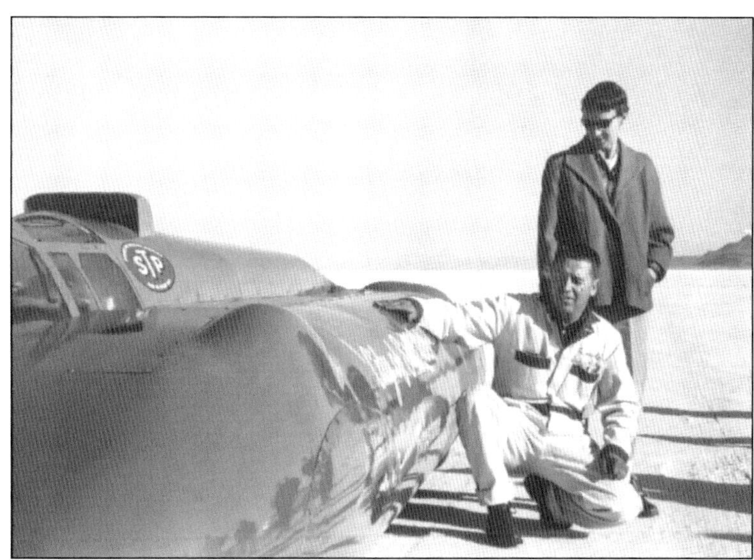

Pictured here are builder and driver Athol Graham with his wife, Zeldine, posing next to the "Spirit of Salt Lake" in 1959. Athol, a Utah native, would later lose his life attempting a speed record, and Zeldine would rebuild the car to shepherd her husband's speed dream forward with another driver. (Courtesy of Zeldine Graham.)

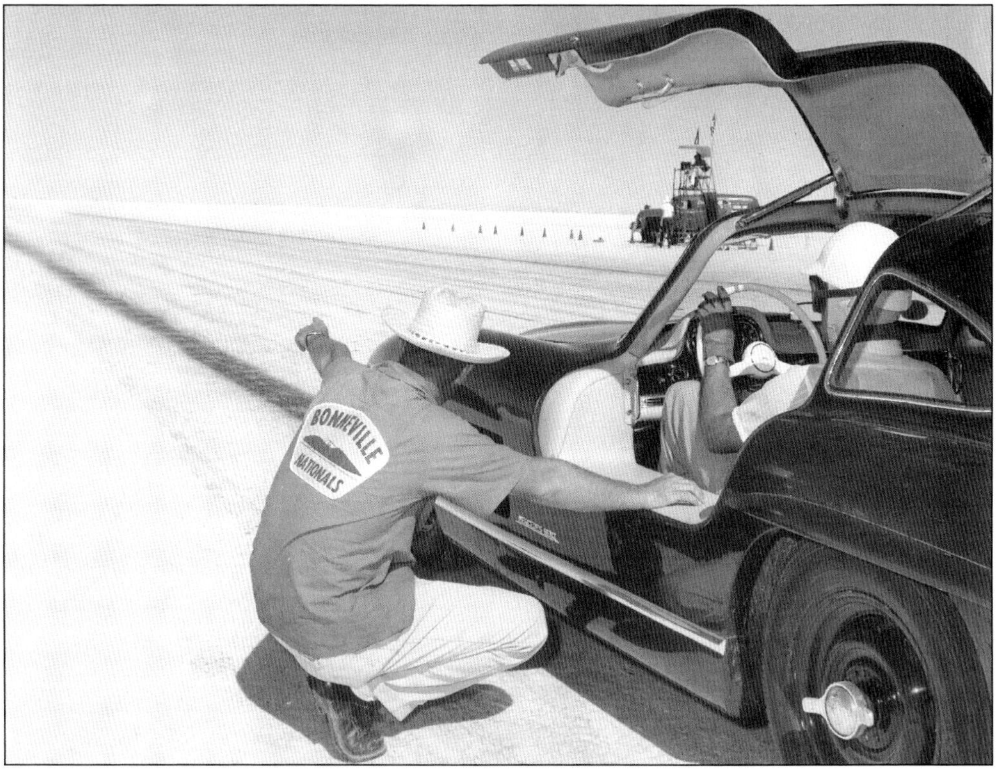

In 1959, Bonneville Speedweek course starter Bob Higbee, with his back to the camera, offers last-minute instructions to No. 120 A/Sports Racing Class driver Albert Schmidt of Cincinnati, Ohio. A few minutes later, Schmidt clocked 180.00 miles per hour in his street-driven Mercedes Gullwing. (Courtesy of Bob Higbee.)

Four

The Jet Age

Axial Flow Blows Off the Reciprocators

Despite the fabulous salt racing surface, there is only so much traction possible before wheel spin takes over. Any wheel-driven machine transferring too much engine power to the wheels too fast wastes the energy needed to record maximum velocity past the timing clocks. Another problem racers encountered was running out of real estate while gradually applying power.

Frustrated speed dreamers in the 1950s searched for an ultimate balance and discovered that pistons are primitive in comparison to the sophisticated power delivered gracefully, repeatedly from turbines, jets, and even rockets.

First to the salt in 1960 was 49-year-old obstetrician Dr. Nathan Ostitch, who spent $50,000 to build his 28.5-foot-long, brilliant-red "Flying Caduceus" jet car powered by a J47 turbojet engine with a body shaped in California Polytechnic College's wind tunnel.

But not all were ready to rely solely on thrust that year. Britain's Donald Campbell spent millions on a svelte turbine-powered car that delivered power to the wheels fed by a complicated transmission. He arrived with all the bravado of a military operation, but oddly, after carefully ramping up to 240 miles per hour, suddenly got "ants in his pants" and sprinted to 345 miles per hour before crashing dramatically. He survived but made scrap metal out of the multimillion-dollar car.

In 1962, Craig Breedlove's first attempts were disastrous until Lockheed Skunkworks engineer Walt Sheehan (the only other man to ever drive the "Spirit of America") joined the team and shepherded the young California kid to five world marks.

Finally, in 1964, after 16 years of trying to break John Cobb's record, Breedlove succeeded and raised the curtain on the record honors changing hands six times.

Breedlove lost and regained the record repeatedly to Art Arfons, Walt Arfons, and Tom Green until Gary Gabelich drove Reaction Dynamics, Inc.'s "The Blue Flame" rocket car to 630 miles per hour in 1970. It remains the fastest American-built hot rod ever created.

Also emerging were noted female jet car drivers Lee Breedlove, Paula Murphy, and Betty Skelton, who each drove one of the record-setting jet cars.

The thrust-powered cars forced the regulatory authority Federation Internationale de L'Automobile (FIA) to amend its International Sporting Code and establish a category called International Records for Special Vehicles.

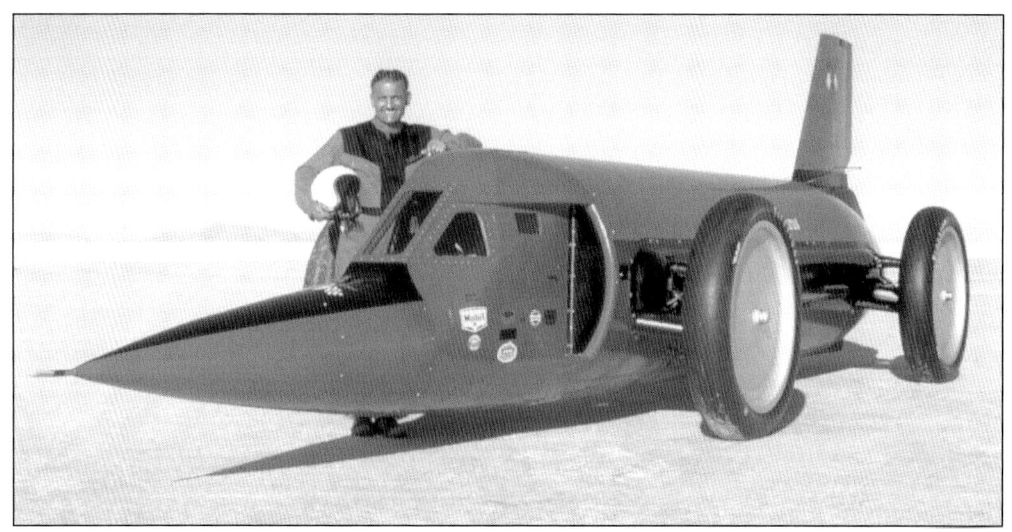

Pictured here is the first man to run a jet on the salt, Dr. Nathan Ostitch, standing beside the "Flying Caduceus" in preparation for a speed run in 1960. Named after the medical emblem taken from Greek mythology, the 7,000-horsepower General Electric J47 turbojet came out of a Boeing B-36 bomber. "To attempt 500-mile-an-hour-plus speeds with the familiar piston engine in the age of jet technology is not practical," Dr. Ostitch stated. In 1962, the doctor clocked 331 miles per hour before the front wheel came off and spun the car three times before Ostitch could pop the parachute. (Courtesy of LPRL/Wally Parks.)

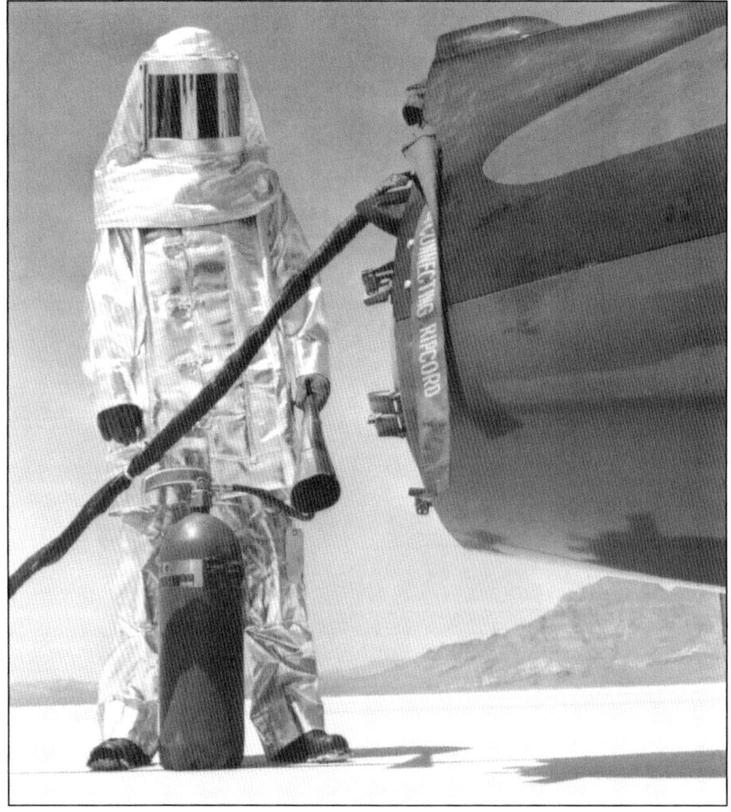

A crewman stands at the ready in safety gear with a fire extinguisher as Nathan Ostitch fires up the 28.5-foot "Flying Caduceus" turbojet fed by a 45-gallon kerosene fuel tank. The four-foot-diameter frame was fabricated as a "birdcage" design, made of round and rectangular steel tubing. Forged from solid blocks, each aluminum wheel weighs 160 pounds, and Firestone tires carry 200 pounds of air pressure and have a scant .020 tread depth. The fire extinguisher was never needed. (Courtesy of Firestone Tire and Rubber Company.)

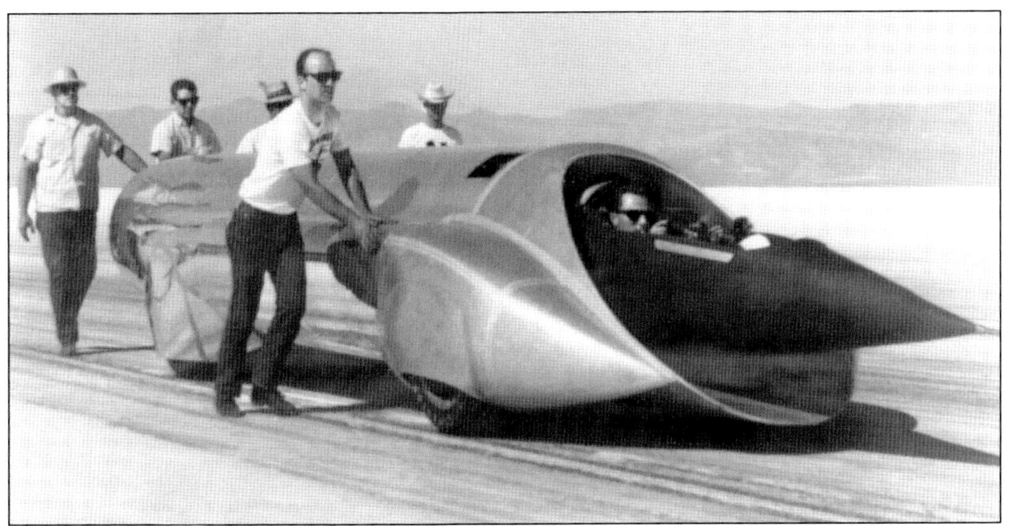

It is 9:00 a.m., and "Infinity" jet car teammates push driver Glenn Leasher to the starting line on Monday, September 10, 1962. Full of hope, owners and builders Romeo Palamides, Vic Elischer, and Harry Burdg planned a leisurely trial run that instead became a rendezvous with death when the car, powered by a J47 engine, crashed at an estimated speed in the high 300s. Leasher, 26, was eager to post big numbers, set a land speed record, and then hurry back to Burlingame, California, where he was to reveal his secret marriage to Lynn Bostic. (Courtesy of Craig Breedlove.)

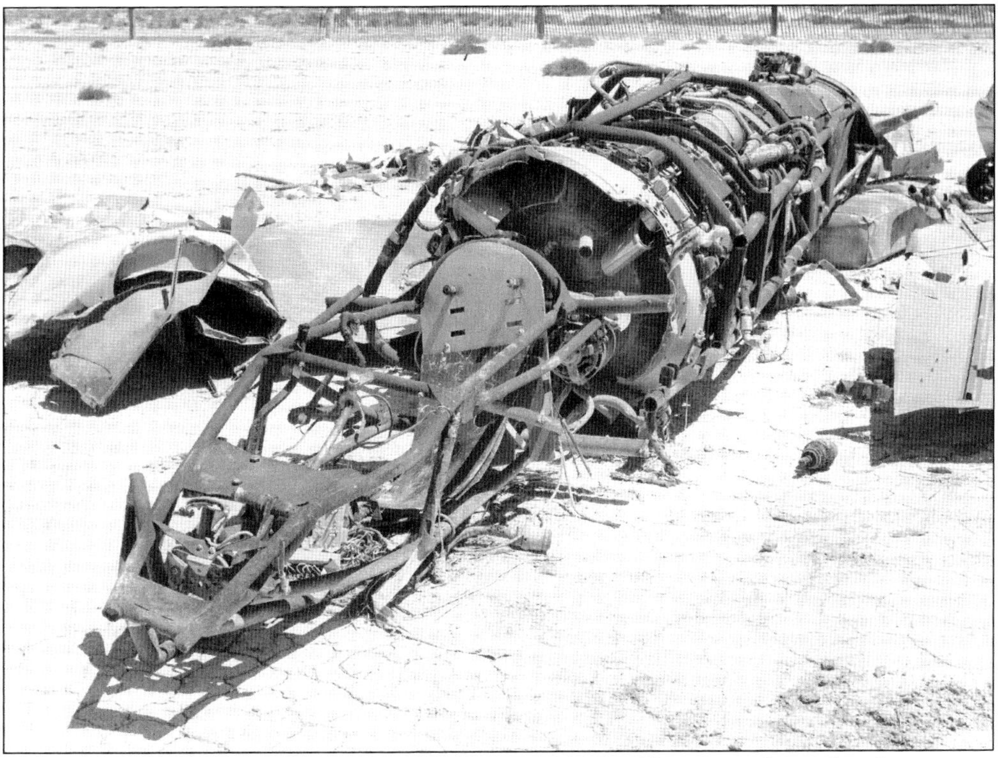

For drag racing driver Glenn Leasher, when things went terribly wrong after only a few practice runs in the "Infinity" jet car, he was killed as the car became a twisted, ripped heap in seconds. Rescue crews had to cut him out of the wreckage. (Courtesy of LPRL.)

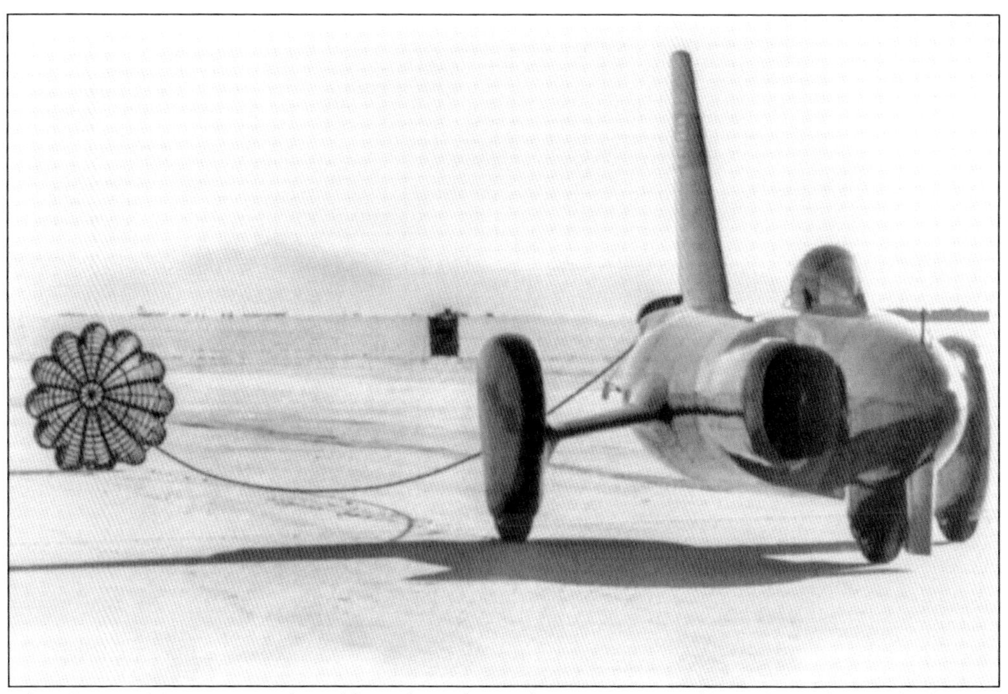

The "Spirit of America" is slowed by a drag chute after setting a world land speed record of 407.45 miles per hour on August 5, 1963. The 26-year-old driver Craig Breedlove of Los Angeles bettered the 16-year-old mark of 394.196 miles per hour set on the same course by the late John Cobb of England. Goodyear and Shell are prime sponsors and believe the car is a capable of 500 miles per hour. (Courtesy of Lee Breedlove.)

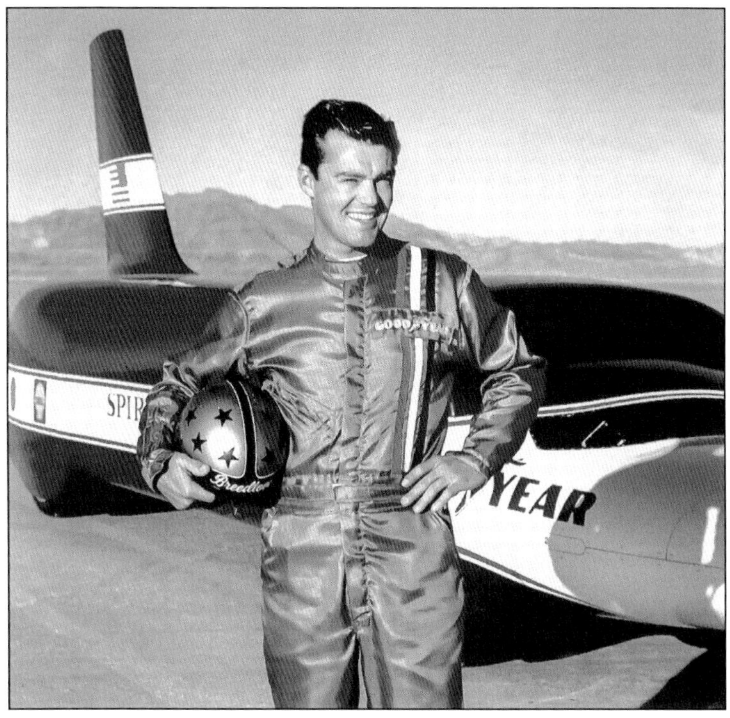

Out of the wheel-driven crowd came hot rodder Norman Craig Breedlove, a skinny kid with the hee-haw laughter of a mule who had it bad for velocity. Driving his J47 jet car named "Spirit of America," he did what others could not—Breedlove brought back the world land speed record to the United States. Atop hero hill, he had plenty of company. Breedlove swapped his crown with Donald Campbell, Tom Green, and Art Arfons. (Courtesy of Goodyear Rubber & Tire Company.)

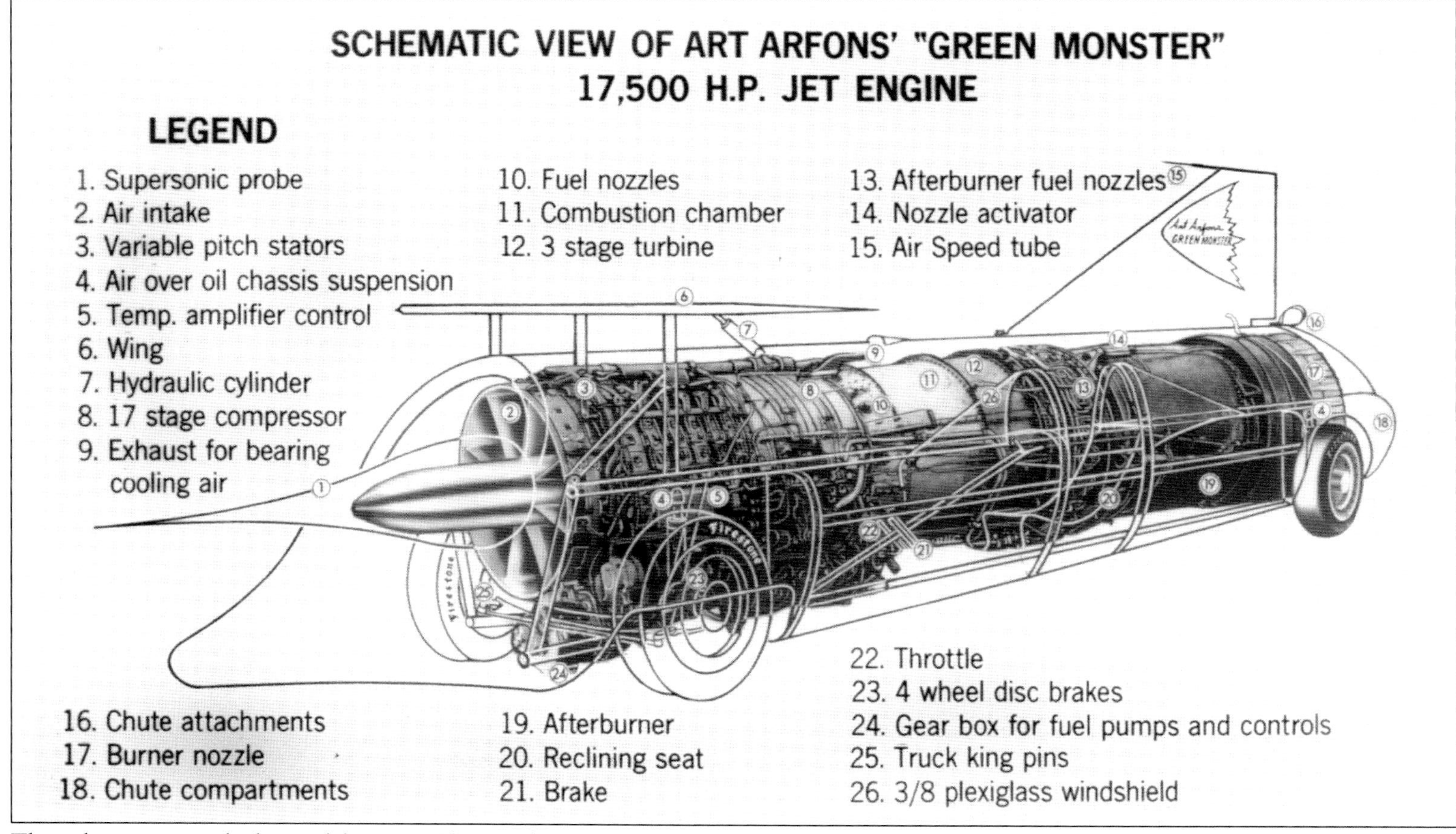

This schematic reveals the modifications Akron, Ohio, resident and racer Art Arfons had made to his "Green Monster" jet car since his record run on November 7, 1965. The major changes were the addition of an air-over-oil chassis suspension to the rear axle and an extension and redesign of the nose section. (Courtesy of Firestone News Service.)

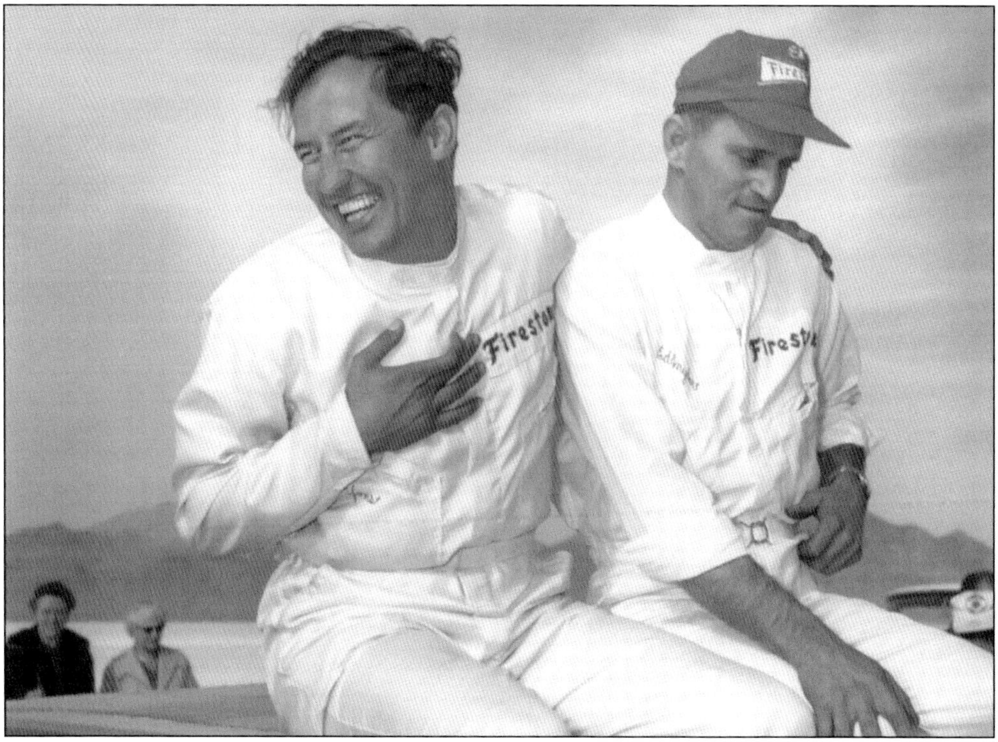

In a moment of joy and relief, world-record setter Art Arfons hugs childhood friend and speed partner Ed Snyder as they sit atop the "Green Monster" on the front aluminum wing at the Bonneville Salt Flats. Snyder was an integral part of every Arfons world-record speed attempt. "Every time the record went higher than mine, it was my greatest personal challenge to try harder," Arfons remarked of the speed chase. "It was all consuming." (Courtesy of the Art Arfons family.)

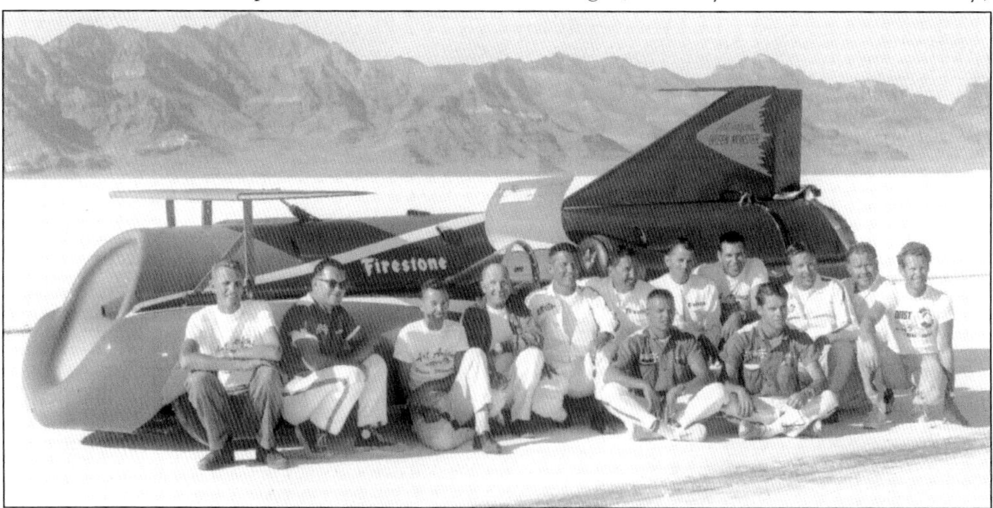

The photographers have gathered the "Green Monster" jet car team for a publicity photograph. Pictured are, from left to right, (first row) two unidentified Firestone technicians; (second row) Henry Butkiewiz, unidentified Firestone employee, Kay Kimes, Bud Groff, Charlie Mayenschein, Art Arfons, Ed Snyder, Les Medveine, Lee Penlenton, Jim Deist, and George Callaway. (Courtesy of Kay Kimes.)

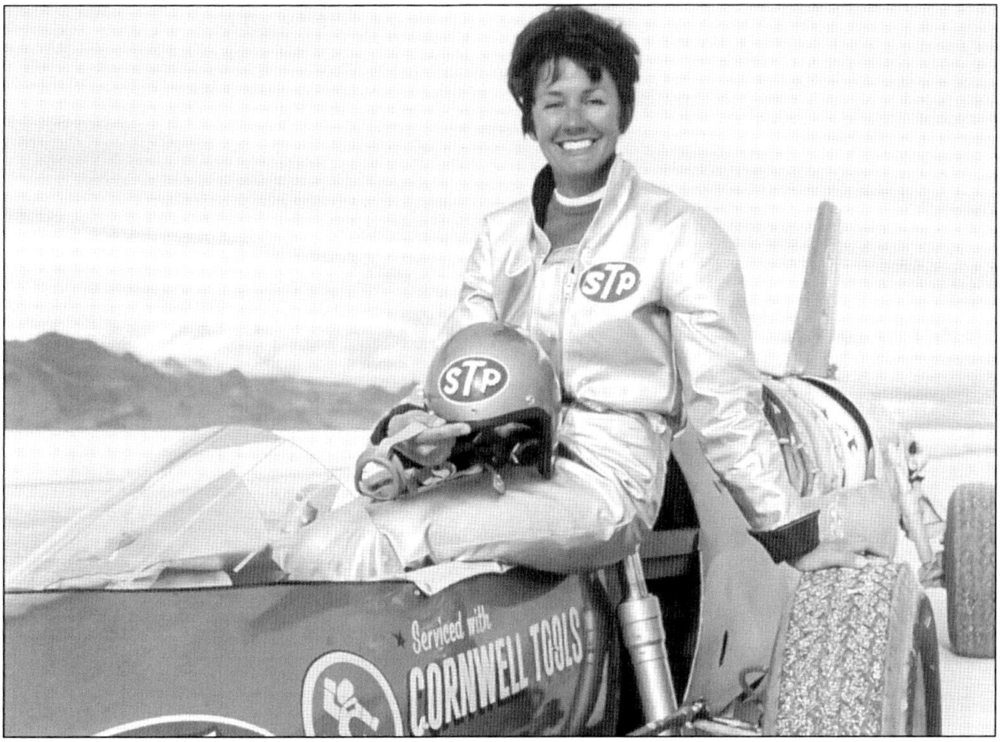

Accomplished race car driver Paula Murphy sits atop Walter Arfons's 10,000-horsepower, J46 jet-powered "Avenger." Already a well-known professional drag racer, road racer, and test car driver, she later drove a rocket car, set stock car records, and was inducted into the International Drag Racing Hall of Fame in 1992, British Drag Racing Hall of Fame in 2016, and Motorsports Hall of Fame in 2017. She led the way for dozens of women in helmets who followed her to the starting line at racetracks worldwide. (Courtesy of Paula Murphy.)

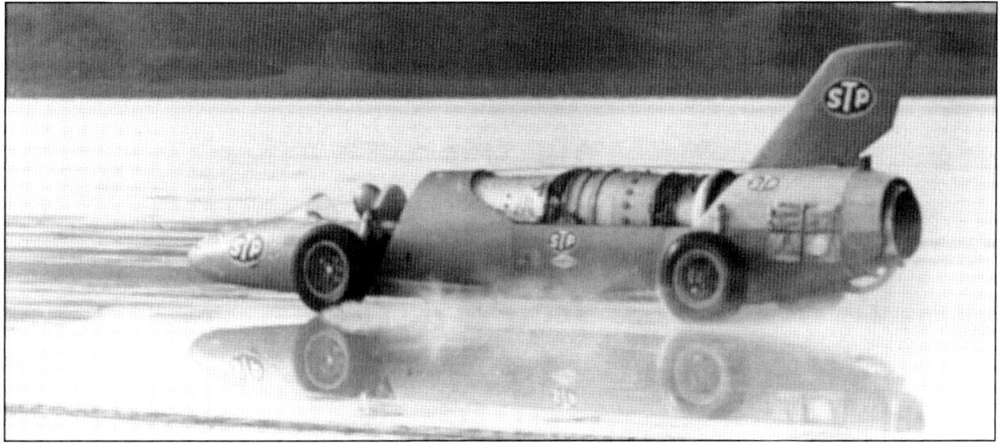

"When I turned up on the salt, I'd never seen it, let alone driven it," recalled driver Paula Murphy of her November 12, 1964, rain-soaked salt run at 243 miles per hour. "I had to sit with a pillow behind me so I could reach the pedals, which meant that my head was sticking out of the cockpit, and at over 200mph the pressure on your neck muscles is incredible. We only had three miles of usable track on the salt. That was a scary ride, but who knows how fast I could have gone with better conditions." (Courtesy of Paula Murphy.)

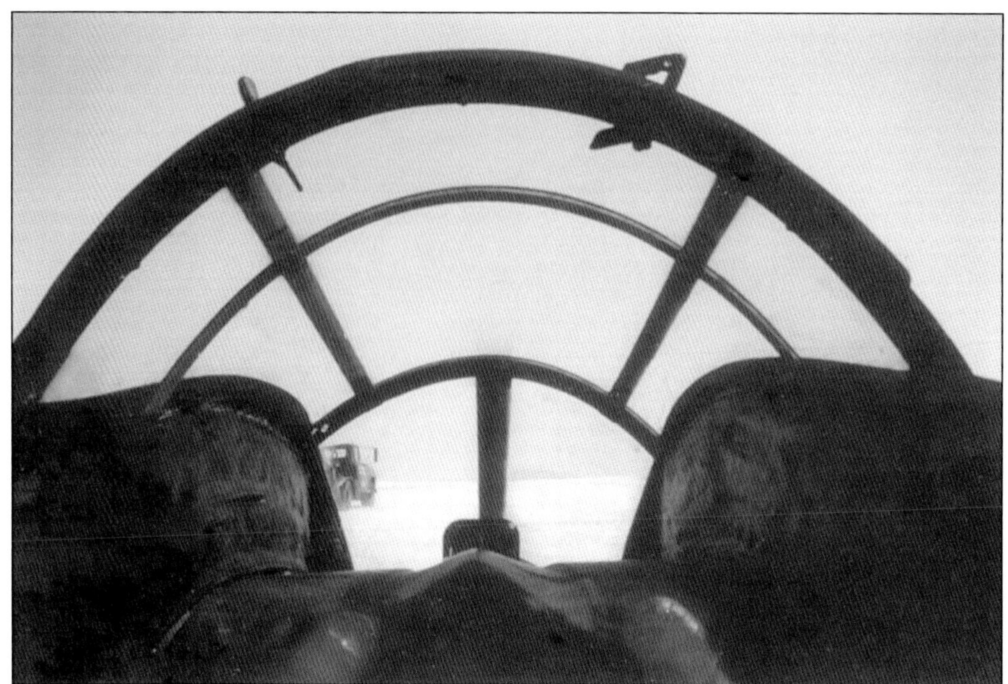

"Green Mamba" jet car driver Doug Rose, a former US Navy photographer, climbed into Walter Arfons's "Wingfoot Express," powered by a Westinghouse J46 jet engine, on the salt flats to capture this rare look out of the canopy. The mountain on the horizon is 25 miles away, but every driver aims straight for it, as did driver Talmadge "Tom" Green on October 2, 1964. "Walter was upset," remarked Green, "He thought I turned off the afterburner in the middle of the measured mile, but I had run out of fuel. It was a tremendous feeling of power and I was fully prepared to see how fast the car could go." (Courtesy of Doug Rose.)

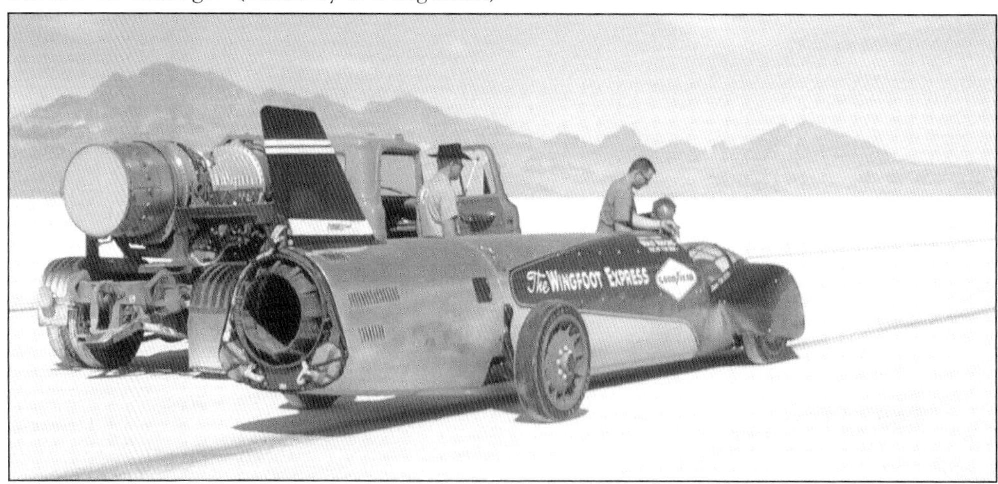

Walter Arfons and his crewman make a last-minute adjustment to the "Wingfoot Express" jet before driver Tom Green makes his first run in the car on the Bonneville Salt Flats in 1964. A heart condition took Arfons out of the driver's seat, giving Chicagoan Tom Green a forever slot in the history books inking a 413-mile-per-hour world record. Supremacy was fleeting, as Arfons's brother Art came along a few days later and snatched the speed crown. That is how it goes in racing, where speed is the deed to stay in the lead. (Courtesy of Goodyear Tire & Rubber Company.)

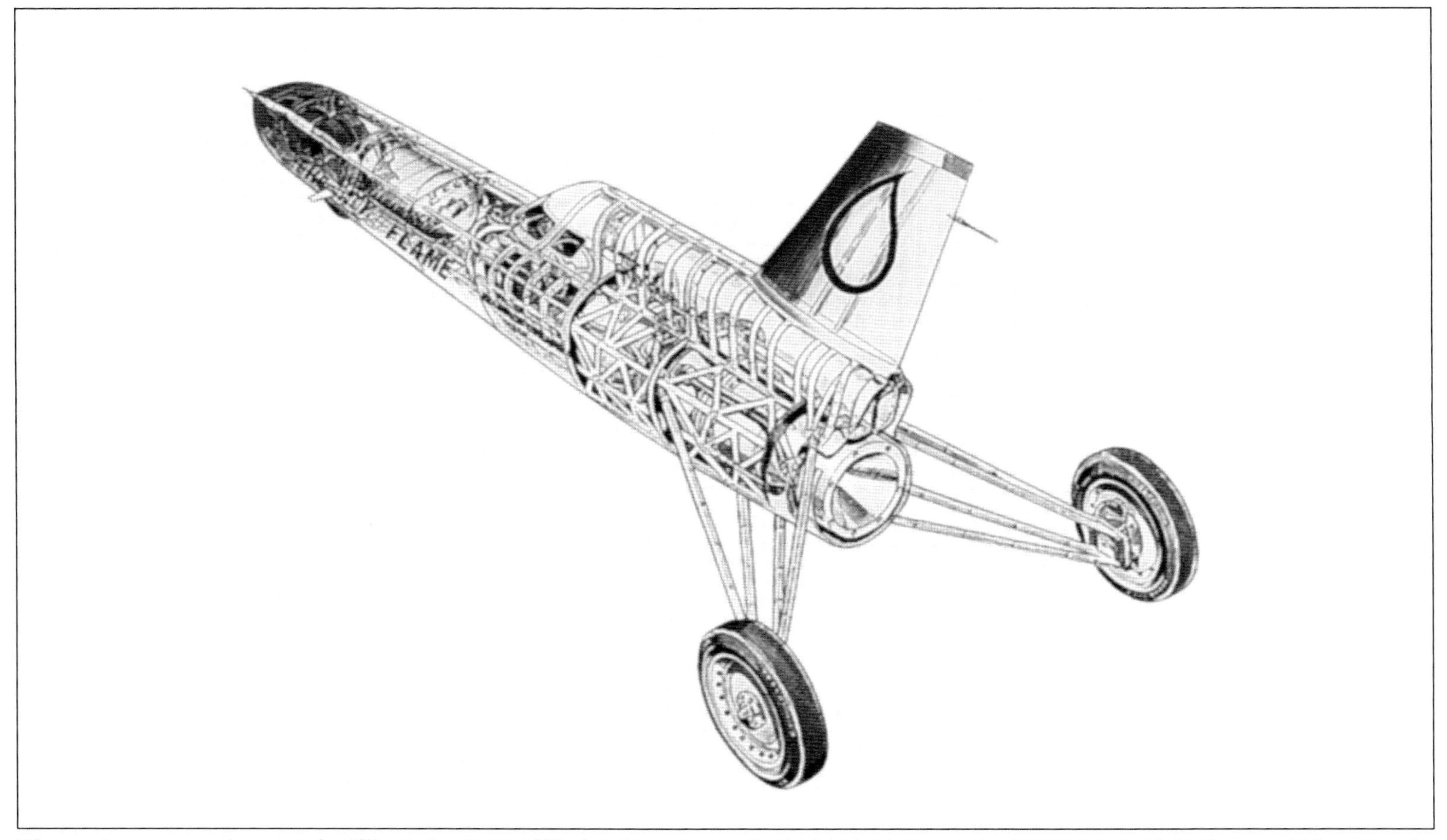

The engineering students at the Illinois Institute of Technology were tasked with designing a single-purpose vehicle that would become the fastest car on earth. This illustration is what they and their professors delivered to Reaction Dynamics, Inc., in Milwaukee, Wisconsin, that Pete Farnsworth and crew fabricated to hold Ray Dausman's throttleable rocket motor—the first of its kind. (Courtesy of Leah and Pete Farnsworth.)

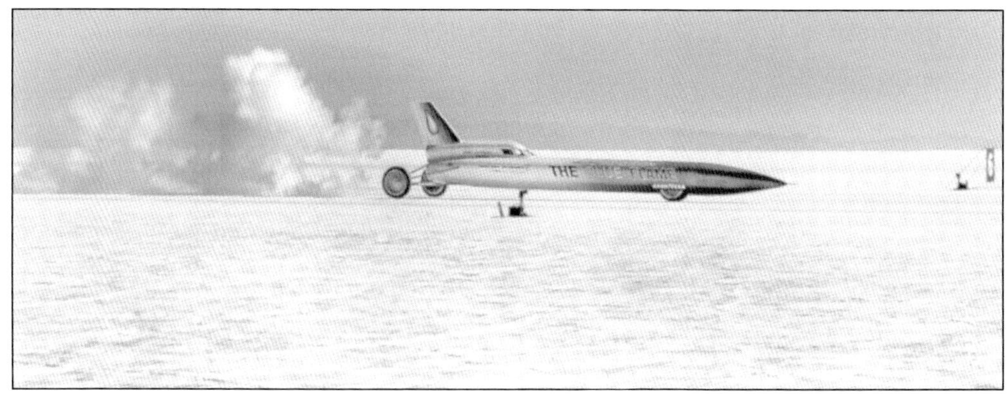

The six-mile marker on the right edge of the frame reveals that the rocket car is on a test run for a measured mile reaching speeds in the low 500s. World records require two passes in opposite directions over the same measured mile within one hour. Driver Gary Gabelich had, only moments before, started a chemical reaction in the catalyst pack that had begun to exit at supersonic speed out the back of the exhaust nozzle. The screeching sound can be considered deafening. (Courtesy of Leah and Pete Farnsworth.)

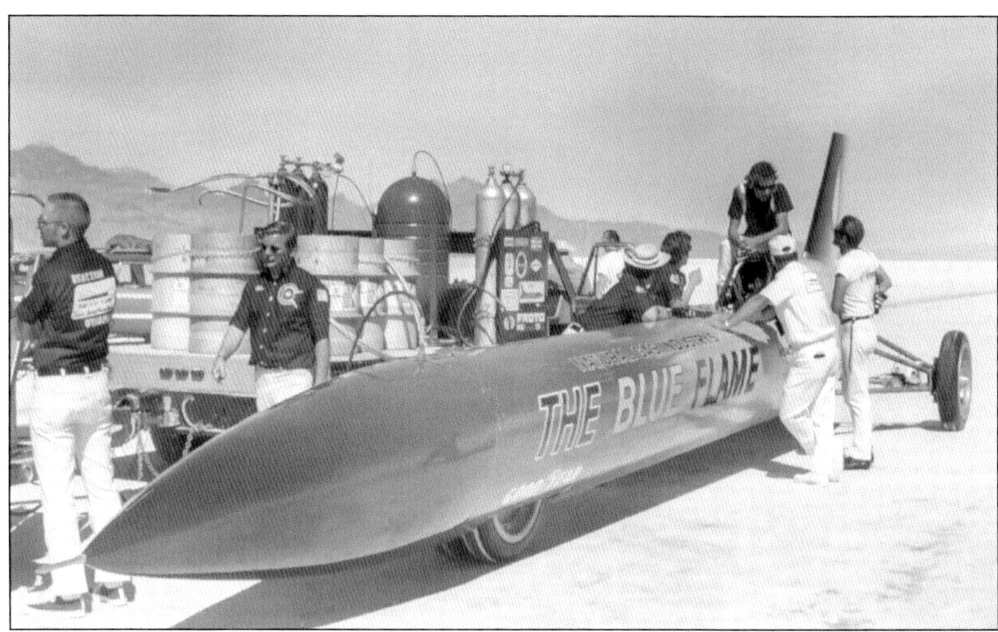

Reaction Dynamics president and crew chief Pete Farnsworth (second from left) walks past the refueling hoses filling the rocket car tanks with hydrogen peroxide, natural gas, and compressed air. "The Blue Flame" crew is talking to driver Gary Gabelich (sitting atop the roll cage). Pictured at left is Dave Bykowski, and behind Farnsworth are Larry Henkel (in the hat) and Mark Neubauer. The man in white wearing a cap is Dean Dietrich. Ready to run, "The Blue Flame" weighed around 9,000 pounds. (Courtesy of Dave Petrali.)

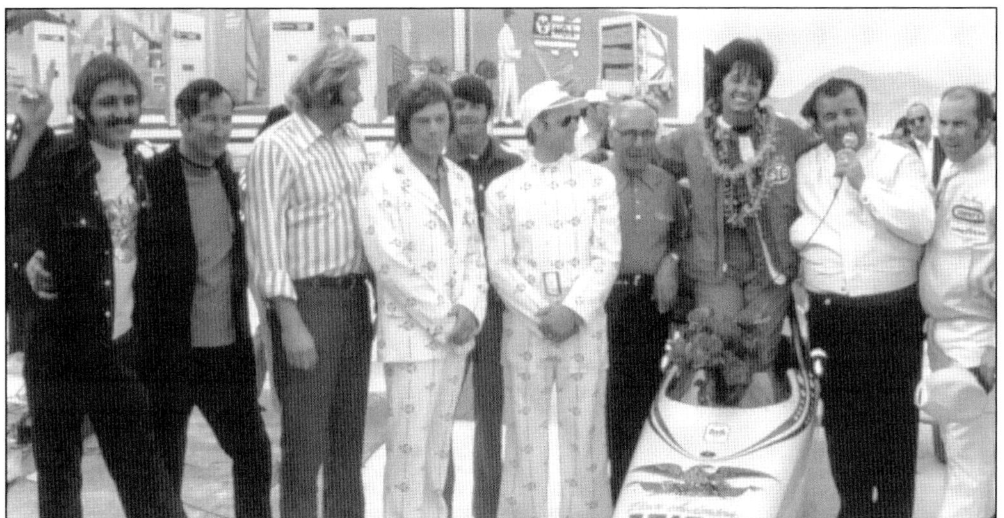

The "Pollution Packer" was already a thrilling drag racing sensation in 1972 when owner Tony Fox brought the team to Bonneville in October for some record setting. With Dave Anderson sharing cockpit time with Paula Murphy, the pair set a number of national and international records. Pictured are, from left to right, "The Blue Flame" rocket car driver Gary Gabelich, "Green Monster" jet car driver Art Arfons, "Green Mamba" jet car driver Doug Rose, "Spirit of America" jet car driver Craig Breedlove, jet car driver Roger Gustin (in back), "Pollution Packer" rocket car driver Dave Anderson, United States Auto Club chief timer Joe Petrali, "Pollution Packer" rocket car driver Paula Murphy, owner Tony Fox, and rocket car driver John Paxon. (Courtesy of Paula Murphy.)

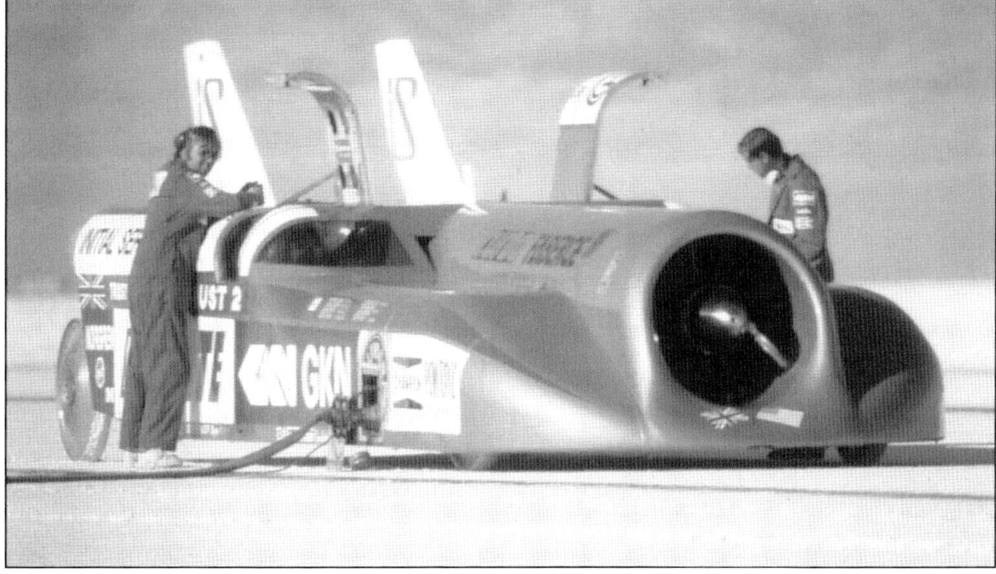

Most all land speed racers know that Britain's Richard Noble, driving his "Thrust2" jet-propelled car, set the world land speed record on October 4, 1983, at 633 miles per hour, ending 20 years of American dominance by eclipsing Gary Gabelich's 622-mile-per-hour mark in "The Blue Flame." The feat also marked the end of absolute world-record setting on the Bonneville Salt Flats, where it had flourished for nearly a half-century, because Noble set the record on Nevada's Black Rock Desert, 330 miles west of the flats. (Courtesy of Glynne Bowsher.)

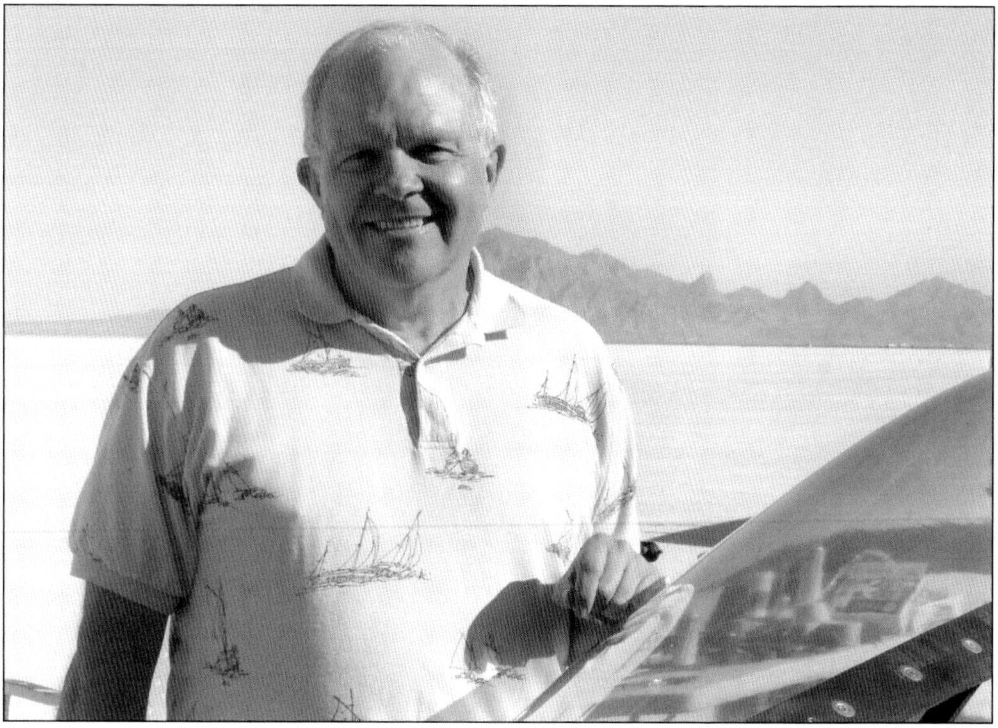

Already a world-famous record setter, James Stephen "Steve" Fossett came to Bonneville in 2006 for driving lessons in advance of his planned world-record runs. He bought and repaired "Sonic Arrow" after its 1996 mishap at 675 miles per hour when owner and driver Craig Breedlove earned "World's Fastest U-Turn" and "World's Longest Skid Mark" honors. Fossett never got to try, as his luck ran out on September 3, 2007, when the small plane he was flying over the Great Basin Desert between Nevada and California crashed—a bitter end for the brave adventure-seeker who set more than 100 records in five different sports. (Courtesy of LandSpeed Louise.)

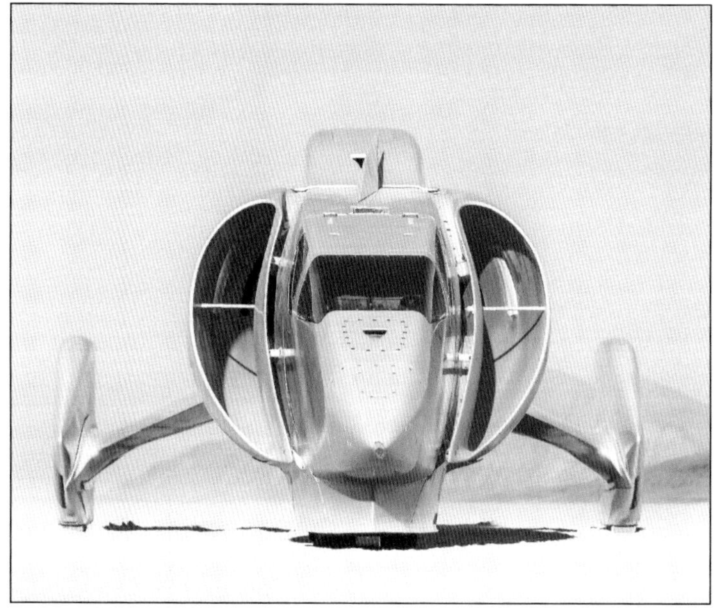

By the time Craig Breedlove brought his five-wheel "Spirit of America" sonic arrow to the salt in the late 1990s, it was merely a charity visit, as poor federal oversight by the Bureau of Land Management had permitted the racing surface to deteriorate so badly in thickness and length that the once-hallowed raceway was not able to safely support absolute world-record attempts. (Courtesy of LandSpeed Louise.)

Five

Women in Helmets and the Record Books

Speed and Courage Are Genderless

Never has any race car, truck, or motorcycle ever operated differently due to gender. All are equally subservient, responsive only to the person handling each. All vehicles, planes, and boats react the same to input from any driver, pilot, or captain.

Good input gets good results. Any inference that gender makes some appreciable difference to the outcome is simply absurd or twisted by trepidation. There is no such thing as a "woman's" or "man's" speed record; it is a record, plain and simple.

However, mix in male ego and prepare to take cover. The idea that a woman can be faster than a man or finish first tends to gnaw at the insecurities of some, and it is why ladies were late to the staging lanes at Bonneville.

From its start in the late 1920s, the sport had always welcomed women to labor for the speed cause, but they were forbidden for decades to take part in the joy of tripping the time clocks on the salty speedway, most any speedway for that matter.

The propaganda was dressed up as fear (real or imagined) that if a woman driver was injured in a race car then the entire sport would suffer. And if she were a mother, the terrifying perceived consequences made men shudder, shake their head, and wince their eyes.

Such parochial wisdom eventually was regarded for what it was: nonsensical. Today, women represent a solid, ever-improving group of land speed racers that ink records in any classification they enter. A fine example is Paula Burns, who raced diligently in 2004 to become the first female SCTA points champion. While drag racing is a very close second, no other form of motorsports—professional or amateur—has more gals with "skin in the game" than land speed racing. This is particularly evident in the motorcycle classes.

"I would have liked to go faster and have a higher record, but the sponsors wouldn't allow it," said Lee (Breedlove) Frank recalling her flawless driving in the "Spirit of America" jet car in 1965. Momentous will be the day when the world speed crown becomes a tiara.

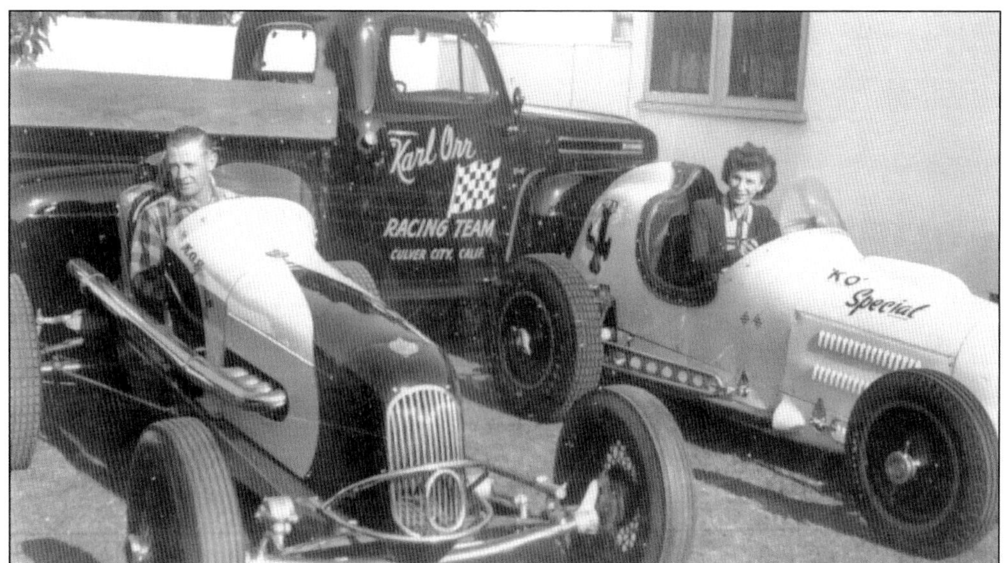

It was back in the 1930s that Veda Orr became the first and, for years, the only woman to compete in the dry lakes time trials. Her best reported speed was 132 miles per hour on California's Rosamond Dry Lake. Together with her husband, Karl, the pair drove roadsters, modifieds, and streamliners, but it is perhaps for her reporting skills that she is best remembered. During World War II, Veda stepped in the editor's role, publishing and distributing SCTA news not only to the stateside members but also to all those stationed overseas. The gesture was deeply appreciated by every recipient. (Courtesy of the Ferguson family.)

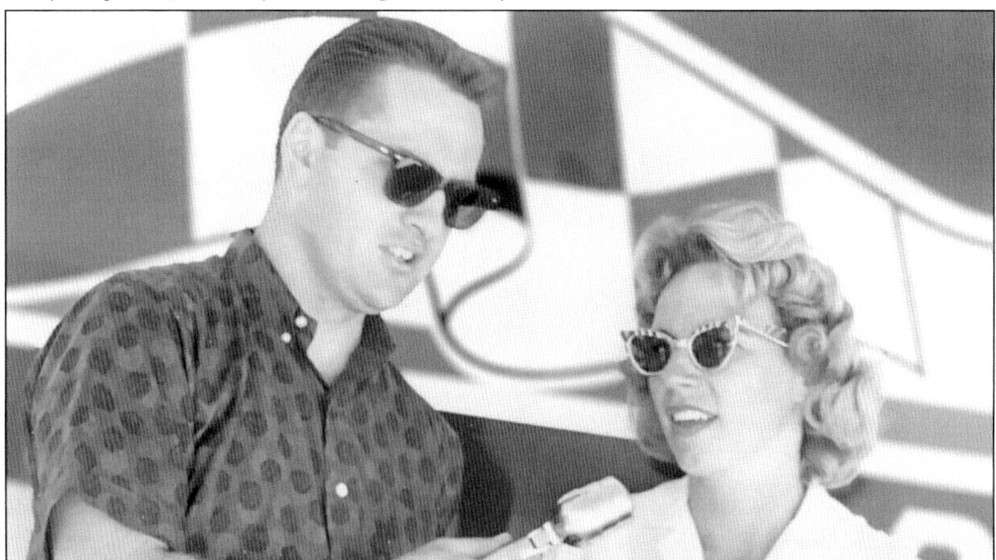

Judy Thompson, being interviewed by Salt Lake City's KSL Radio, was married to Mickey Thompson and was as much a member of her husband's racing team as any man, contributing heavily to every Bonneville record attempt. Whether it was porting engine parts or repairing Mickey's leather driving suit, she got it done and done right. In 2018, at age 90, despite a stroke a month before son Danny's speed runs, she announced: "I'm gonna do, what I wanna do, and I'm going to Bonneville." Danny replied, "Yes, ma'am." And she watched the kid set a 448-mile-per-hour record driving his dad's fully refurbished "Challenger II." (Courtesy of Judy Thompson.)

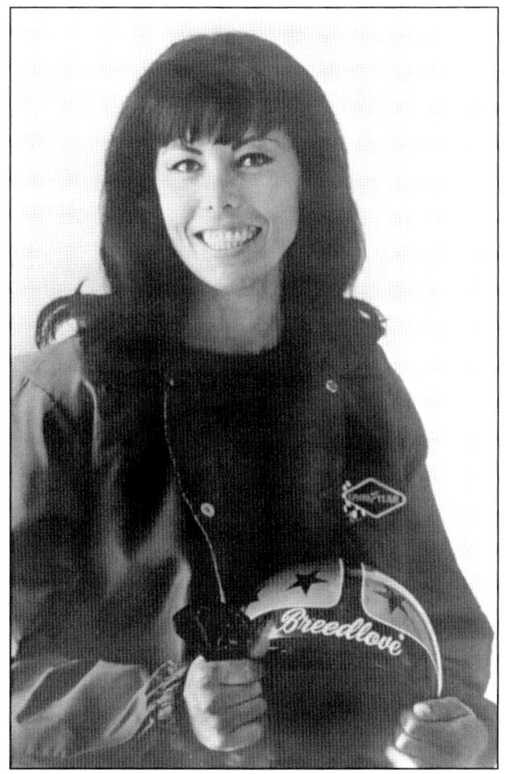

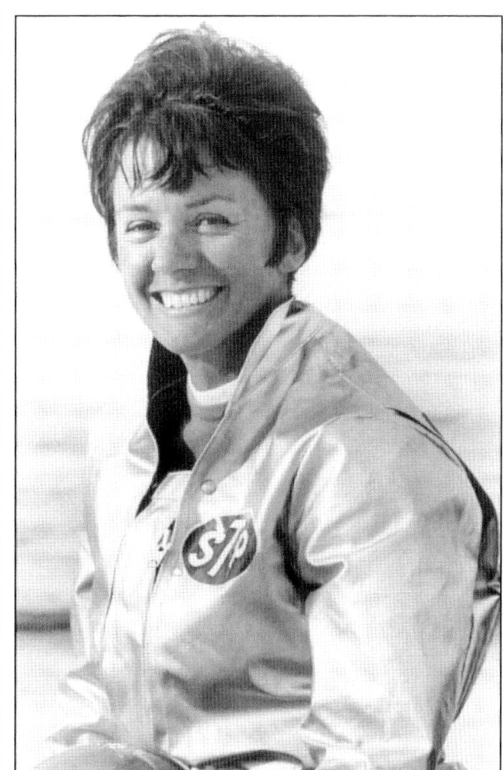

At left is Lee Breedlove, who at 28 drove the "Spirit of America Sonic 1" jet-powered car to a two-way average of 310.14 miles per hour in 1965. Sponsors insisted the mechanics detune the jet engine so that Lee could not erase her husband's mark even if she wanted to do so. Paula Murphy, at right, won the first race she entered. "Shoot, I can do this!" thought the woman whose father never learned to drive. "You are either a driver, or you are not. You will figure that out pretty quick, but you have to try." (Left, courtesy of Lee Frank; right, courtesy of Paula Murphy.)

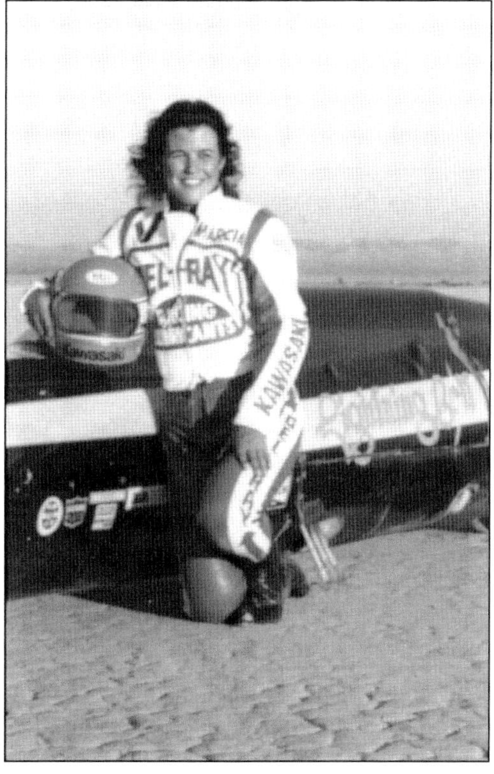

World motorcycle record champ Don Vesco thought offering his 21-foot motorcycle streamliner on a dare would be a great way to romance stuntwoman Marcia Holley in 1978 as well as shatter the all-boys lock on the prestigious Bonneville 200 MPH Club. He was right on both counts. Holley recorded a 229-mile-per-hour average riding "Lightning Bolt" and became the first woman to earn life membership. To this day, her accomplishment mentors the aspirations of many women who try on a helmet and fireproof clothing to find out how fast they can go. (Courtesy of Don Vesco.)

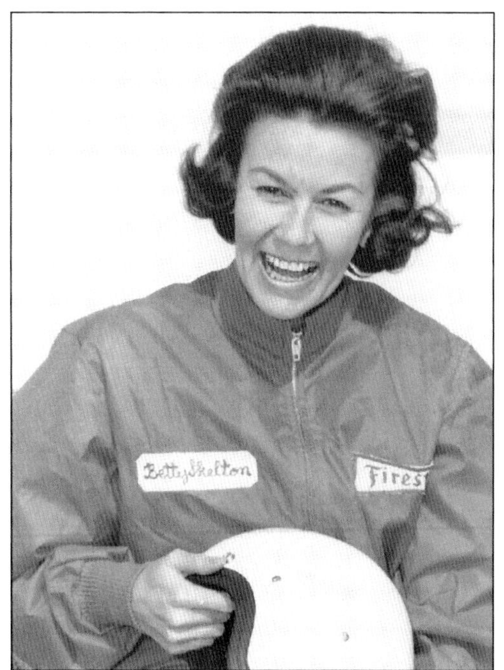

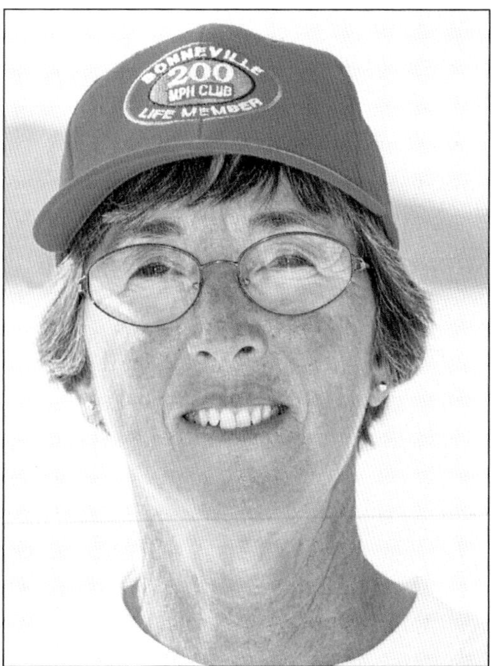

Betty Skelton of Detroit, Michigan, stands in the cockpit of the "Cyclops" jet car moments before she clocked 277 miles per hour in 1965. Note the open-face helmet in her hands, the standard head protection that required the use of goggles as an eye shield before full-face helmets were available. When not busy racing the family 450-mile-per-hour streamliner, Betty Burkland, 63, of Great Falls, Montana, likes to climb into speed machines herself. In 2003, the grandmother of three drove the "Trackmaster" competition coupe to a Class E Blown Fuel record of 263 miles per hour. (Left, courtesy of Firestone Tire and Rubber Company; right, courtesy of Bill Taylor.)

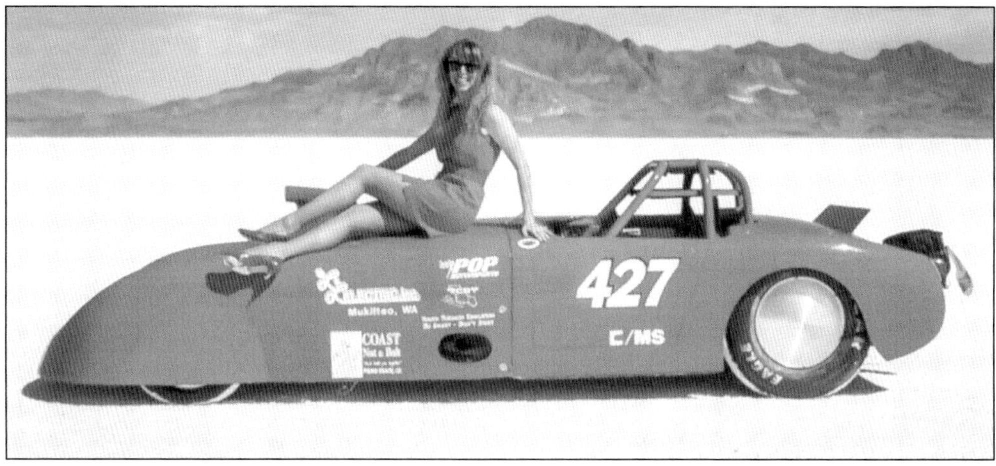

Whether at Bonneville or Australia's Lake Gairdner, Dry Lakes Racing Hall of Fame member Gail Watson Phillips has proved herself repeatedly behind the wheel of speed machines since 1995. Entering the Bonneville 200 MPH Club in 1999 driving 202 miles per hour in a modified Austin Healey Sprite, she inked a 205-mile-per-hour record in 2001, becoming the first female to set a record "down under" over 200 miles per hour. In 2007, she drove her 1999 C-5 Corvette 202 miles per hour on Bonneville, followed by crashing a 25-foot streamliner at 242 miles per hour in 2008, rolling gently enough for her to walk away! (Courtesy of POP Motorsports/Gail Phillips.)

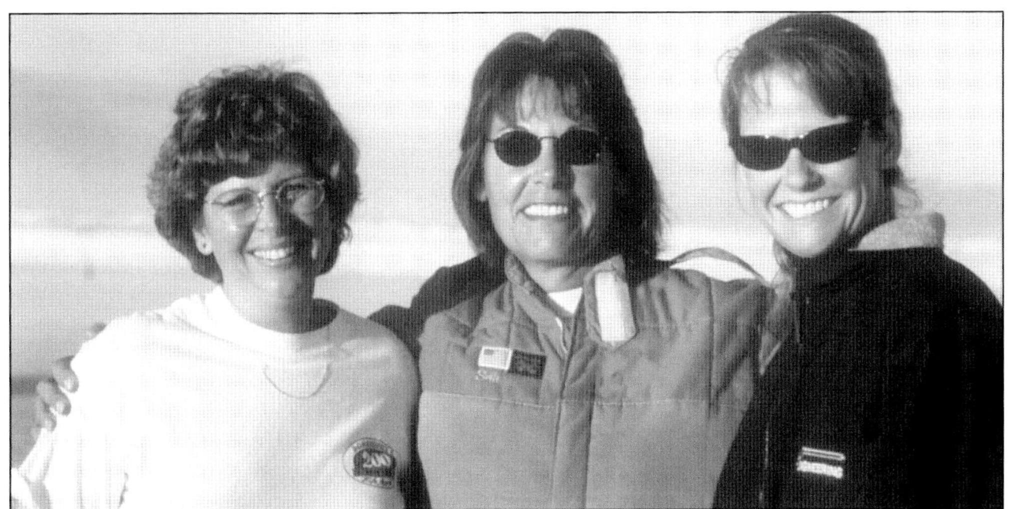

Susan Christophersen's (left) first race came after she married Steve and they went to the Bonneville Salt Flats for their 1994 honeymoon. She spent the next decade racing the Doll-Fox-Christophersen 1982 Camaro, with which she earned her Bonneville 200 MPH Club red hat in 1998 with 214-mile-per-hour record. Tanis Hammond (center) was the mother of three when she became the first woman to earn a Bonneville 200 MPH Club blue hat, worn only by those in the chapter who ink a land speed record north of 300. She did so driving her husband Seth's lakester to a 304-mile-per-hour record before earning her helicopter pilot's license in 2001. Using the same car Tanis drove, Dr. Jeannie Pflum (right), the engine builder's daughter, gave Tanis some company when she inked a 302-mile-per-hour record in 2002 and then went on to race motorcycles in between delivering newborns. (Courtesy of LandSpeed Louise.)

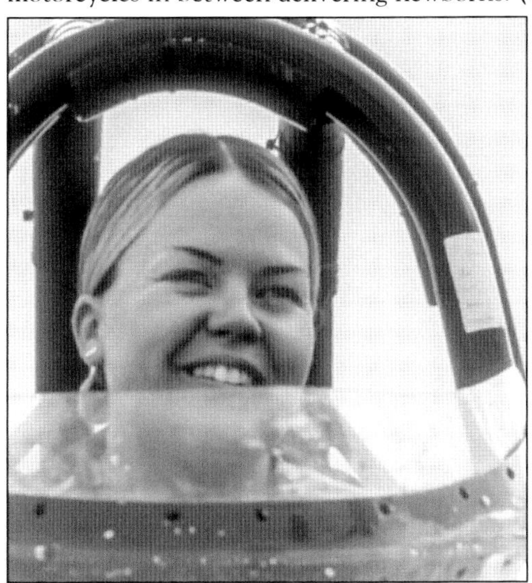

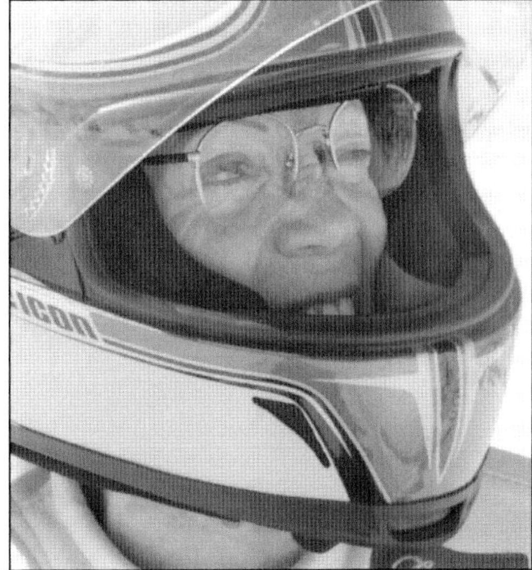

Allison Volk, left, was born into racing and at age 23 climbed into the family roadster and embarked on what was part destiny and part sibling rivalry. She set the highest speed record in the Volk family, 236 miles per hour, yet was a bit nervous as she took her thrilling rookie rides. Connie Sulu Beavers-Nicolaides is possibly the fastest female senior citizen to date. At 74, jaws dropped when she rolled off the starting line on her Suzuki Hayabusa making 200-plus-mile-per-hour speed runs. The Gear Grinders Racing Club member had a color-coordinated helmet and leathers that matched her two-wheel mean machine. (Both, courtesy of LandSpeed Louise.)

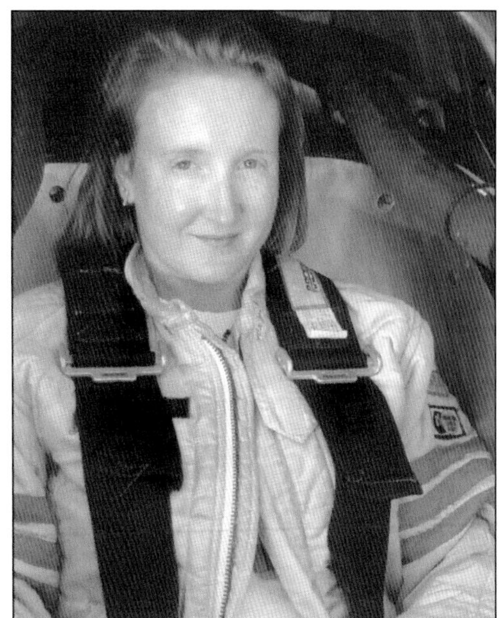

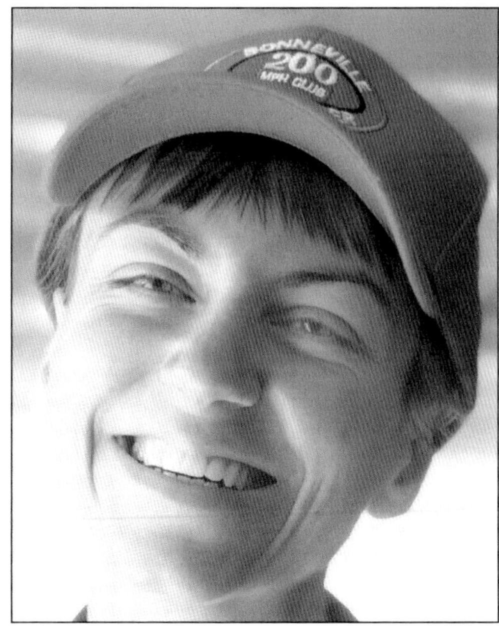

At left is novice driver Tricia Kisner, 26, who humbled all by setting top speed of the meet at 325 miles per hour. Driving the "Grumpy Ole Men" lakester, she became the first woman and rookie to earn the prestigious *Hot Rod Magazine* Top Time trophy, reminding all "it's not a man's sport." With no previous high-speed training, Zofi Peda-Proffitt, right, climbed into the Fergusen family's No. 76 red and white streamliner and drove from zero to 280 miles per hour in a handful of runs. Peda-Proffitt is the only Polish citizen in the Bonneville 200 MPH Club. *Twoje zdrowie!* ("Cheers!" in Polish). (Both, courtesy of LandSpeed Louise.)

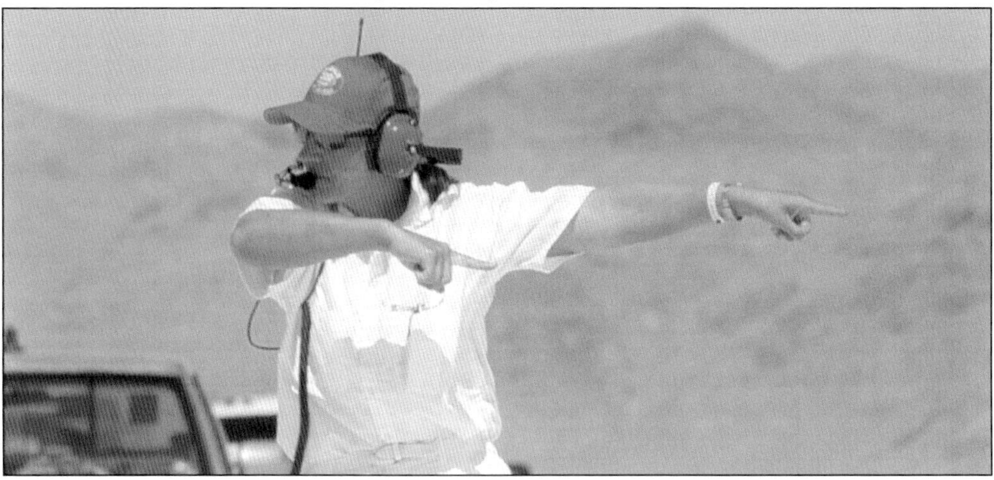

New Zealand native Miriam MacMillan is an unquestioned role model for the sport from both racing and volunteer perspectives. She was the 2012 Bonneville National, Inc., chair (the first woman to occupy the role), Southern California Timing Association (SCTA) vice president, Rod Riders Racing Club president, and a Save the Salt Advisory Board member. MacMillan built her own race car to earn her Bonneville 200 MPH Club life membership at 204 miles per hour and was 2010 SCTA points champion. "Running at over 200 mph is a real buzz," MacMillan recalled, without mentioning that her side window blew out past 200, but she never lifted her foot off the throttle. (Courtesy of Zane McNary.)

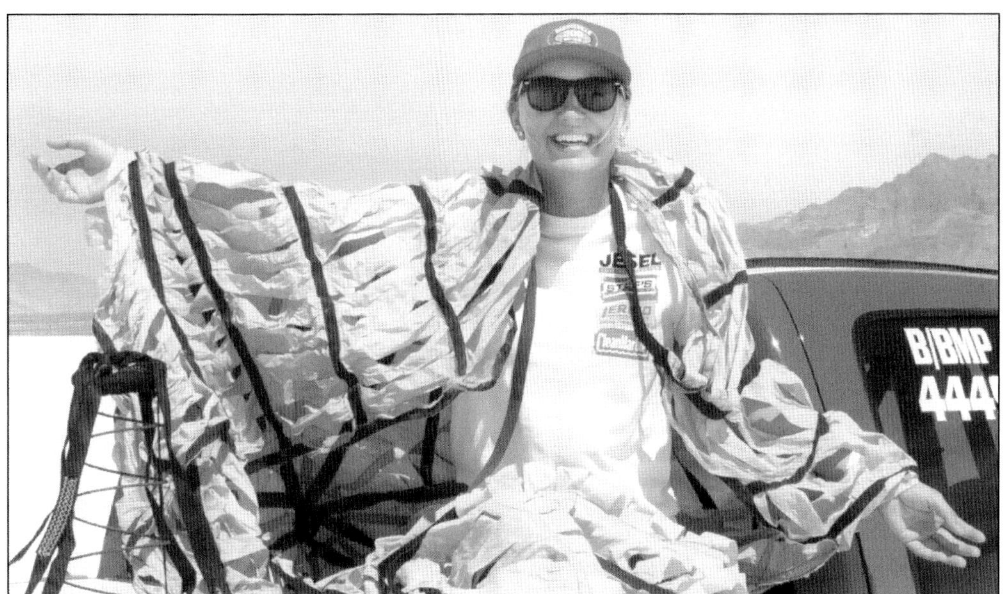

Kaylin Stewart, 18, is wearing her brand-new fast hat earned with a 224-mile-per-hour land speed record in Class B Blown Modified Pick-up. She joins the Bonneville 200 MPH Club with a speed greater than her father's, and he could not be happier. "I was running out of race track," she explained about conquering fear and replacing it with skill. "It's just as important to practice slowing down and turning off the race course safely as it is to go fast. I was focused on staying safe, straight and oriented and didn't pay much attention to the speed." (Courtesy of LandSpeed Louise.)

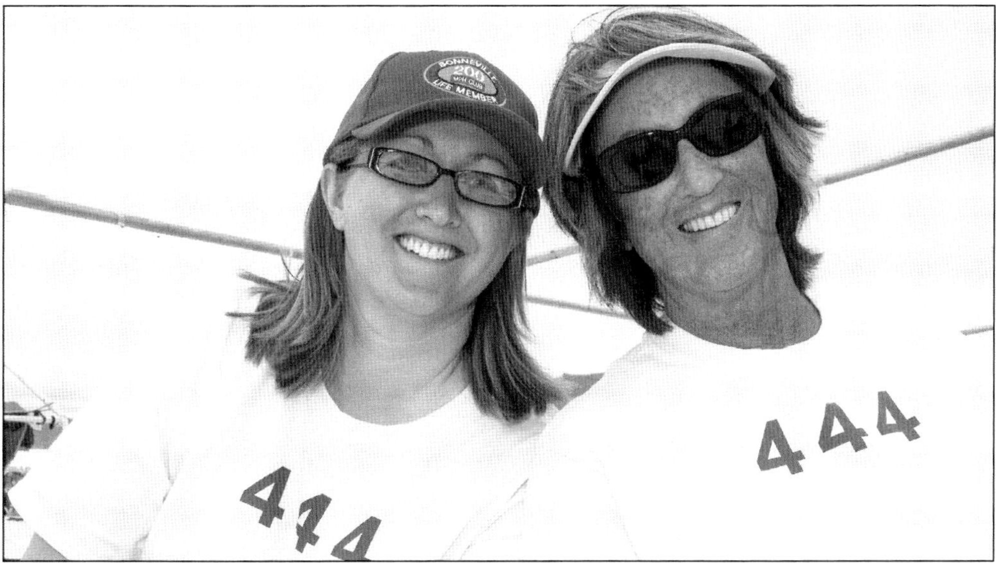

Jinx Vesco (right) beams with daughter Rhonnie Vesco, who, in 2008 as a 24-year-old rookie driver, earned the Utah Salt Flat Racing Association's Fast Lady trophy, clocking 233 miles per hour in the family's 51-year-old historic "Little Giant" streamliner. Ditto in 2011 with a 310-mile-per-hour record that collected her another trophy. Jinx is the diamond glue that holds TEAMVesco together. Single-handedly, she curates the family and team archives, is web mistress of the team's website, and generally puts elected officials and government staff on notice when they fall down on the job. Cross her path at your peril! (Courtesy of LandSpeed Louise.)

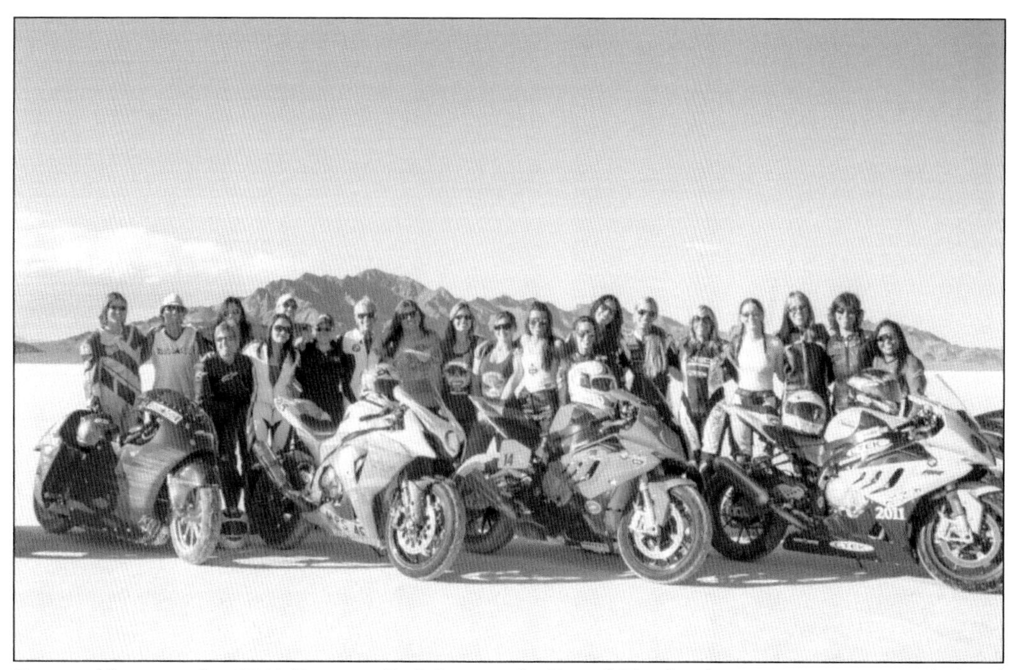

Pictured here at the 2011 Bonneville Motorcycle Speed Trials, the premier motorcycle land speed racing event on the salt each year, are 20 women who, over many years and events, have recorded more than 250 land speed records! From left to right are Kathleen Cooke, Jody Perowitz, Julianna (Wallingford) Williams, Belen Wagner, Delissa Bartholome (in white), C. Tucker Allen (behind in hat), E. Hakansson, Erin Sills, Christine (Freeman) Howard, Michelle Mielke, Tiadra Simmermon, Erica Cobb, Karlee Cobb, Laura Klock, Leslie Porterfield, Valerie Thompson, Karena Markham, Tracey Snyder, Kim Krebs, and Lucille Dunn. Scooter Grubb set up the shot. (Courtesy of LandSpeed Louise.)

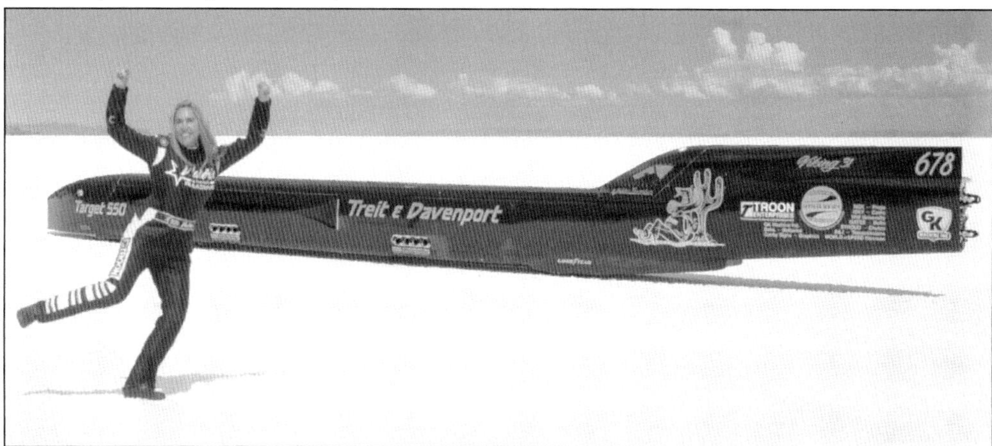

Valerie Thompson, 53, is an eight-time land speed record holder who can honestly claim "World's Fastest Female Motorcycle Racer" bragging rights. In 2018, she inked a 328-mile-per-hour record piloting a motorcycle streamliner as well as multiple records riding traditional two-wheelers. In 2018, the Dry Lakes Racers of Australia gave Thompson the Fastest Lady on the Lake award for the Class 3000 S-BF mark. Thompson is the first woman appointed to the board of the Bonneville 200 MPH Club. In 2019, she became an automobile driver of the "Target 550" streamliner and hopes to exceed 500 miles per hour. (Courtesy of LandSpeed Louise.)

Six

DRAG RACING DRAIN 1961–1983

THE NEED FOR SPEED GOES CLOSER TO HOME

As motorsports matured and engines became more sophisticated, the racers wanted to run their speed machines more than once a year in August. The rise of organized drag racing provided the needed outlet as quarter-mile drag strips opened in multiple locations across the country.

At the start of the 1950s, because both were straight-line acceleration challenges, the racers would race on the salt flats during Speedweek and then alter the engine, transmission, and tire setup to be able to enter drag events closer to home. A few later built bespoke racing vehicles for each discipline, but most never had the extra disposable income to maintain more than one machine, and slowly the drag strips became the chosen outlet over the Bonneville Salt Flats.

This shift did not kill the long-distance speed sport, though. It only caused a distinct slowing of its growth for some years because it was very hard for some to eschew the allure of a multi-mile chance to run with the throttle wide open. The abiding question resonated: "How fast will it go?" and it could only be answered with a ripping trip at speed down the surveyed miles and past the certified clocks.

By the mid-1970s, the State of Utah stopped prepping the federal land racecourse, and the Bureau of Land Management (BLM) had no intention of helping either, so it fell to the racing organizer to ensure competitors had a safe surface upon which to make speed attempts.

Next, as the sport celebrated its 25th anniversary, the BLM put the racing community on notice that holding a single, one-week event per year was no longer enough if they wanted the speedway to be protected the remaining 51 weeks. This prompted the founding of the Utah Salt Flats Racing Association (USFRA), which held two events annually—a July date, if the salt dried out by then, and the World of Speed in September. The SCTA added the World Finals in October, and suddenly there were four time trials instead of one.

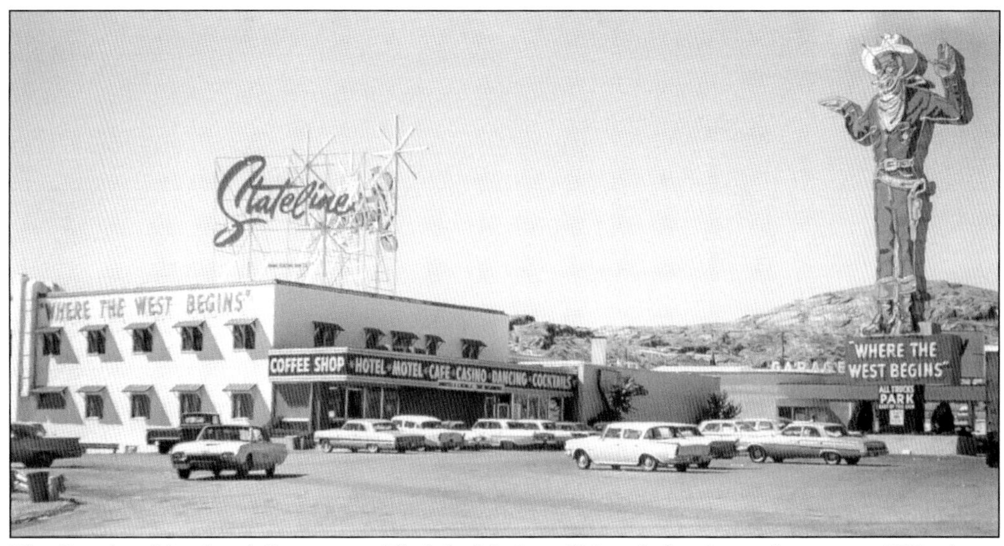

The Stateline Hotel and Casino straddled the Utah and Nevada border in the towns of Wendover and West Wendover. The idea was visitors could sleep and eat on the pious Mormon side but walk in air-conditioned comfort to the gambling, drinking, and rabble-rousing side. For years, a line was painted right across Wendover Boulevard marking the state divide. (Courtesy of Just Hallen.)

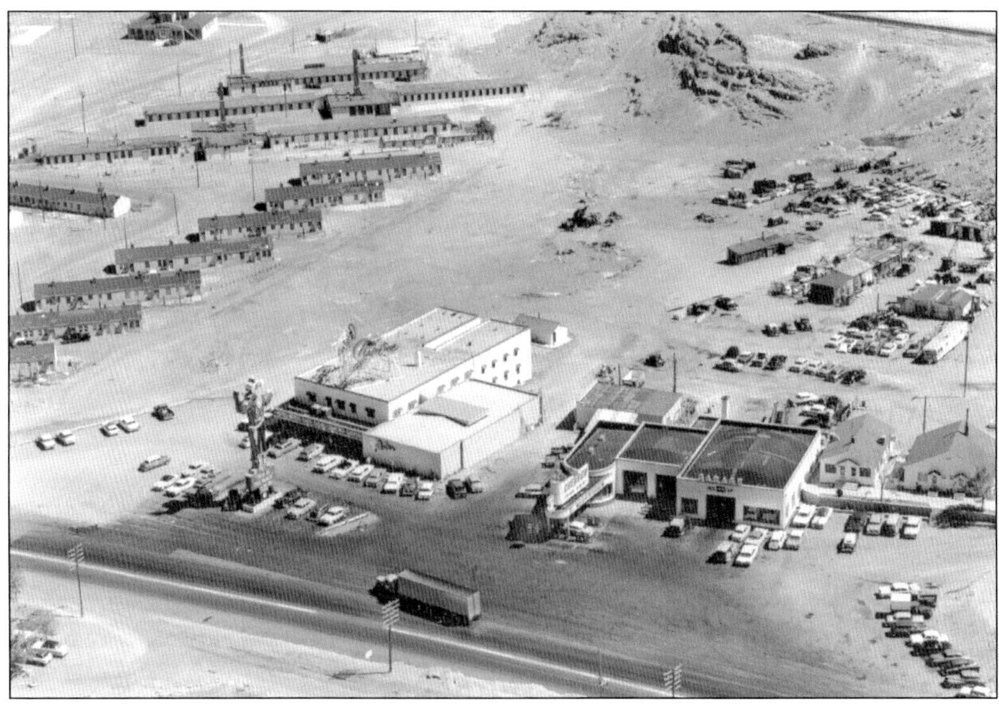

The Stateline Hotel and Casino was doing a brisk business in 1950. Proprietor W.F. Smith insisted the establishment was located directly on the Utah–Nevada state line. Next door was his Cobble Stone Service Station, the place where he found a job after jumping off a train a few miles up the road. (Courtesy of the Utah Historical Society.)

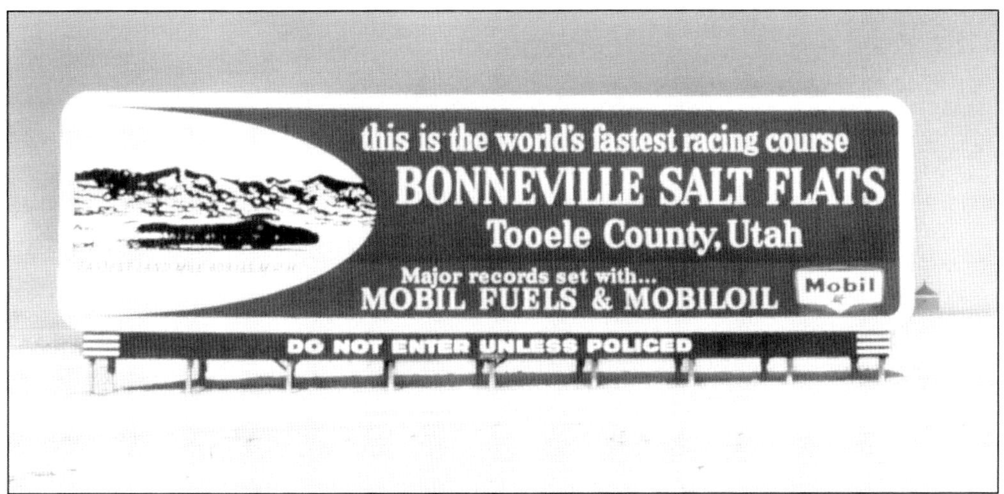

This immense billboard greeted those who came to the salt flats. For years, it painfully reminded American hot rodders that the top speed honors belonged to British driver John Cobb, the first man to ink a 400-plus-mile-per-hour one-way pass. When Craig Breedlove drove his "Spirit of America" jet car 407 miles per hour for a new world record, it remedied the long-standing ache, and the sign got a new paint job the following year. (Courtesy of Kay Kimes.)

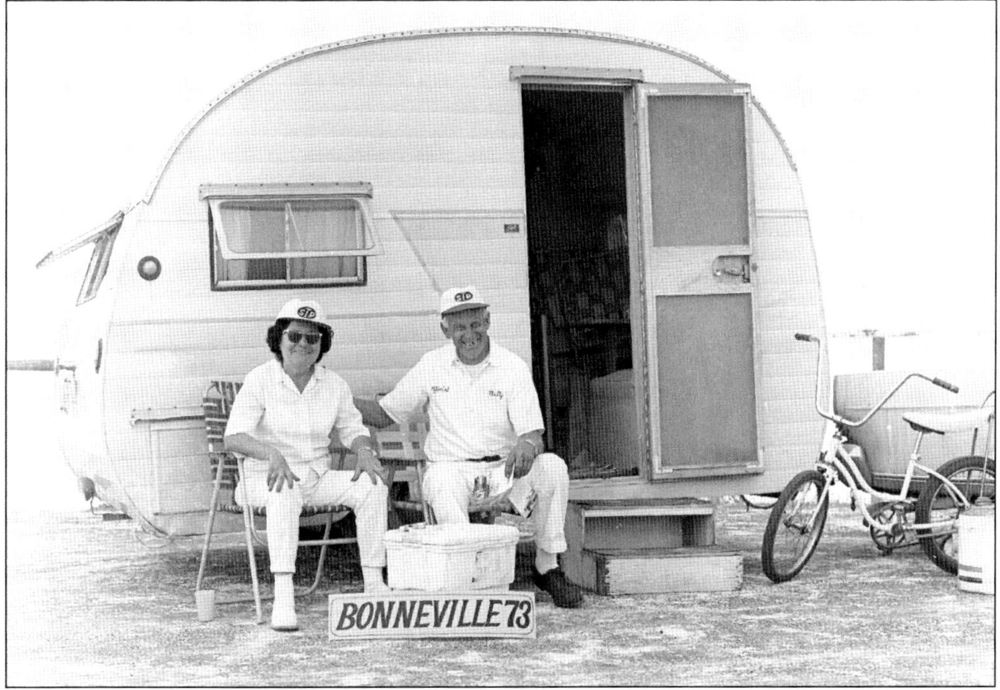

Pictured here are Vera and Roy "Multy" Aldrich in front of their strategically located camper so they could cheerfully greet all comers to the salt. The valued pair had gold business cards from event organizers designated "Hospitality" and were several times voted the Meb Healy Memorial Trophy, given annually to a man or woman who contributes more than his or her share to racing. Racing since the 1930s, Multy entered the first time trial in 1949 with his 1922 four-cylinder Model T. From 1950 until 1972, he volunteered as safety inspector, continually improving the checklist used by the sanctioning body. (Courtesy of LPRL.)

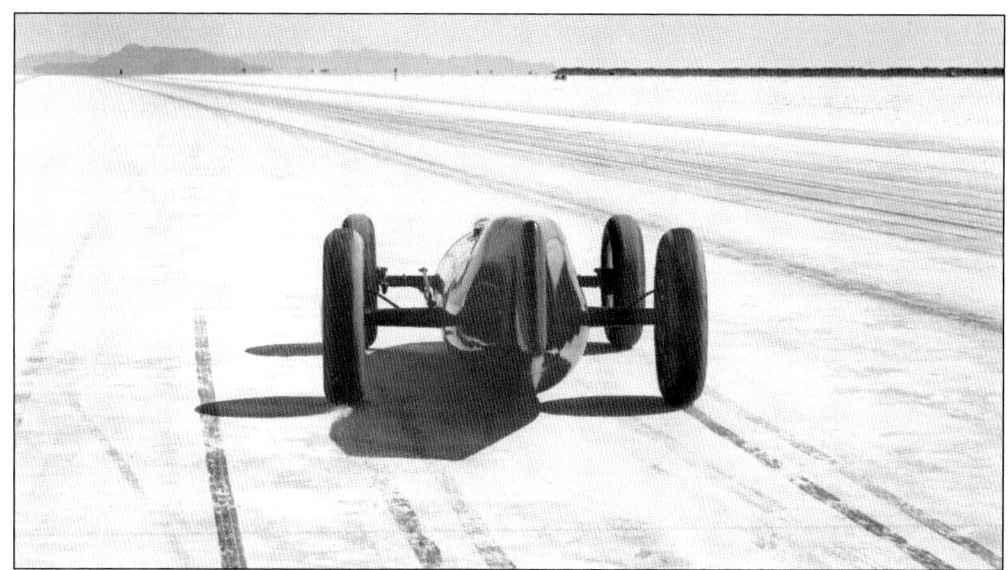

"I enjoy turning money into noise," fierce competitor Timothy Mortimer Rochlitzer often remarked. Pictured here hustling off the starting line in 1962 driving his handcrafted belly tank lakester, he was the youngest launch director at Vandenberg Air Force Base. He quit to open True Radius Bending, which was responsible for shaping dozens of race car frames. Widowed young, he made sure sons Brad and Brian got to earn life membership with him in the Bonneville 200 MPH Club. (Courtesy of Dean Batchelor.)

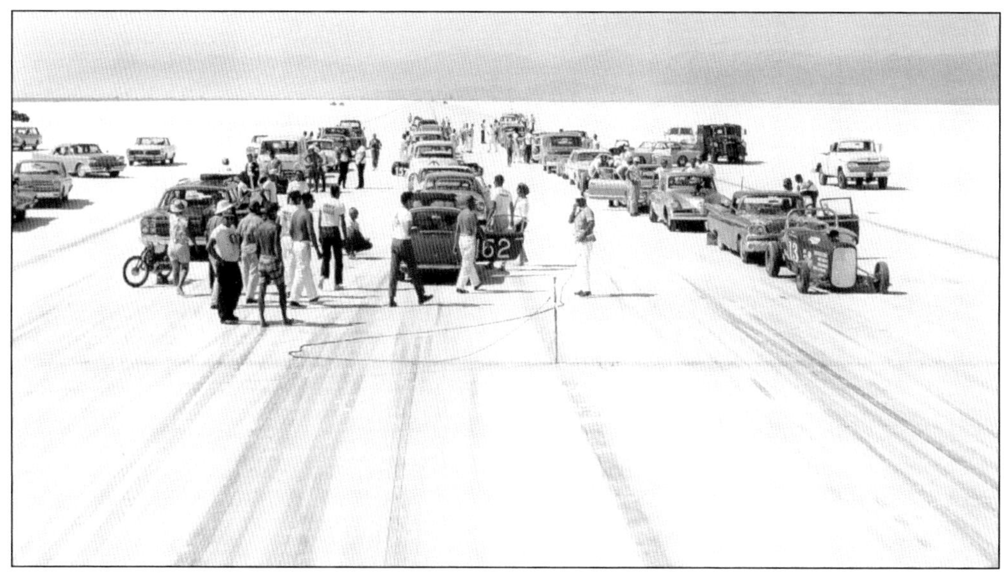

The racers in the staging lanes wait for their chance on the starting line at Bonneville Speedweek. Seeing the first machines in line, one can tell anything goes, with a motorcycle in lane one, a Porsche in lane two, and a roadster in lane three followed by a Studebaker. (Courtesy of Tim Rochlitzer.)

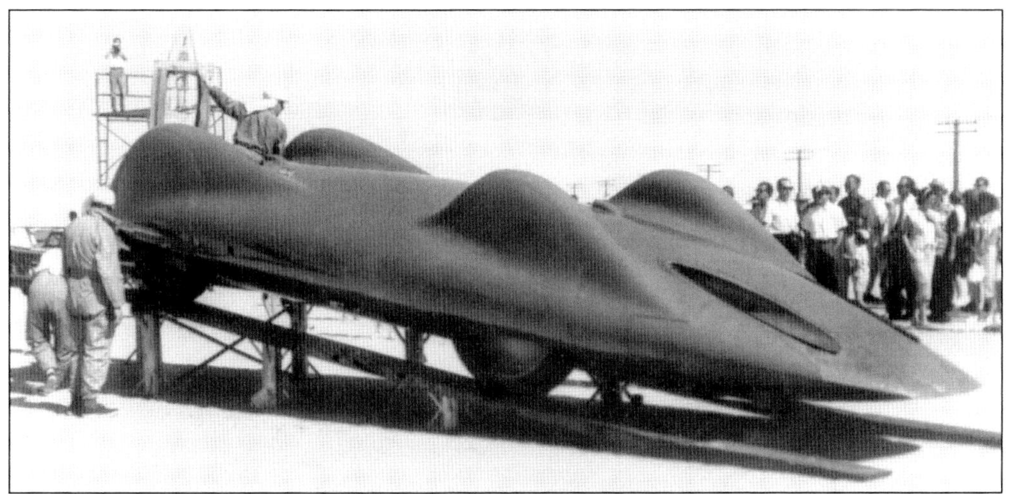

Arriving in 1960, Donald Campbell's "Bluebird Proteus" streamliner car is unloaded in the pits with great hopes of world-record speeds to come. "Campbell simply was in much too big a hurry and is alive solely by the grace of God," wrote respected journalist and on-site observer Griff Borgeson in the January 1961 *Sports Car Illustrated* issue. Many felt Borgeson was sending a veiled message to others about taking their time about going fast. (Courtesy of the Utah State Historical Society.)

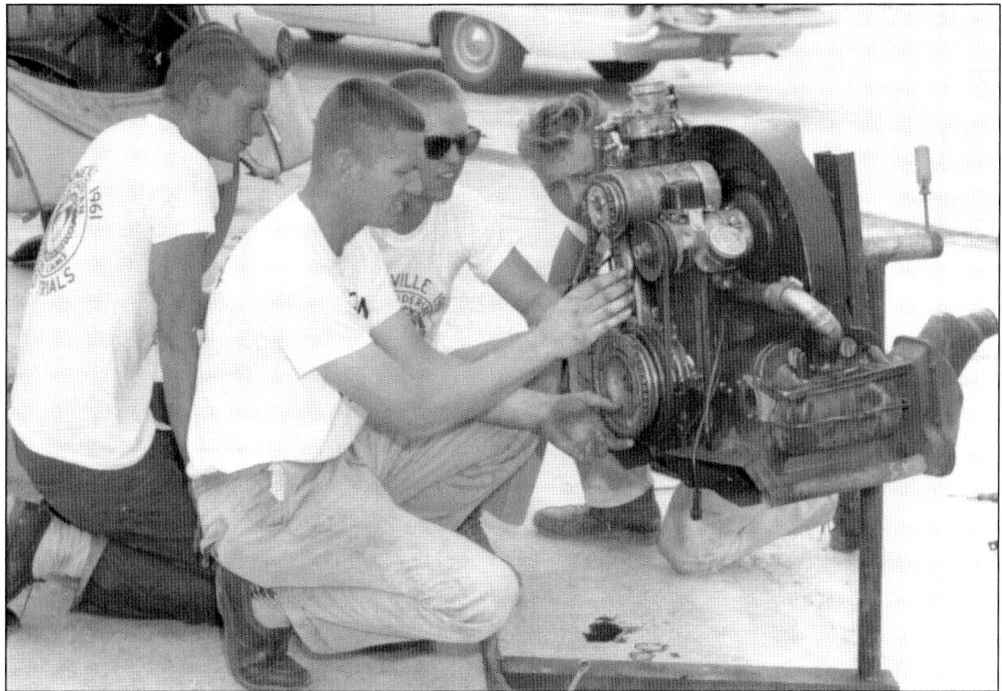

Many connect Dick Beith as the founder of E-T Mags, a respected aftermarket wheel manufacturer. But here, the schoolteacher from Pittsburg, California, wearing the light pants, explains the details of the 36-horsepower, air-cooled Volkswagen engine he and his students mildly modified for the 1960 salt racing season. Beith was the first competitor to set a record with German engines in his 1958 Beetle at 77 miles per hour (and a top speed of 80 miles per hour fitted with his homemade dual carburetor system). He would return years later with a tiny streamliner. (Courtesy of Lester Nehamkin.)

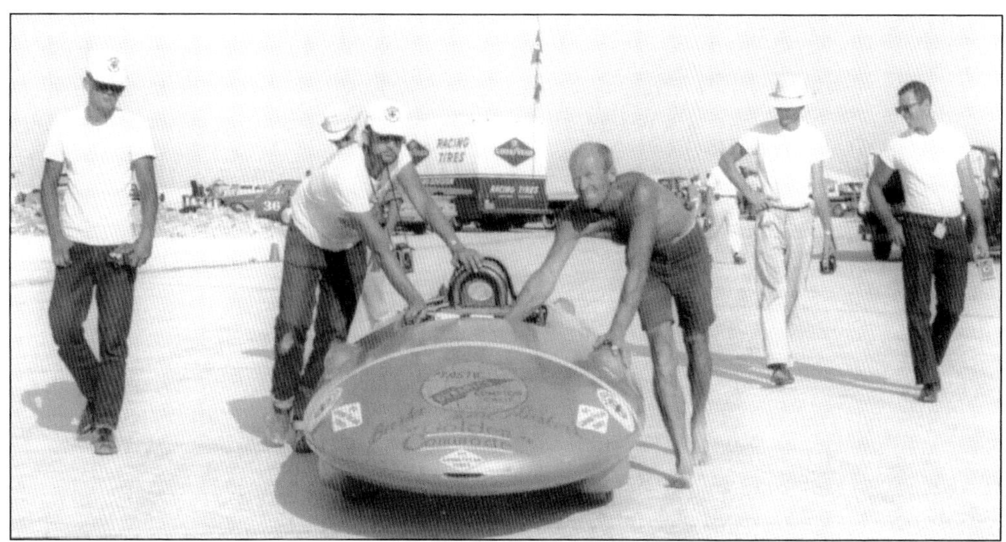

Barefoot Bill Burke and crew push the "Golden Commode" through the pits past curious onlookers. Measuring around 32 inches from the ground, the car was a tight fit, even for the smallest of drivers. Bill was six feet, two inches and sat semi-reclined. Later called the "Pumpkin Seed," it carried Burke to glory in August 1960, recording a record that gave him life membership in the prestigious Bonneville 200 MPH Club. The car was rejuvenated to meet modern speed demands, set several more records, and is now part of the Museum of American Speed collection in Lincoln, Nebraska. (Courtesy of Bill Burke.)

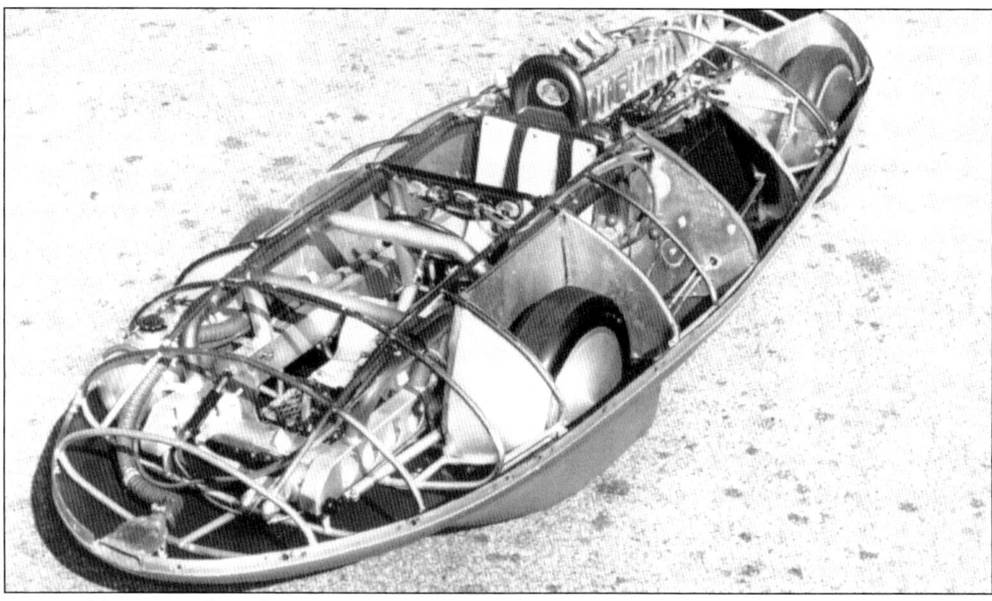

Pictured here is Bill Burke's streamliner with the top body panels removed. The instrument panel lifted out to allow driver egress. The fiberglass body panels were supported by the steel conduit tubing supports attached to a chassis made from mild steel box tubing through which holes were cut to allow feeding of wires and lines. This kept critical parts protected from salt and driver mishaps. Built before the days of roll cages, note the driver protection is only a mild steel tubing hoop. The "hoover" style collector up front was designed for ram-air cooling of the driver's compartment. (Courtesy of Bill Burke.)

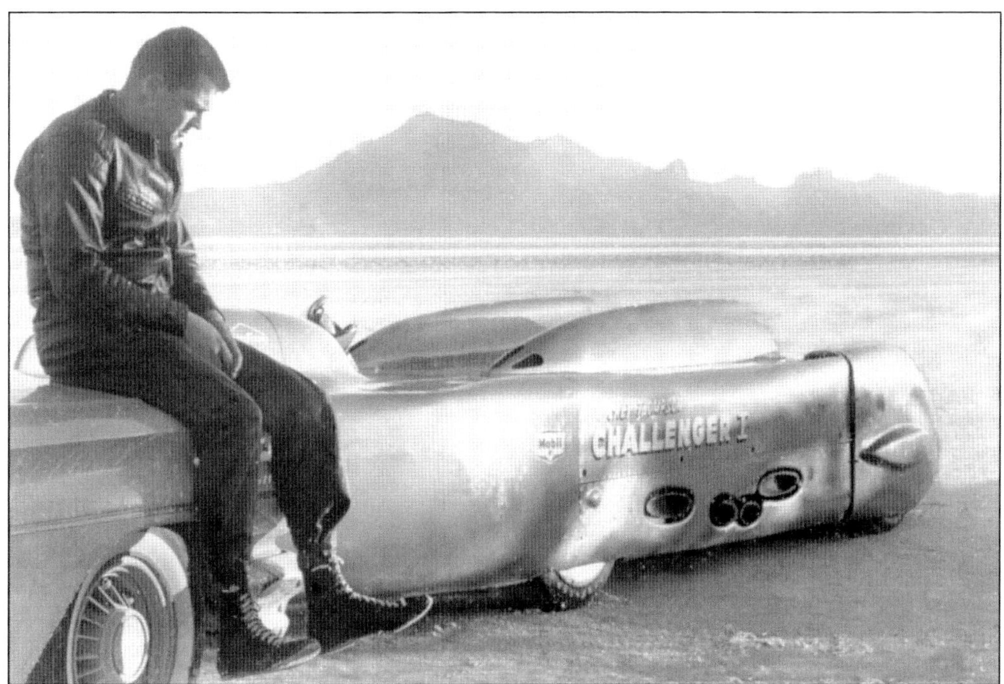

"I am betting my ingenuity against my own life," hot rodder Mickey Thompson told *Time* magazine in September 1958. "Hot rodding is an addiction, like dope or alcohol. I couldn't leave it alone if I had to. The car will do 400. It's a challenge." (Courtesy of Judy Thompson.)

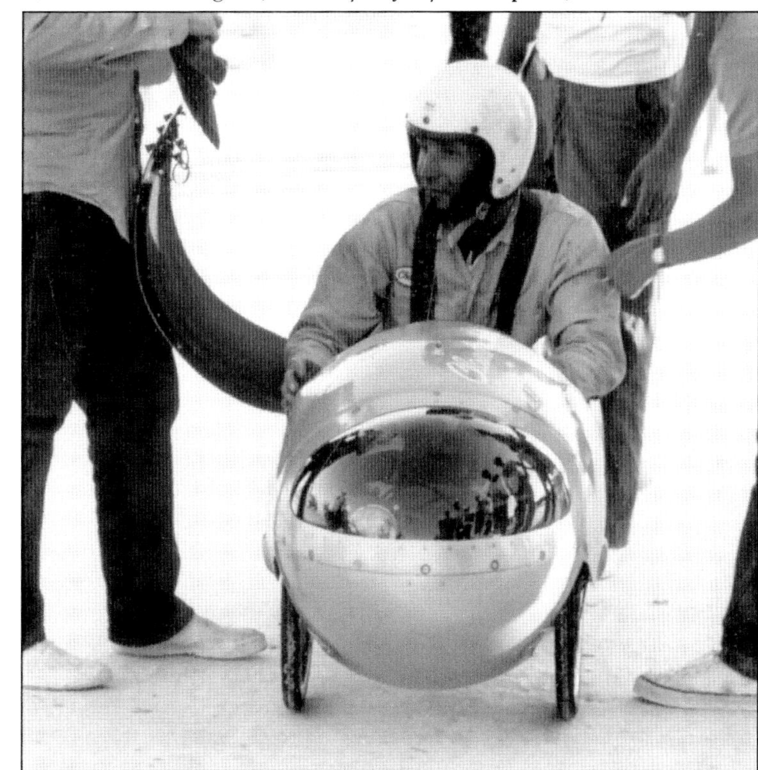

Alan Richards built the smallest car to ever crunch the salt crystals. Aptly named, the 200-pound "Claustrophobia" mystified most as to how the hell anyone could fit in it, let alone drive it. The aluminum bug had a 32-inch wheelbase and 18-inch tread and was powered by a 2.8-inch Garelli engine that recorded 55 miles per hour but had more speed than Richards could use. (Courtesy of LPRL.)

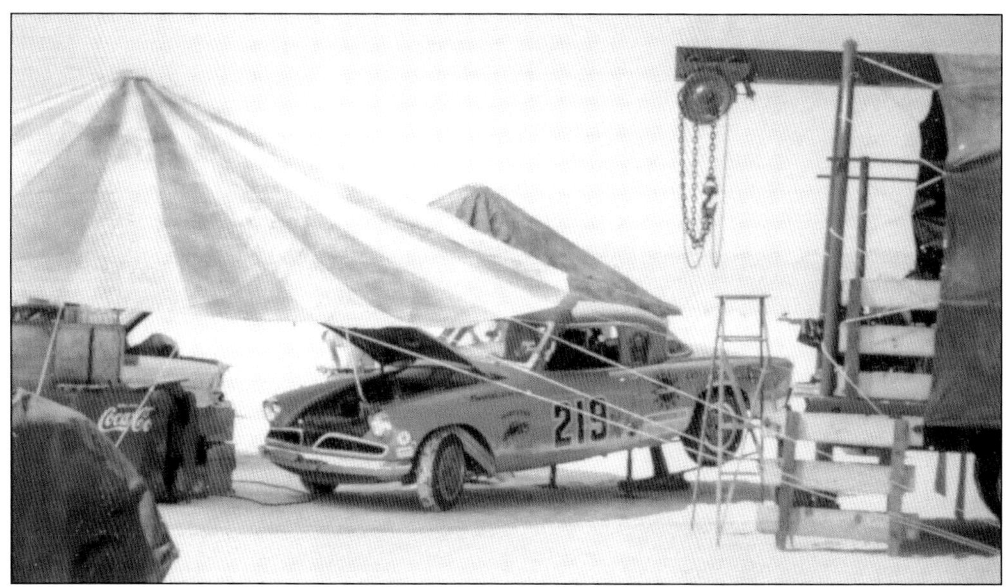

Bruce Geisler and his partner Gary Vail are the recognized power and persistence that brought the No. 219 "Hanky Panky" 1953 Studebaker to the salt for decades, setting more than 80 records. The aerodynamic design of Raymond Loewy found itself earning world's fastest passenger car honors, running on pump gas while simultaneously holding upwards of a dozen records at one time. (Courtesy of LPRL/Bruce Geisler.)

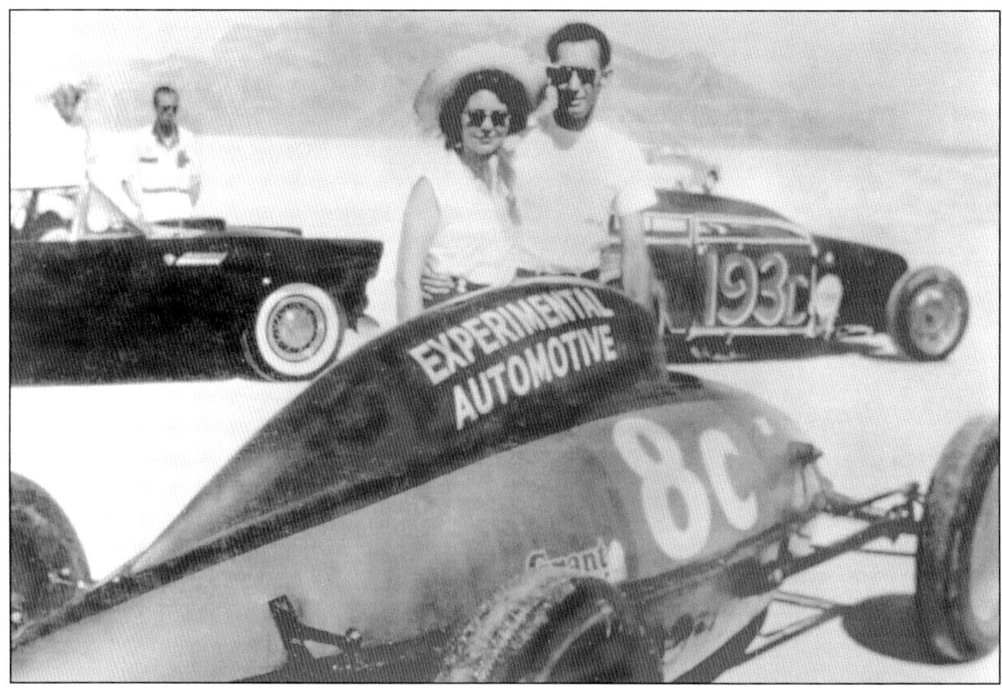

Standing behind their belly tank lakester, Frankie Beatty and her husband, Tom, spent years on the salt experimenting with supercharging various engines. When everything went well, the speeds and records came easily, but when things went wrong, the engine destruction was spectacular. (Courtesy of the Beatty family.)

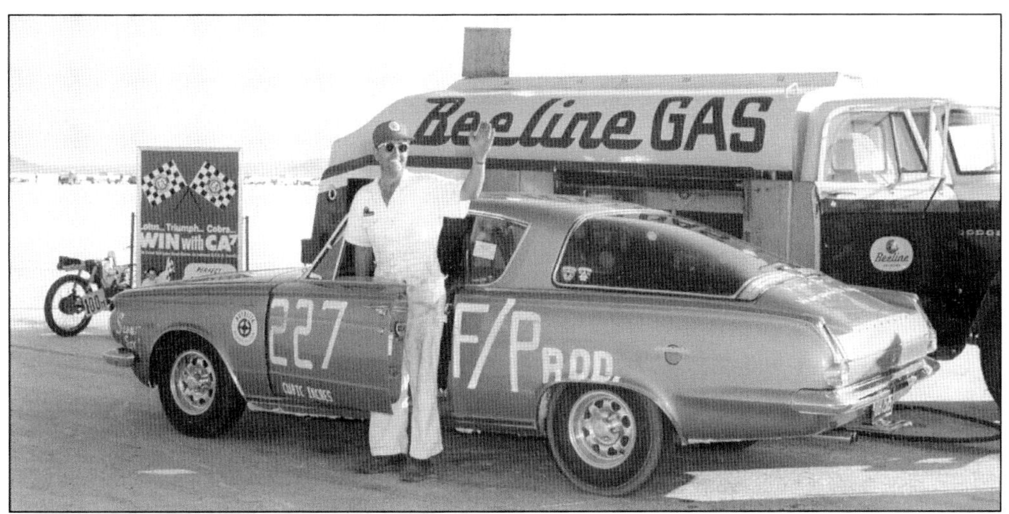

New record holder Wilford Day, 34, of Cedar City, Utah, waves from his 1964 Plymouth Barracuda. The happy Mormon had just set an F/Production record at 143 miles per hour using a 227 CID slant six Dodge engine in 1966. (Courtesy of Wilford Day.)

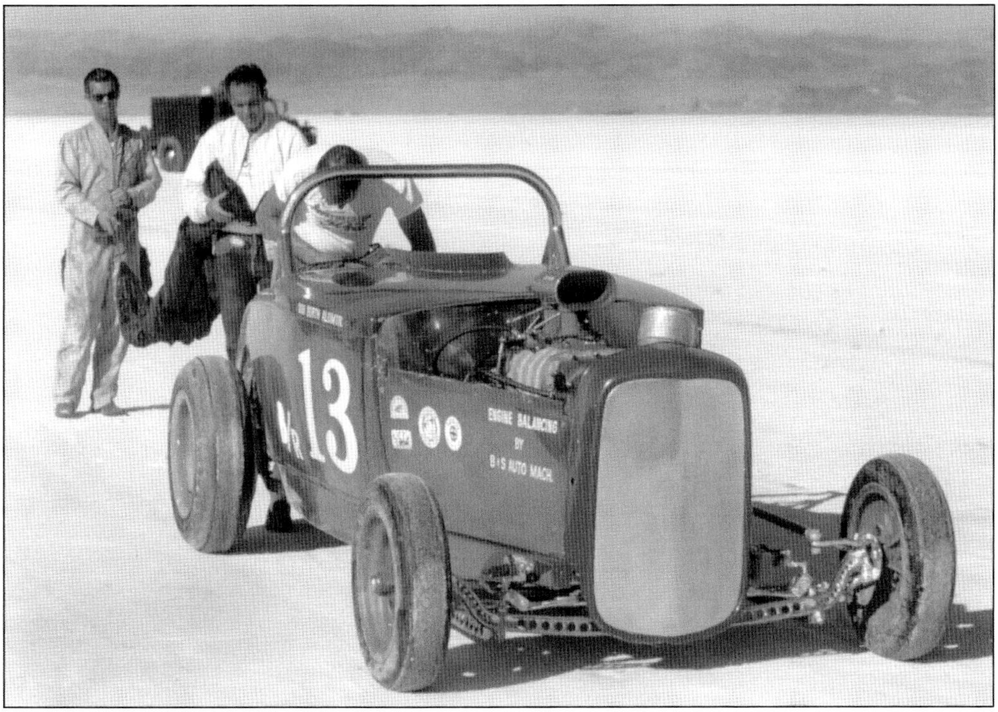

Fred Willert's red roadster needs more than brakes to stop because the three men working behind it are repacking the ring-slot parachute. The man at the back holds the spring-loaded "pop chute" that propels the main parachute (held by the middle man) out of the rear mounted, four-flap sack into which the front man is carefully folding the riser lines. (Courtesy LPRL/Lynn Yakel.)

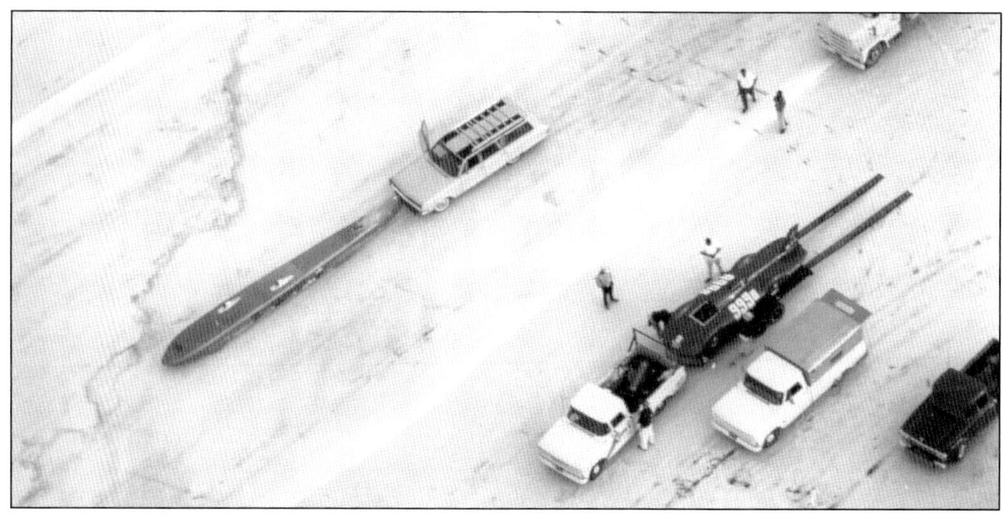

A racer turned writer and photographer, Dean Batchelor captured this great 1965 aerial view of the ready-to-be-push-started Summers brothers "Goldenrod" streamliner with Bob Herda's "999" crew unloading its absolute engineering marvel. That car could have easily passed aircraft-quality building standards, and it arrived with a 311-mile-per-hour world record in the books. (Courtesy of LPRL/Dean Batchelor.)

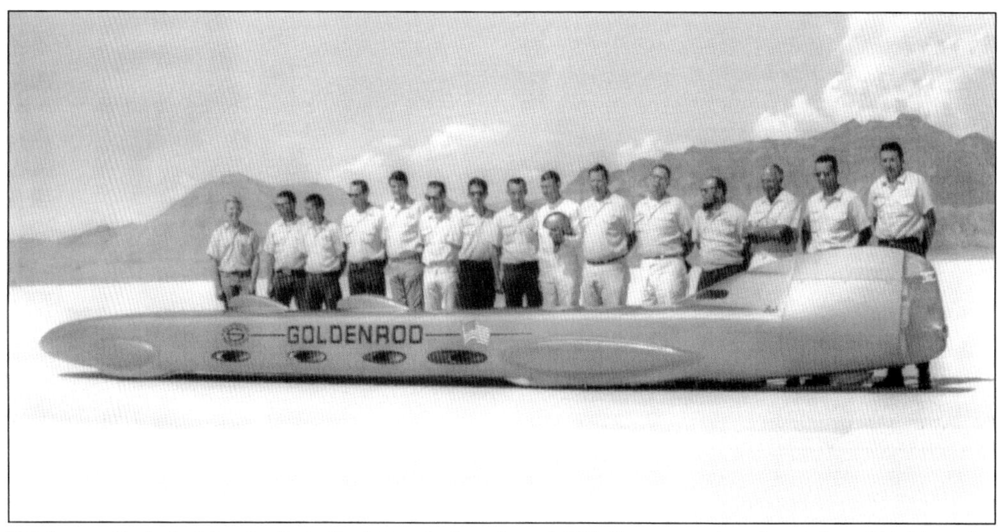

Without all their friends, Bob (holding helmet) and Bill Summers (to the right of Bob) , who had been racing on the salt since the 1950s, would never have realized their dream of setting a world record. The "Goldenrod" used four naturally aspirated Chrysler Hemi engines to record its 409-mile-per-hour mark that stayed put until 2010! (Courtesy of John Baechtel.)

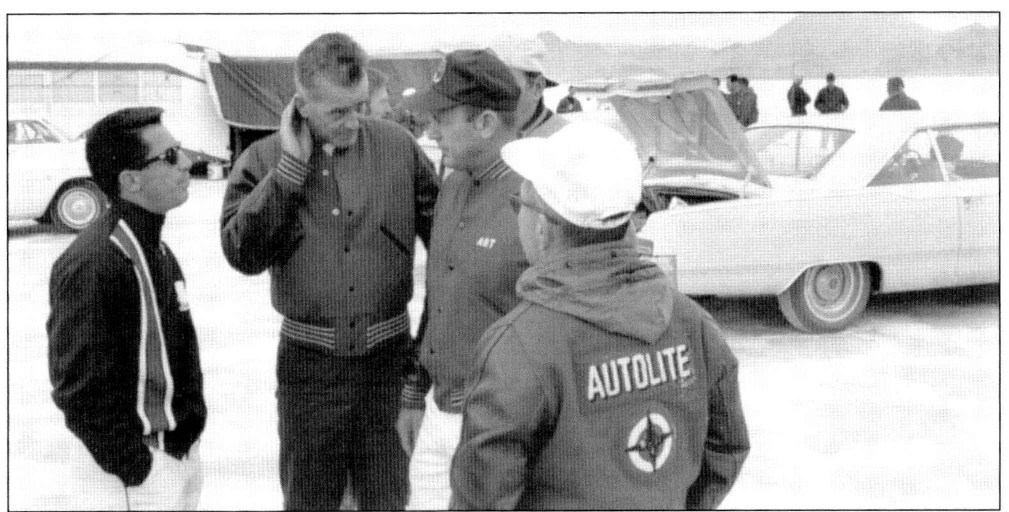

The man on the left is a very young Mario Andretti talking with his Autolite sponsor representatives, from left to right, Danny Eames (scratching his ear), Art Chrisman, and Chick Hiroshima (back to the camera), on the Bonneville Salt Flats. Andretti drove a specially prepped 1967 Ford Mustang fastback, running on straight alcohol, to a couple of minor records. When the crew later poured in nitromethane, he was able to achieve a top speed of 175 miles per hour before a piston blew apart, ending the fun in November 1966. Andretti also learned the fine art of parachute release, a skill he never needed in other race cars. (Courtesy of Ed Justice Jr.)

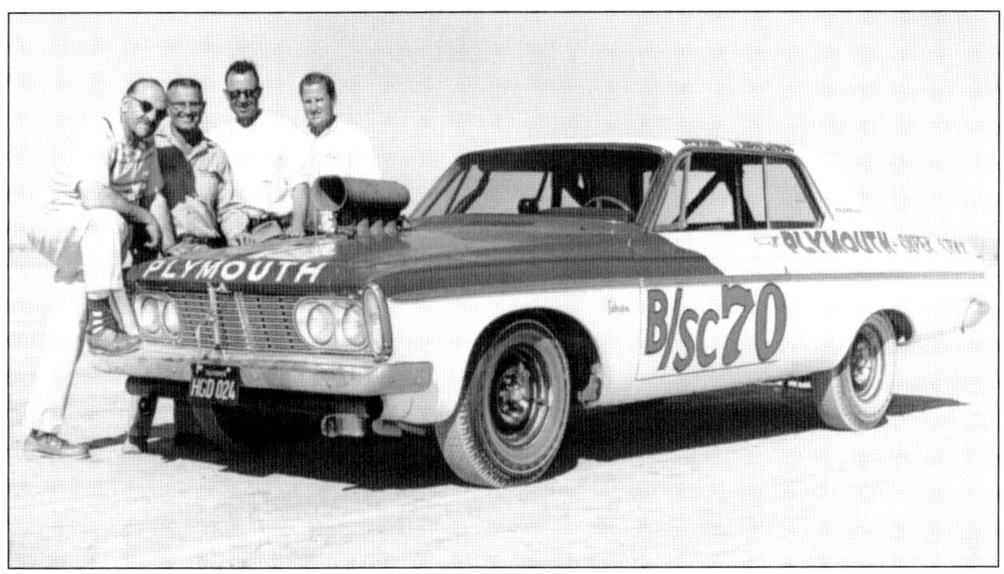

In the mid-1960s, out of Van Nuys, California, came Norm Thatcher, 66 (left), with seemingly no end to his record-setting streak. Next to Thatcher are, from left to right, Bill LaRoy, Gene Cadenhead, and Doug Lovegrove. Of his 200-mile-per-hour racing, the grandfather remarked, "I have one system, I put my foot in it and never lift once I get going. If I go into a little skid, I either go into a bigger one, or bring it out of it." (Courtesy of Josh Ackerman.)

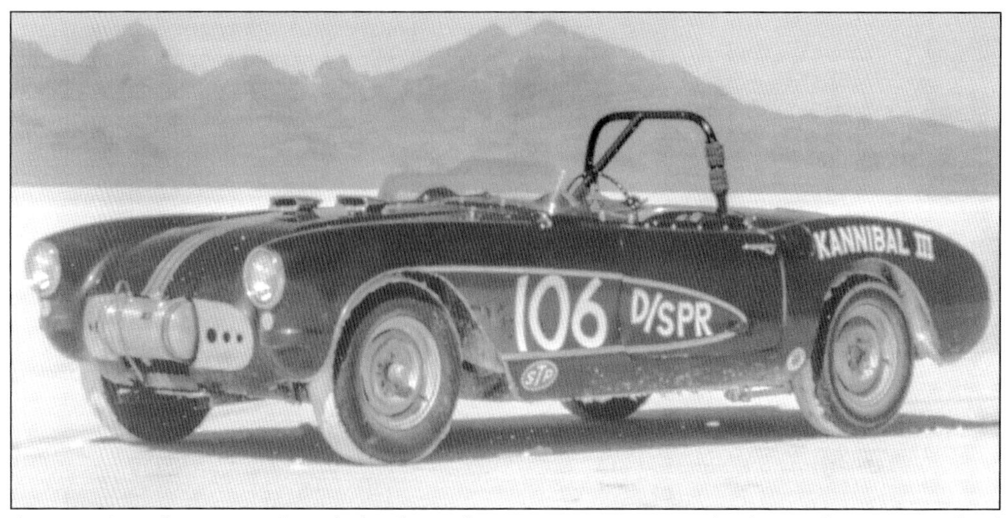

As was often the case with early land speed teams, no one person had enough money to fund an entire racing operation, so a group of guys would band together, usually as a car club, and start hunting for class records. This 1958 Corvette was the 1965 entry for the Knights Car Club from Oakland, California. Some team members—Gary Hartsock, Bruce Cameron, and Jack Solomon—still race at Bonneville today as the 554 Racing Team. (Courtesy of Gary Hartsock.)

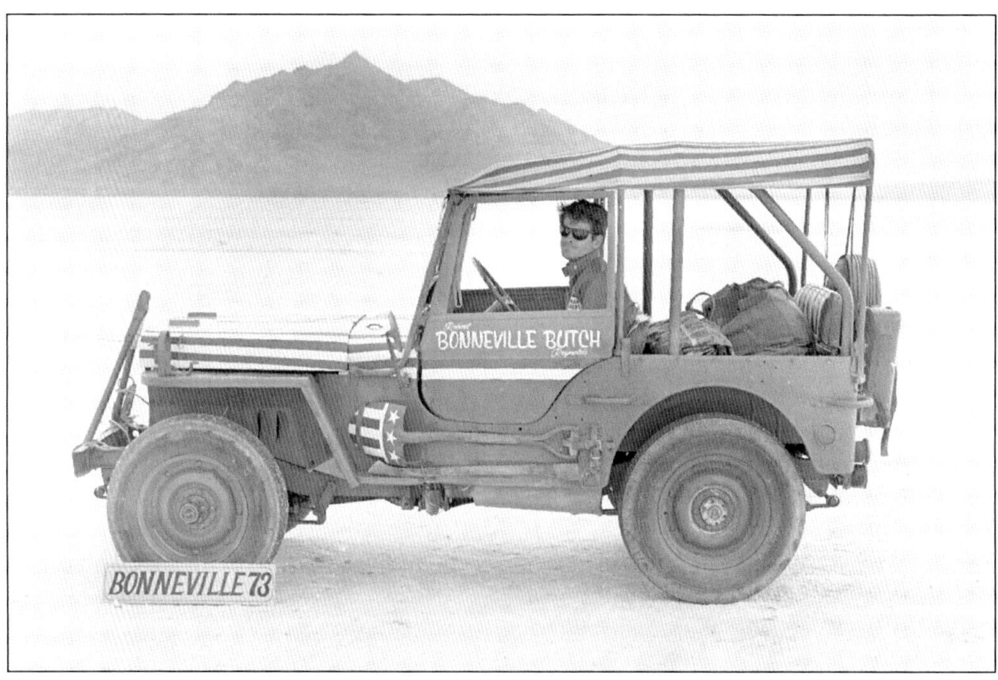

Robert "Bonneville Butch" Reynolds is in his jeep built for him by George Callaway in 1973. Many said he could make ten pounds of parachute fit in a five-pound pack. Reynolds was kin to safety wizard Jim Deist of Deist Safety, who for decades was highly skilled at packing high-speed parachutes. (Courtesy of Jim and Marian Deist.)

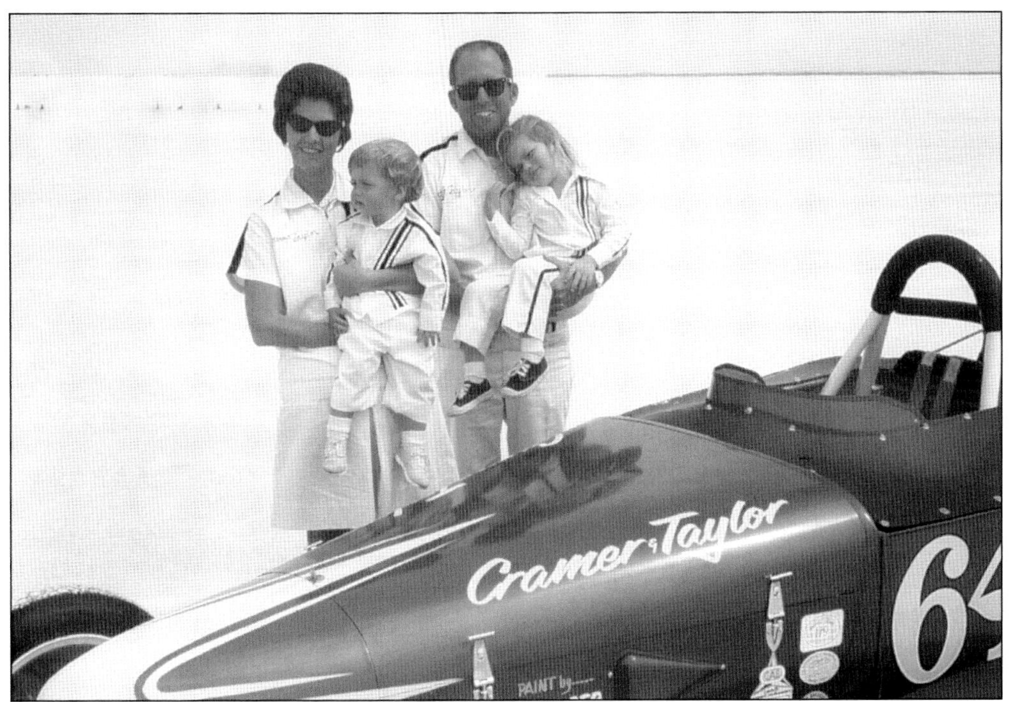

Push car driver and parachute packer Dwianna Taylor holds son Scott while driver and husband Bill holds their squinting daughter Candi behind the 1927 steel-bodied No. 64 T-Roadster in 1970. Dwianna made matching clothes for the kids. Bill was involved in land speed racing from 1954 until retiring in 2011. The car was nicknamed "Dwianna's Mink." (Courtesy of Dwianna and Bill Taylor.)

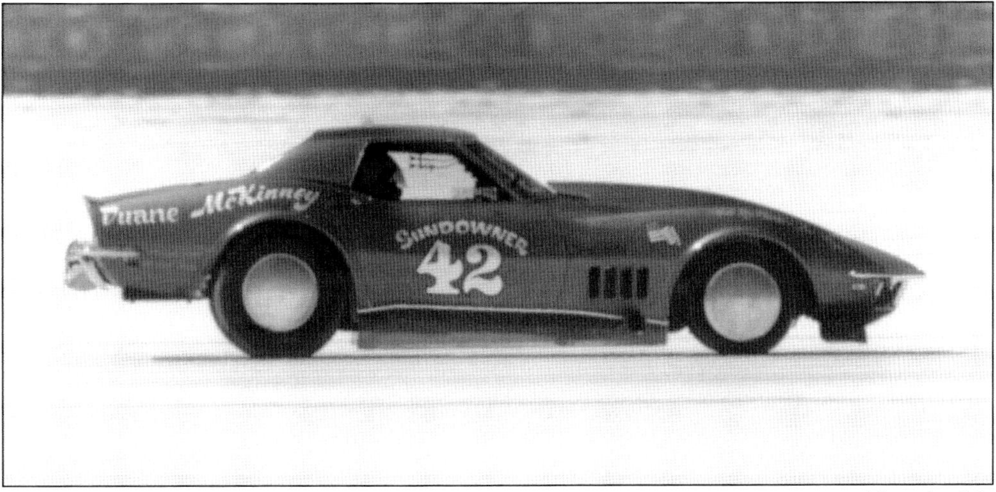

The "Sundowner" Corvette roars across the Bonneville Salt Flats in 1976 powered by a highly modified Chevrolet engine bolted into a nearly all-stock chassis. Owner and driver Duane McKinney set a 240-mile-per-hour record to become world's fastest production car in 1981. McKinney was one of the original pioneers, attending the first 1949 hot rod meet. (Courtesy of Duane McKinney.)

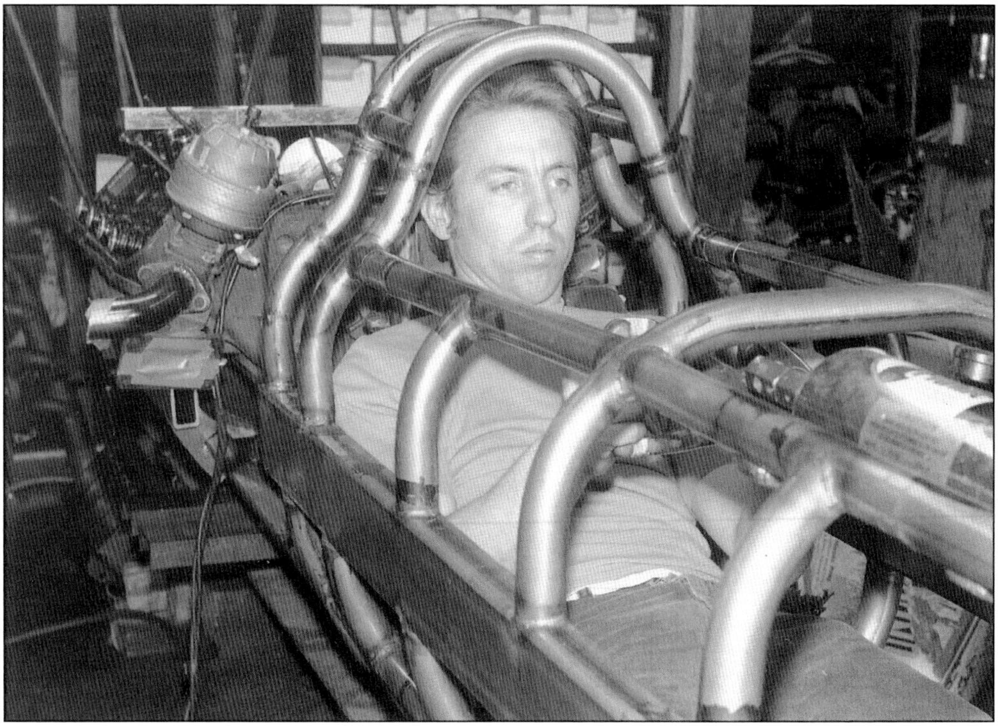

Beginning on January 1, 1975, Elwin "Al" Teague worked for months in his mother's two-car garage building his lakester. He would rise steadily in speed, rebuilding and altering this basic structure until he recorded world-record speeds. Before he departed for the salt, his mother, Margaret, would require he cut the lawn. (Courtesy of Jim Richards and Al Teague.)

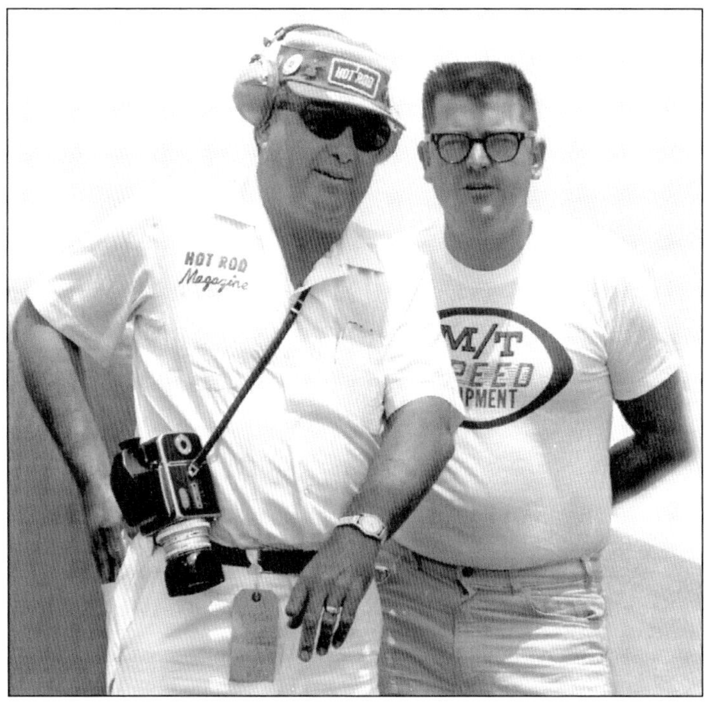

For some 40 years, anyone reading *Hot Rod Magazine* saw photographer Eric "Rick" Rickman's work. The man behind him on the right is Mickey Thompson, who not only gained renown on the salt but also worldwide acclaim in many professional motorsports segments. Rare indeed is it to see this hard charger with spectacles on in public. (Courtesy of Ed Justice Jr.)

Seven

Passing the Wrenches, Helmets, and Records 1984–1997

The Next Generation Grasps for Glory

Age is superfluous at Bonneville. Young or old, it is all the same: wide-eyed wonder of a regal place constantly swirled with a riot of color; cackling thunder propelled from homebuilt metal magic; and the indescribable feeling of being so incredibly lucky to be there, to take part, and to bear witness to the heart of motorsport still so pure and so welcoming.

Some might think to fill the racer ranks the mindset should be "get 'em while they're young!" That is certainly one way, but youthful exuberance remains available at any age, and the gee-whiz wonder of salt virgins (a first-time racer or spectator) provides an entertaining and educational opportunity for both sides.

By now, there were many members of a second-generation wave filling the staging lanes, breaking records of family members and dreaming up new ways to go fast and stay safe. In some cases, third-generation youngsters, destined for remarkable speed deeds, were also found in the pits. The last name might be the same as in 1949, but the first names were rewriting the historical timeline with deeds of their own making.

Although the amateur land speed racers had firmly dominated the world stage from a speed perspective, very little attention was paid to them; recognition was given to those who had accomplished stunning milestones—on and off the speedway. The Gold Coast Roadster & Racing Club, located in Santa Barbara County, California, established the Dry Lakes Racing Hall of Fame in 1993 to preserve the sport's historical timeline, paying homage to racers, their speed machines, historians, and manufacturers of speed equipment whose contributions enhanced the speed quest.

Where once automakers came with regularity to prove the merit of their vehicles to the buying public by setting internationally recognized speed records, that marketing interest waned and was replaced by the curious professionals from other segments of motorsports. The lure of the salt brought big name drivers who were joined by engineers, mechanics, tire changers, and even team owners looking to scratch their speed itch at the controls.

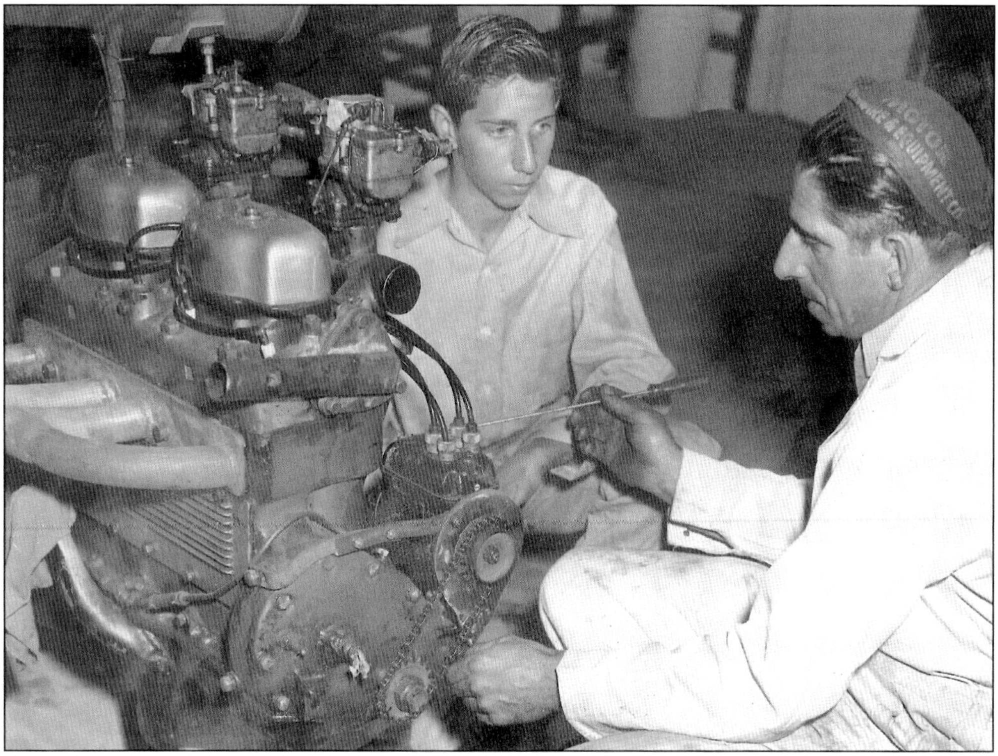

John Vesco shows his son Don the fine points of four-cylinder tuning in 1953. Note the bicycle chain drive off the magneto to the crankshaft and the finned side covers on the engine block. Young Vesco would grow to capture three world land speed motorcycle records as well a variety of speedway accolades, but when he unseated Britain's Donald Campbell in 2001 with a 458-mile-per-hour world mark, he also enjoyed the distinction of being the first man to have set both motorcycle and automobile top marks. (Courtesy of the Vesco family.)

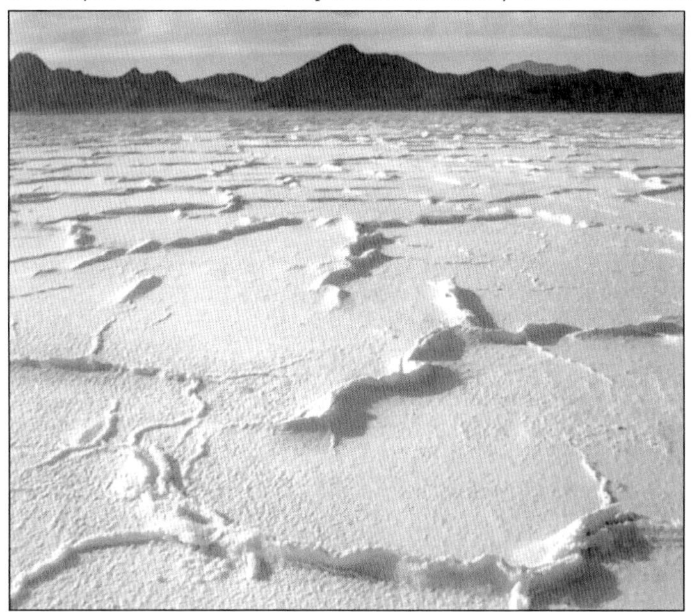

This is what greets the racing community each summer: raw salt with delicate but rigid pressure ridges that need to be dragged, skimmed, and smoothed into a usable speedway without any bumps to permit safe, high-speed runs. As federally permitted potash mining continued unchecked, the thick salt crust thinned little by little every year, eventually allowing cars to easily break through and get mired in mud, just like the Conestoga wagons in the 1800s. (Courtesy of Bob Higbee.)

Standing behind the sports car is Steve Burke, awaiting the driver, his legendary father, Bill, to issue the next instruction as the duo prepare for a run on the salt. The youngster grew up to set a number of his own speed records and help other family members do likewise. Land speed racing is the only form of motorsport were multigenerational racing is common. (Courtesy of Bill Burke.)

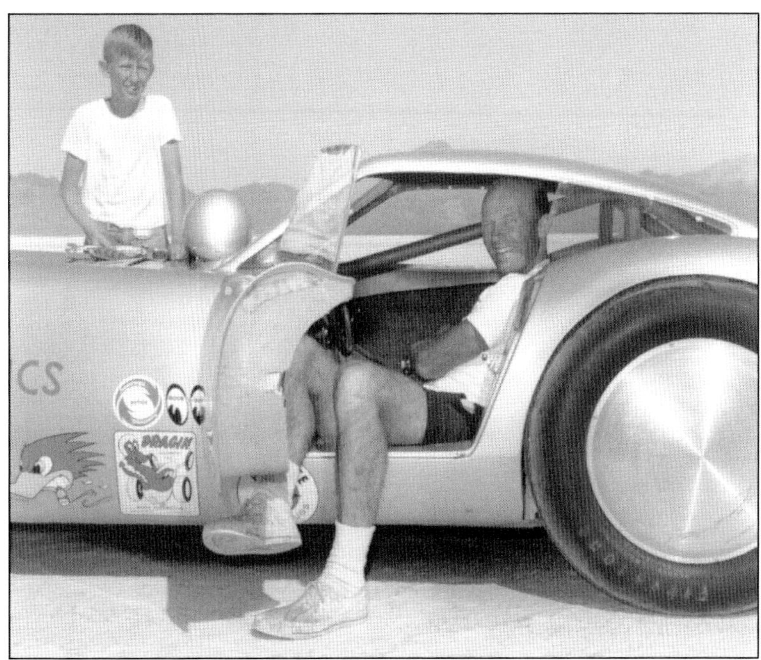

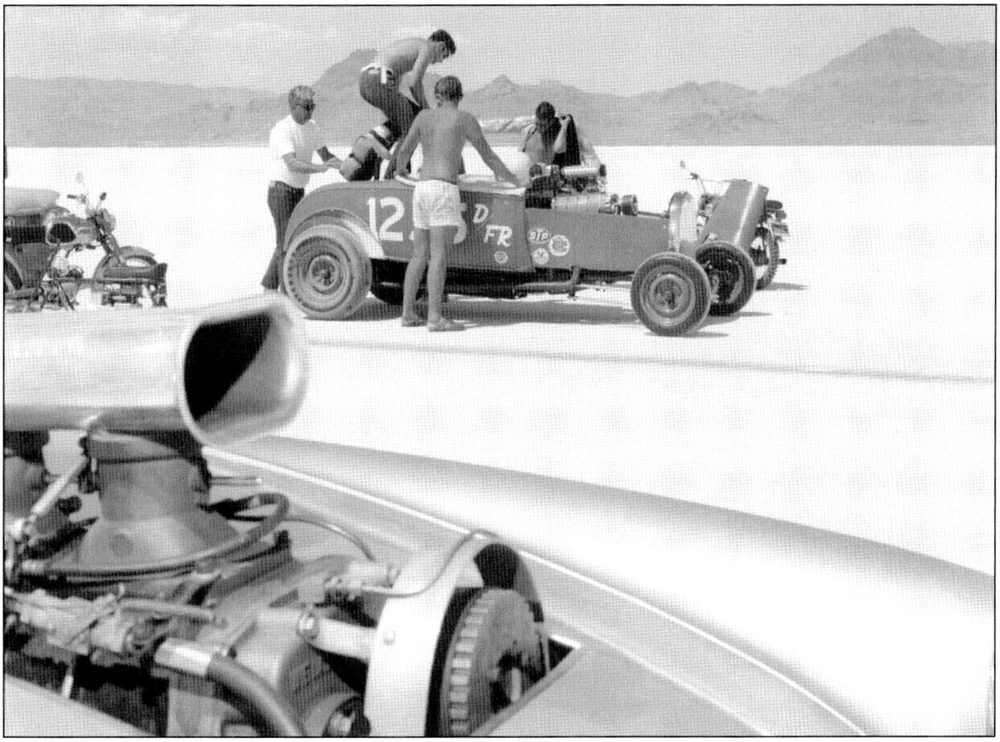

Long before there were four-hour waits in the staging lanes, teams would simply roll up to the starting line, casually make last-minute adjustments, suit up, climb in, and take off. Note that the supercharged engine in the foreground looks much like the engine in the roadster in the background—both rely on a special fuel mixture instead of pump gas. (Courtesy of Eric Dahlquist.)

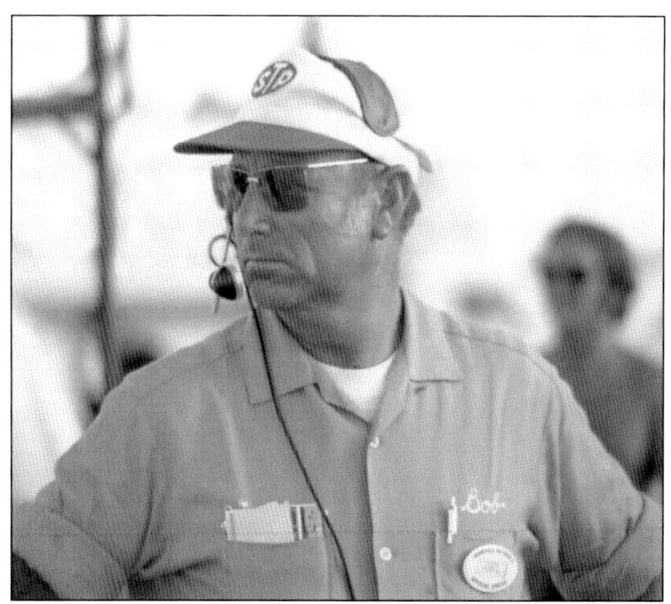

This is the face of more than a half-century of volunteer service. Bob Higbee, pictured here in 1971, had already devoted two decades to the sport and was now the chief starter. He controlled when each competitor would gain solitary access to the speedway. Every driver (or rider) and his or her speed machine received his personal safety inspection before getting the signal to go. Racers believe Higbee saved more lives on the starting line than the ambulance crews after a crash. (Courtesy of Gary Hartsock.)

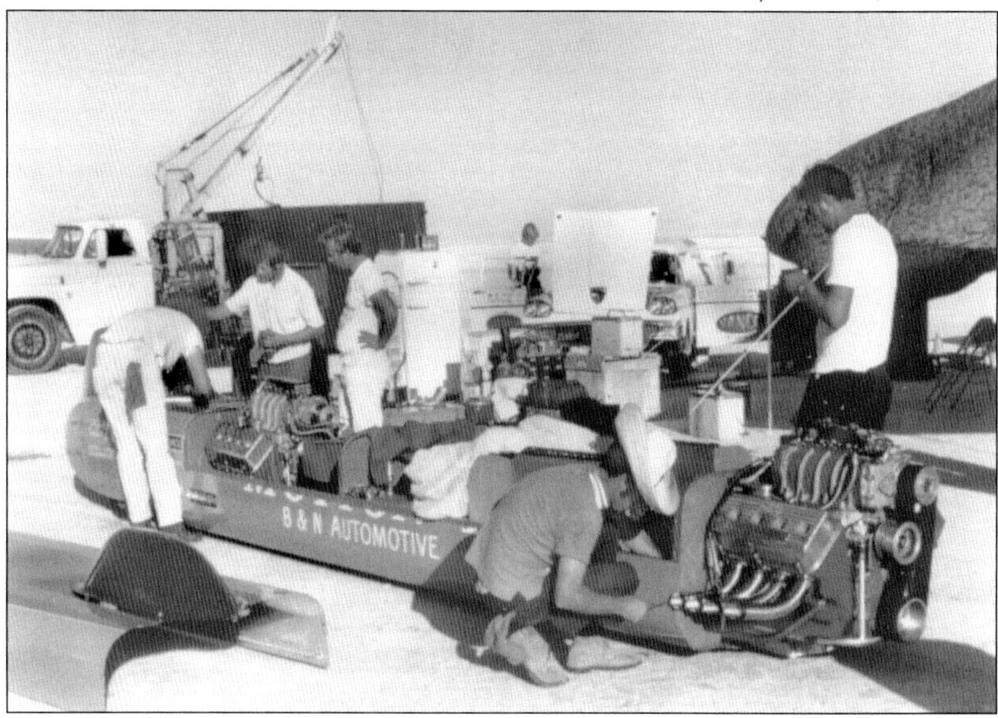

Working on the racer in 1970 is co-owner Bert Petersen (standing at far right) of the B&N Automotive "Motion I" streamliner. Crouched by the front wheel is crewman Clarence Zeitler, with driver and co-owner Noel Black (hands on hips) discussing changes with crew. After safe 300-plus-mile-per-hour runs, calamity chimed at 380 miles per hour. When Black cleared the fourth mile, the car wiggled, slid, lifted into the air, and disintegrated through repeated rolls, coming to rest past the five-mile marker. Flown by air ambulance to a Salt Lake City hospital, the respected competitor and genius at making do with limited resources did not survive the night. (Courtesy of John Sprenger.)

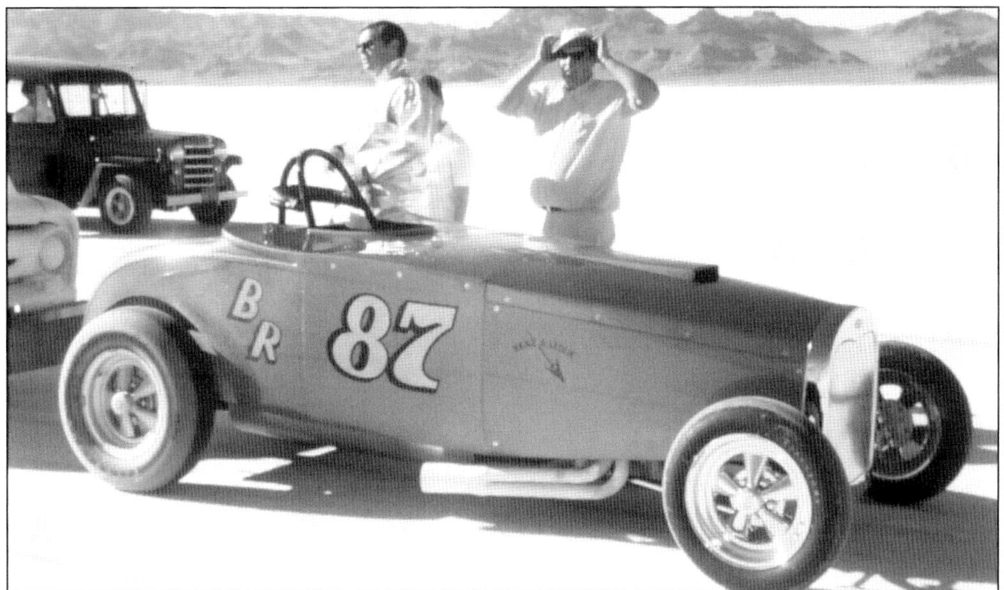

In August 1968, the Peek brothers from Littleton, Colorado, brought their groovy little powder-blue metallic roadster to the salt, and *Hot Rod Magazine* photographer Eric Rickman put it on the cover of the December issue. Driver Jerry Peek is at left with brother Michael, but from their expressions, neither knows where brother Greg might be. The brothers raced the car for seven years and set a pair of records every time they went out. They sold the car in 1978, but Greg bought it back in 1995 and restored it to concourse race quality. (Courtesy of Bob Higbee.)

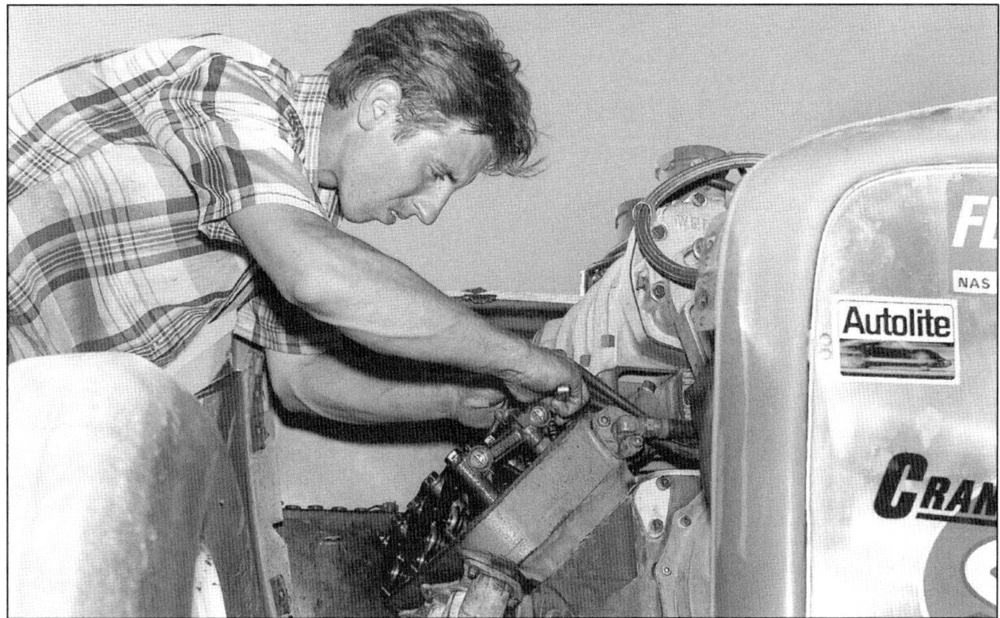

When William Teague took his seven-year-old son Al to a speedway motorcycle race close to their home in East Los Angeles, he had no idea it set afire a passion to last lifetime. Here, Al works on the engine in the Sadd, Teague, and Bentley roadster, a car that dominated national competition for years and gave young Teague solid driving experience to confidently enter international competition years later. (Courtesy of Al Teague.)

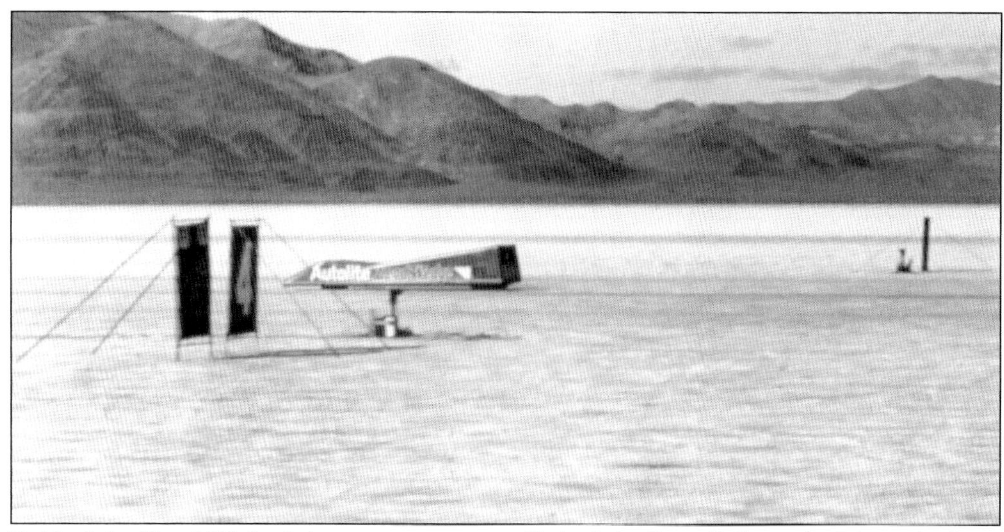

Dubbed the "Lead Wedge," this racer was originally built by Dean Jefferies for Mario Andretti to drive. However, the project shifted, and Jerry Kugel drove the car using 20 special Autolite car batteries, setting a 138-mile-per-hour record on November 19, 1968. A variety of automotive journalists also got to pilot the car. All Kugel's kids have raced on the salt. (Courtesy of LPRL/ Dean Batchelor.)

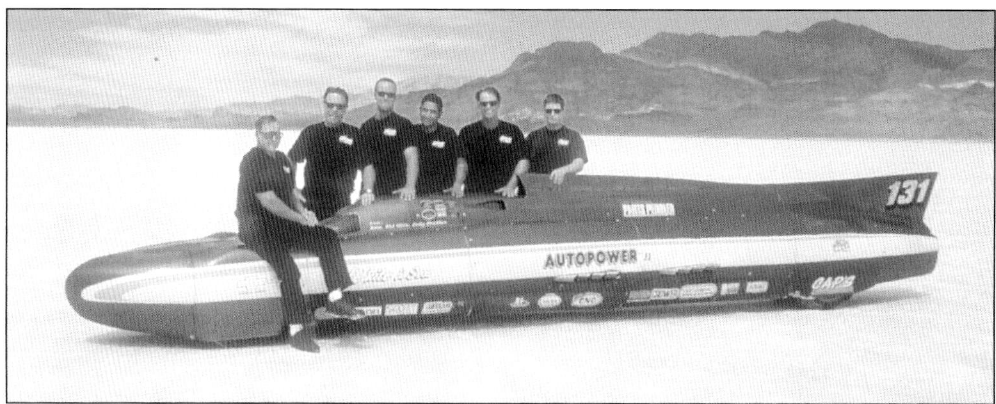

As tough a competitor as ever there was, the 2002 "Spirit of Autopower" race team was led by Nolan White (left), who is seated next to son Rick (second from left) and grandson Brad (third from left). From left to right, friends Julio Hernandez, John Hartwell, and son Ryan Hartwell fill out the crew. "The family is made of something different," said a competitor. "Not that the rest of us are chickens, it's just they run on a different octane than the rest of us." In August, Nolan, 71, clocked a top speed of 434 miles per hour while setting a 413-mile-per-hour class record. Unfortunately in October, the car rolled above 400 miles per hour, and Nolan died three days later surrounded by family. (Courtesy of LandSpeed Louise.)

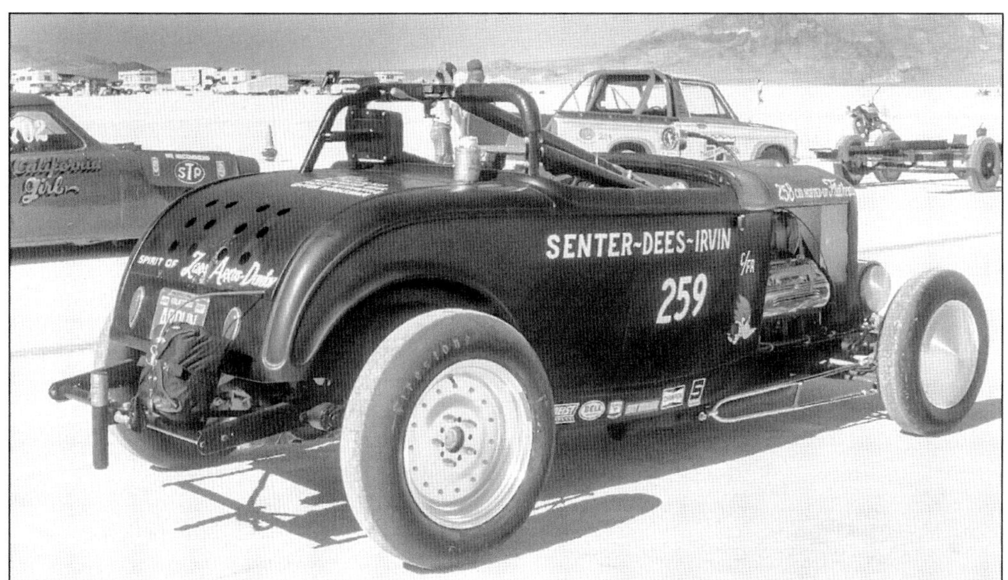

Jack Senter, a production designer in Hollywood, spent eight hours hand lettering his son Tom's flathead Ford roadster for its trip to 1978 Speed Week with partners Mark Dees and Jeff Irvin. Tom, known for his wry smile and splendid automotive journalism, was off somewhere making recordings of engines roaring down the racetrack to play back while working in his family garage and annoying the neighbors back in California. (Courtesy of LPRL/Betty Burkland.)

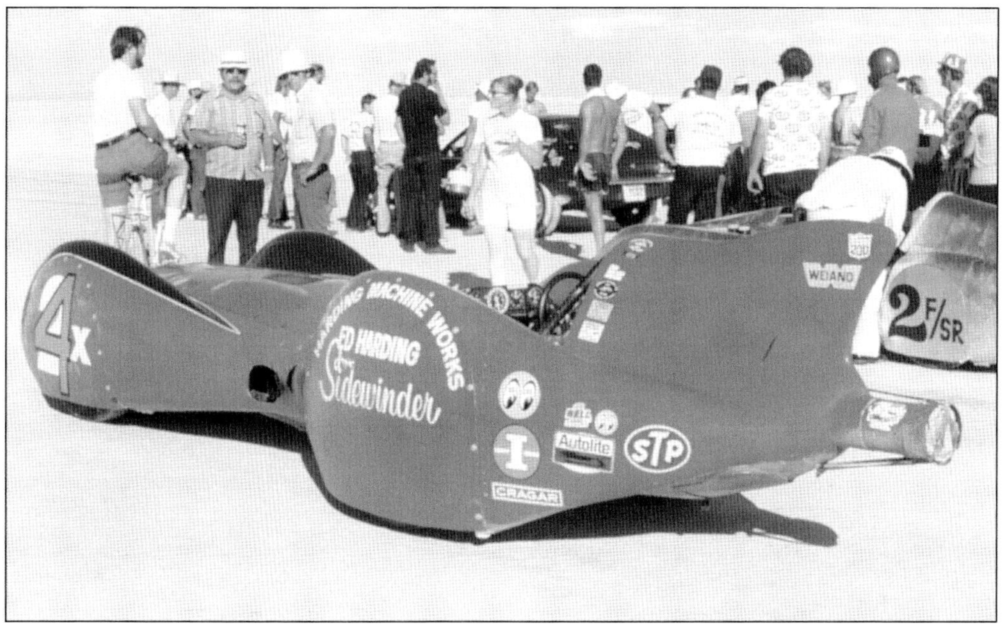

This exquisite, unusual streamliner has changed hands many times through the years with each owner trying to slap another name on it. Nothing stuck except "The Redhead," just like Clayton Moore will always be The Lone Ranger no matter who tries wear the mask. (Courtesy of Betty Burkland.)

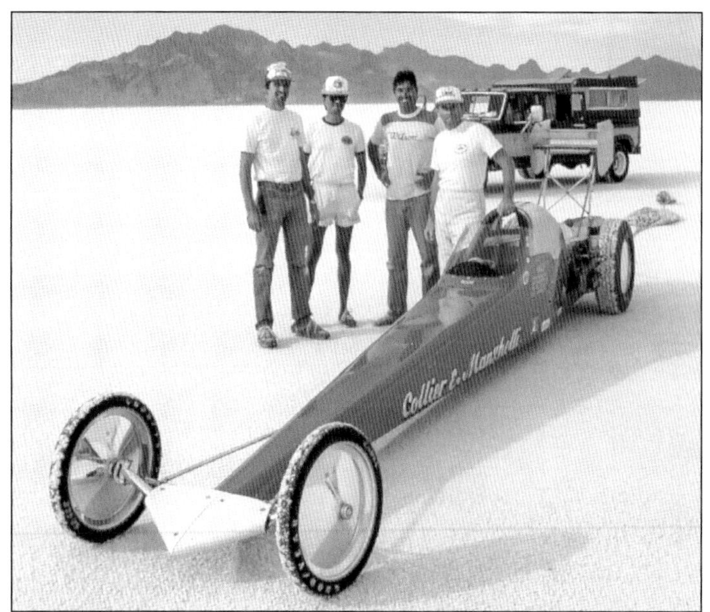

Pictured are, from left to right, Mike Manghelli, Steve Garcia, Steve Cantelli, and driver Jerry Collier. The last three men had been friends since the fourth grade at Our Lady of the Holy Rosary Catholic School, adding Manghelli to their mischief when they built this four-cylinder, air-cooled, three-liter Volkswagen engine that roared to a 189-mile-per-hour record in 1988—the fastest a VW had ever gone on the salt. (Courtesy of Burly Burlilie.)

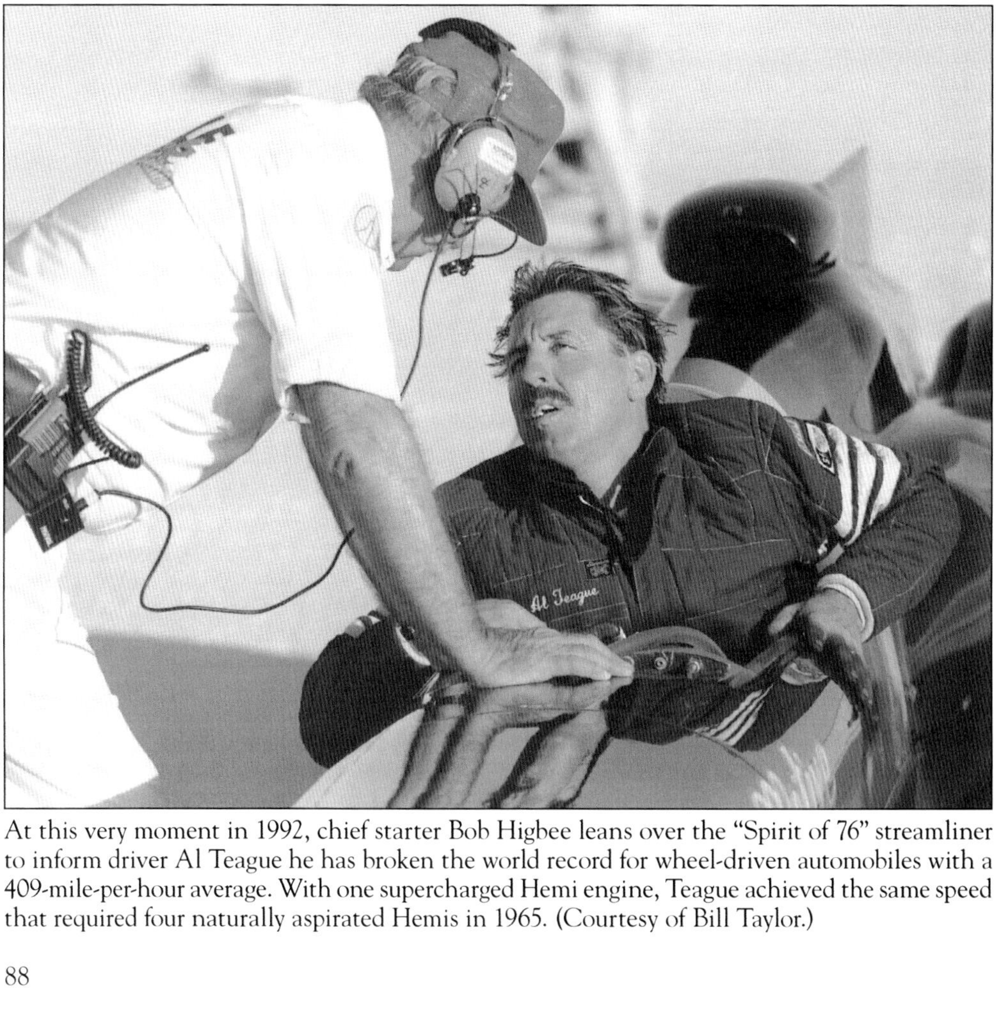

At this very moment in 1992, chief starter Bob Higbee leans over the "Spirit of 76" streamliner to inform driver Al Teague he has broken the world record for wheel-driven automobiles with a 409-mile-per-hour average. With one supercharged Hemi engine, Teague achieved the same speed that required four naturally aspirated Hemis in 1965. (Courtesy of Bill Taylor.)

Eight

Motorcyclists Make Their Mark

How Fast Will It Go?

No matter the speed on the time slip, there is always more to get, and some prefer adventuring forth on two or three wheels instead of four. Marvel at those who, utterly gleeful, work with the smallest engines, from which they squeeze out speed numbers thought impossible. Applaud the mechanical geniuses who stuff multiple engines into sheathed tubular frames that resemble mechanical fish trying to hook a 400-mile-per-hour record.

In between are those that enjoy riding "naked" bikes, machines without any air-cheating body panels, as well as riders with a bevy of bespoke pieces fabricated to allow them to almost crawl under the paint and zing through the wind. All display potent perseverance mated to calculated derring-do with an attitude of gratitude when the time slip verifies their thinking.

Spectators require nothing but curiosity when in the pits or on the starting line. The visual treat is elevated to sensory alert when the ignitions wake up the bazillion screaming bumblebees that roar out of the exhaust pipes. Only crazy people forget to bring ear protection.

Because motorcycles were always subservient in organized automobile time trials, the tenacious spirit of bikers was elevated when the BUB meet was granted a permit for an all-motorcycle event in 2004. The new "Run Watcha Brung" class allowed anyone who showed up—even street bikes—the chance to tease the timing lights and earn a time slip.

The event was well attended annually, offering not only national American Motorcycle Association (AMA) record opportunities but also Federation Internationale de Motocyclisme (FIM) world marks because it was easy for organizers to allow bikes to safely make the required two-way runs within the prescribed time allotment.

Longtime manager of the BUB meet event Delvene Manning assumed ownership in 2014, rechristening it the Bonneville Motorcycle Speed Trials (BMST), which continues to the present day. She not only purchased the necessary equipment but also became fully responsible for securing funding, planning operational tactics, and leading promotion duties—all while a single mother of a six-year-old child.

Unquestionably, there is just as much passion behind the scenes as astride the bikes!

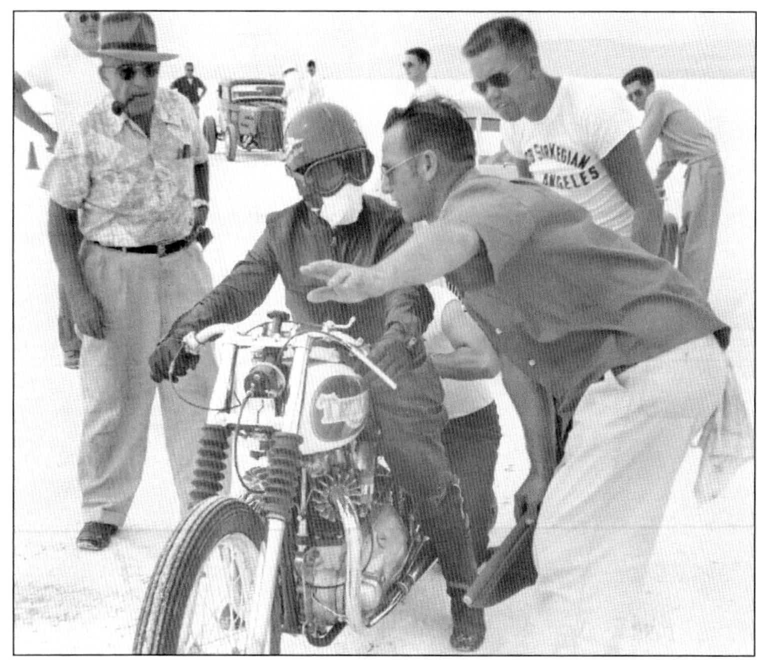

Astride a 1949 Triumph 6T Thunderbird, 13-year-old Californian Bobby Sirkegian gets last-minute instructions from a teammate before twisting the throttle grips of the 649cc engine up to 122 miles per hour in 1953. It was not a record-setting pass, yet the schoolboy was given a special award for being the youngest rider ever on the Bonneville Salt Flats. (Courtesy of Tom Medley.)

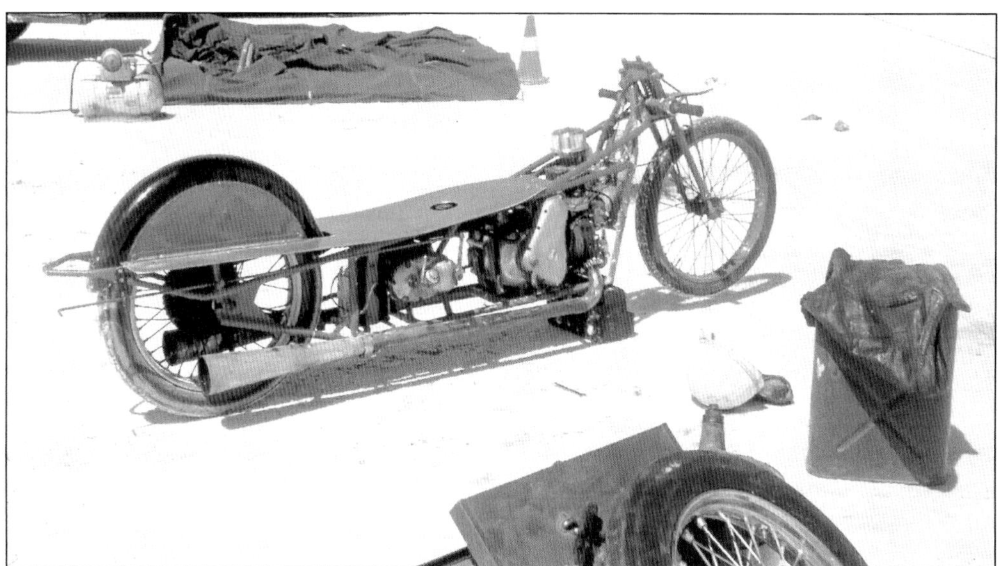

Once Bud Hare got ahold of this Triumph and modified it for salt racing, it bore little resemblance to what dealers sold. Experimenting with the trend of the era, where riders tried to emulate Rollie Free's daring runs stone prone, clad only in a pair of bathing trunks, bikes like this were inevitable. In 1951, Hare was one 10 motorcyclists invited to Speed Week. Note the odd engine placement; it is rotated 90 degrees forward and uses a custom two-barrel downdraft carburetor. Hare set a 125-mile-per-hour record lying prone on his fabricated "ironing board" plate. (Courtesy of LPRL/ Bud Schmitt photograph.)

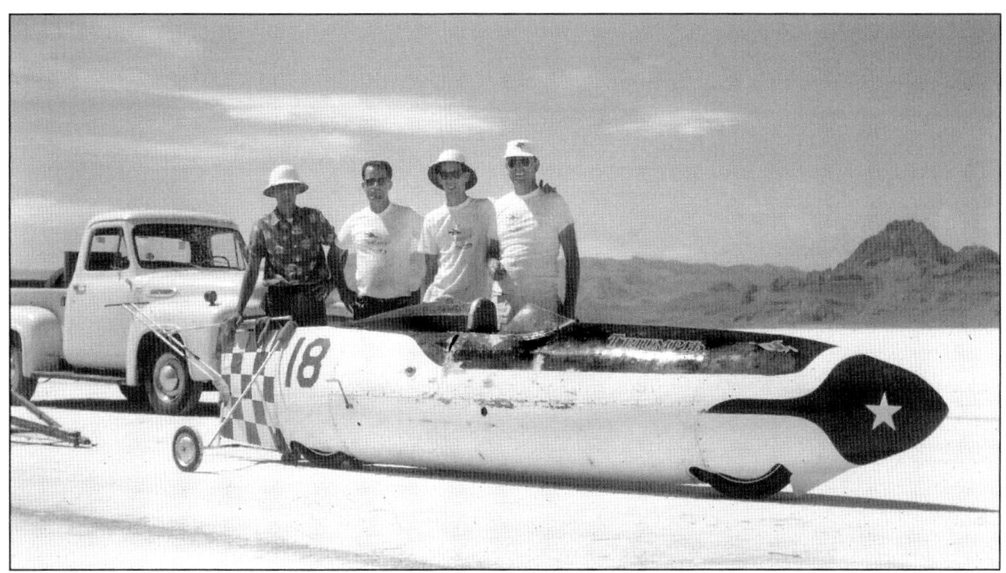

Out of Smithfield, Texas, came Stormy Mangham with his fully streamlined Triumph "Texas Cigar." Mangham was considered the first to use a braking parachute on a motorcycle streamliner. Stored in the tail section, it was spring-loaded for quick deployment. In 1956, powered by a naturally aspirated 650cc Triumph Thunderbird engine, rider Johnny Allen recorded a 214-mile-per-hour average, knocking the well-financed German NSU factory team record out of the books. It was also the first time America had held the record since 1921, and it earned Allen entry into the Bonneville 200 MPH Club—the first American motorcyclist to do so. (Courtesy of Tony Waters.)

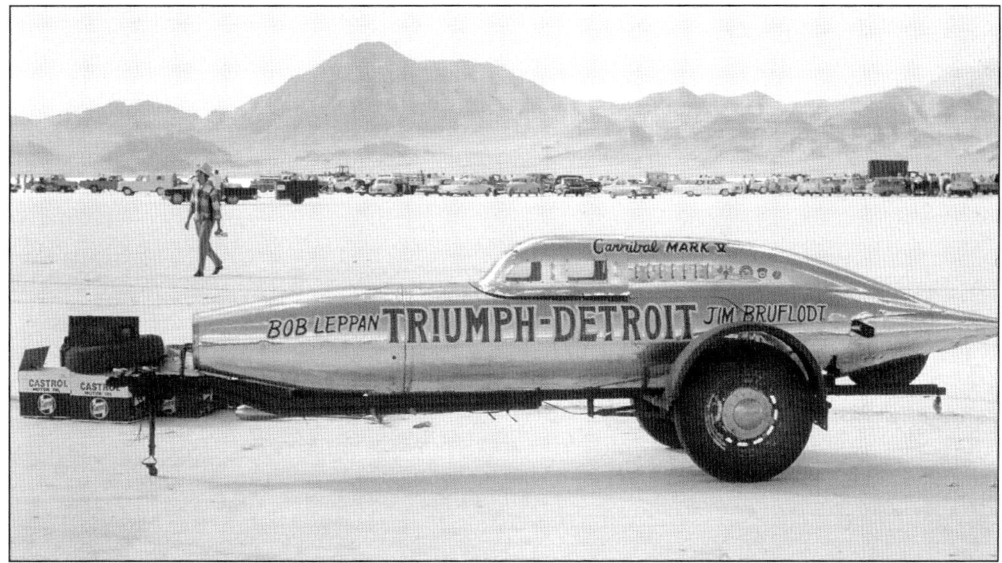

Long before the world knew Bob Leppan's bike as the "Gyronaut" it was, in 1963 the "Cannibal Mark V" arrived wrenched by Jim Bruflodt. It was here that Leppan joined forces with noted auto industry designer and stylist Alex Tremulis. By 1966, the bike, now radically improved by the pair, set a new national record of 245 miles per hour with Leppan as the rider of record. Even fitted with innovative safety equipment for the time, including a roll cage and fire suppression, when the streamliner crashed on the salt in 1970 near 270 miles per hour, Leppan was seriously injured in the accident. (Courtesy of LPRL.)

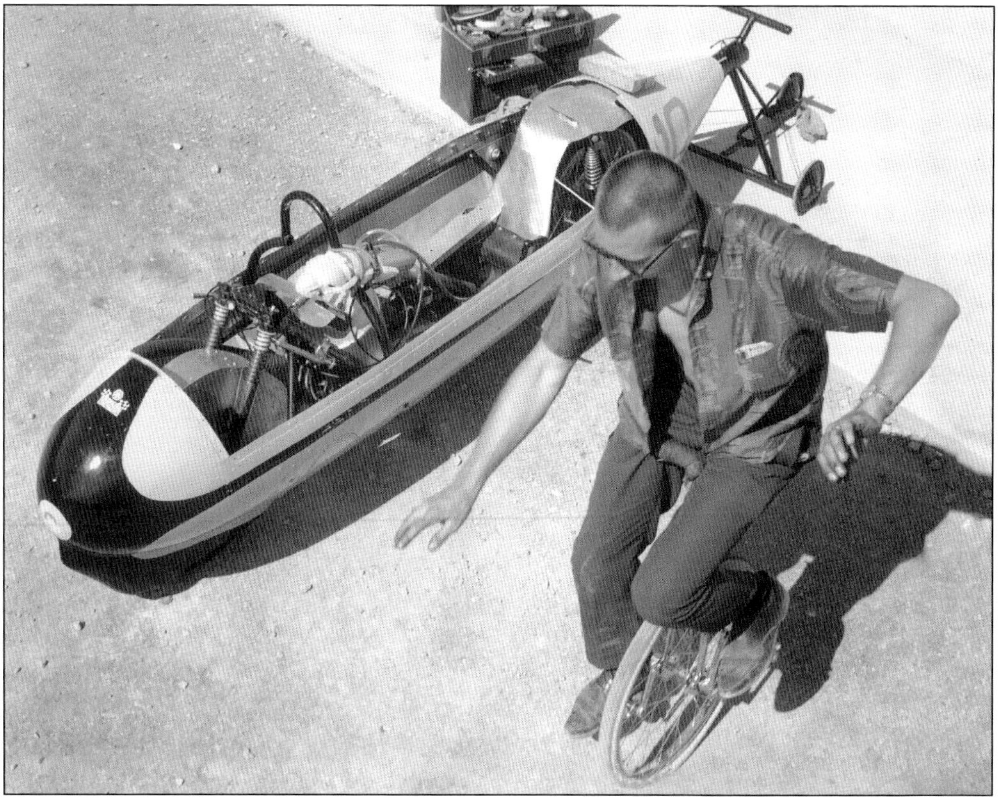

The late Don Vesco is pictured here in 1965 using Ralph LeClercq's unicycle to teach himself how to better balance a motorcycle streamliner at low speeds—the sport's hardest vehicles to control. Nearby is an early version that brought a broken collarbone when a practice run went sour. Vesco turned adversity into life lessons that saw him later pepper world record books with 18 motorcycle and 6 automobile world records; he was the first motorcyclist to exceed 200 and 250 miles per hour and was inducted into the Motorcycle Hall of Fame and the Motorsports Hall of Fame of America. (Courtesy of Don Vesco.)

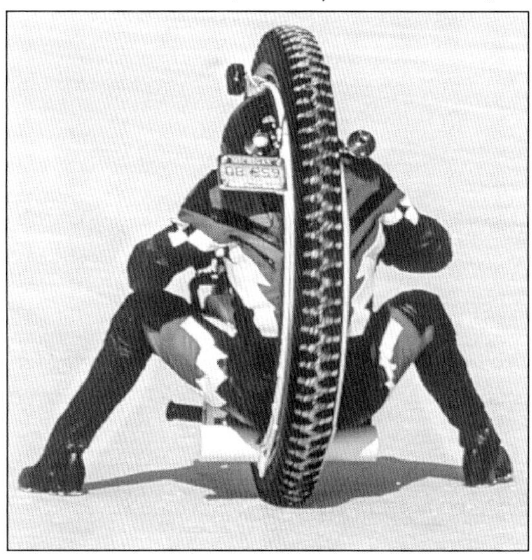

Ingenious is a single word to characterize Michigan resident Kerry McLean. Pictured here in 2000, he is just beginning to roll off the starting line riding his handcrafted monowheel. On the monowheel, which is licensed for the street, McLean managed a timed average of 53 miles per hour. Although most observers were waiting for him to fall over, he never did and flawlessly went wherever he wanted—even on the highway. "It is important to be innovative and follow your dreams," stated McLean. "Besides, it makes life a lot of fun." Powered by a 40-horsepower snowmobile engine, the monowheel is four feet in diameter, but McLean sits within a three-foot circle. (Courtesy of LandSpeed Louise.)

Pictured here is salt virgin Roosevelt "Rosey" Lackey, 32, astride a Triumph 3 open-frame motorcycle in 1969. He is being pushed off the starting line by Triumph Corporation mechanic Ted Rivard (in white) and fellow rider David Early (black T-shirt). Lackey clocked a Class A-750 record of 115 miles per hour. There were a multitude of bikes thanks to the promise of bonus money from Birmingham Small Arms (BSA), Triumph, and Kawasaki for any rider setting a record with their particular brand. Lackey, now 83, races on the salt more often after retiring from the GM Tech Center after 26 years as an engine development engineer. (Courtesy of Bob Higbee.)

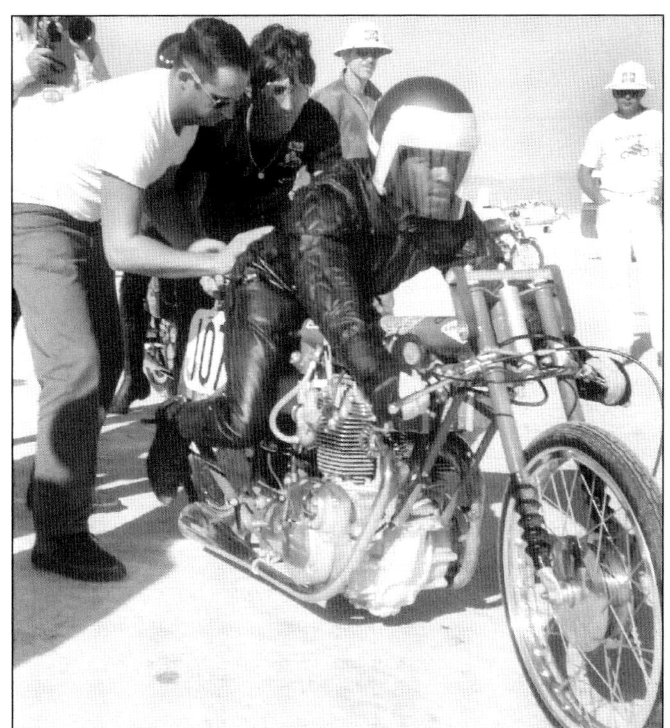

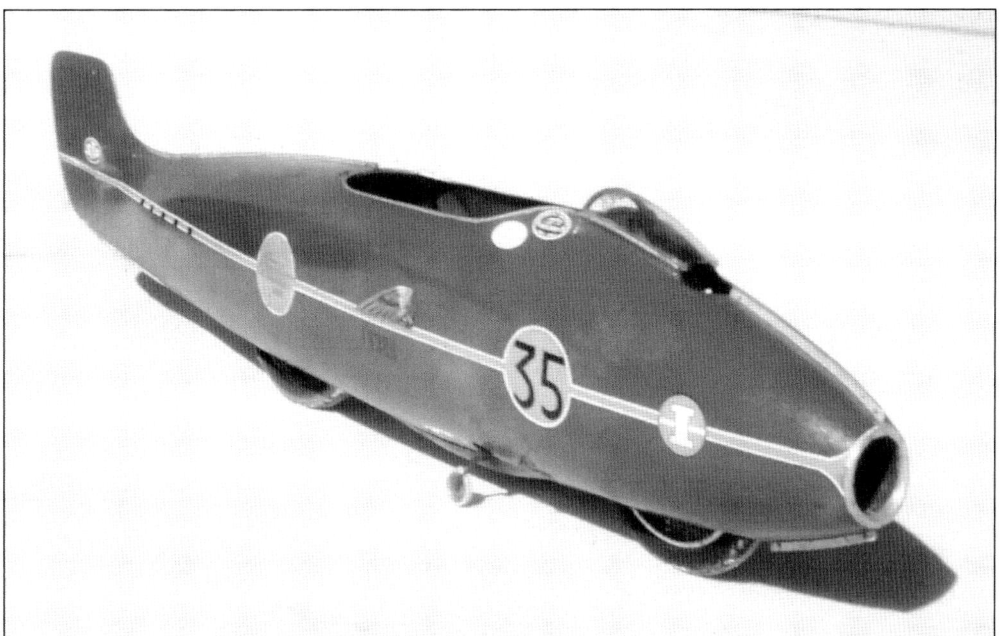

New Zealander Burt Munro was a hands-on racer with little money but incredible talent, perseverance, and ingenuity. Munro bought the 1920 bike new and spent decades improving its 55-mile-per-hour factory speed capabilities. Pictured here is the 1968 hand-built streamliner version that was such a sensation in the 1960s it inspired the film *World's Fastest Indian* starring Anthony Hopkins, who never rode a motorcycle in real life. Munro last raced in 1967 at age 68, setting a 184-mile-per-hour record that still remains intact today. (Courtesy of Bob Higbee.)

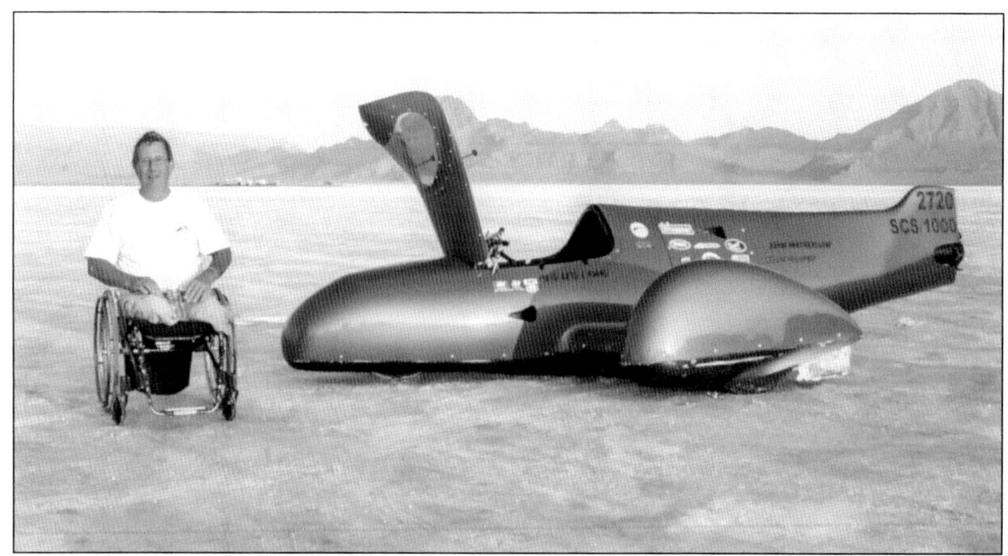

"Peg Leg" Craig Anderson, 55, is the world's fastest optimist and oozes potential and possibilities. In 2006, the salt virgin demonstrated that one does not need knees, ankles, or toes to be a Bonneville record setter. Pictured here in 2011, the two-time land speed record holder set another record at the BUB Motorcycle Speed Trials with his 1,000cc sidecar, achieving a personal best of 190 miles per hour. "I grew up loving motorcycles," he said. "I can't imagine life without them. They are an integral part of my body." (Courtesy of LandSpeed Louise.)

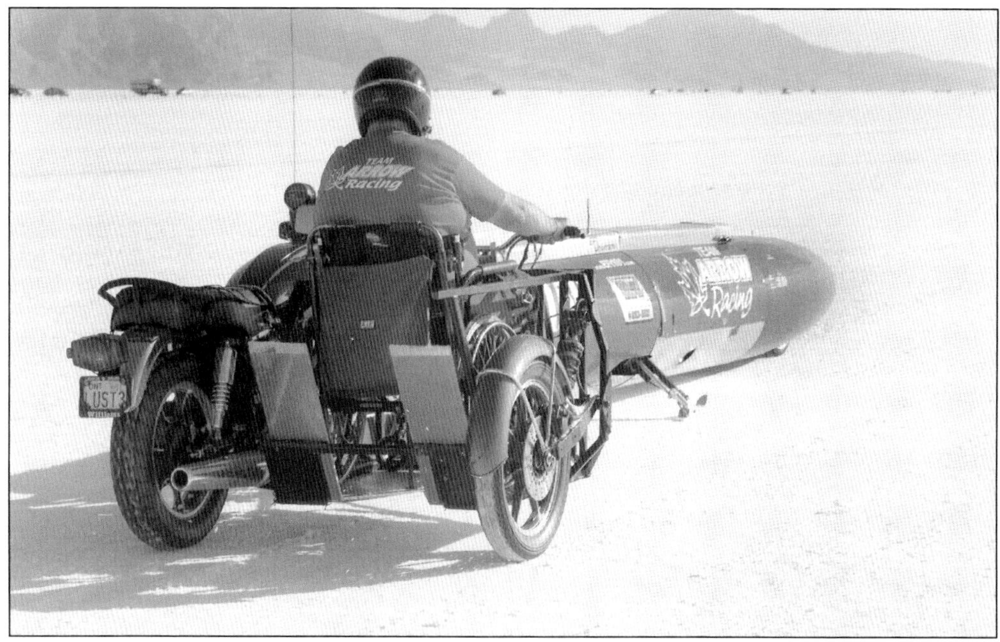

It was more than 40 years after Bob Williams turned down a chance to crew with world-record-setter Bob Leppan that he bought an F-14 fighter jet drop tank and got to work building his own streamliner—from his wheelchair. His son Jeff and Gary Hensley guided the Arrow Racing bike after being pushed up to starting speed by Bob in his custom, repurposed Honda 750, now a sidecar motorcycle with the handlebars moved to the sidecar. If one thinks Williams anything but serious, note the license plate on his push machine. (Courtesy of LandSpeed Louise.)

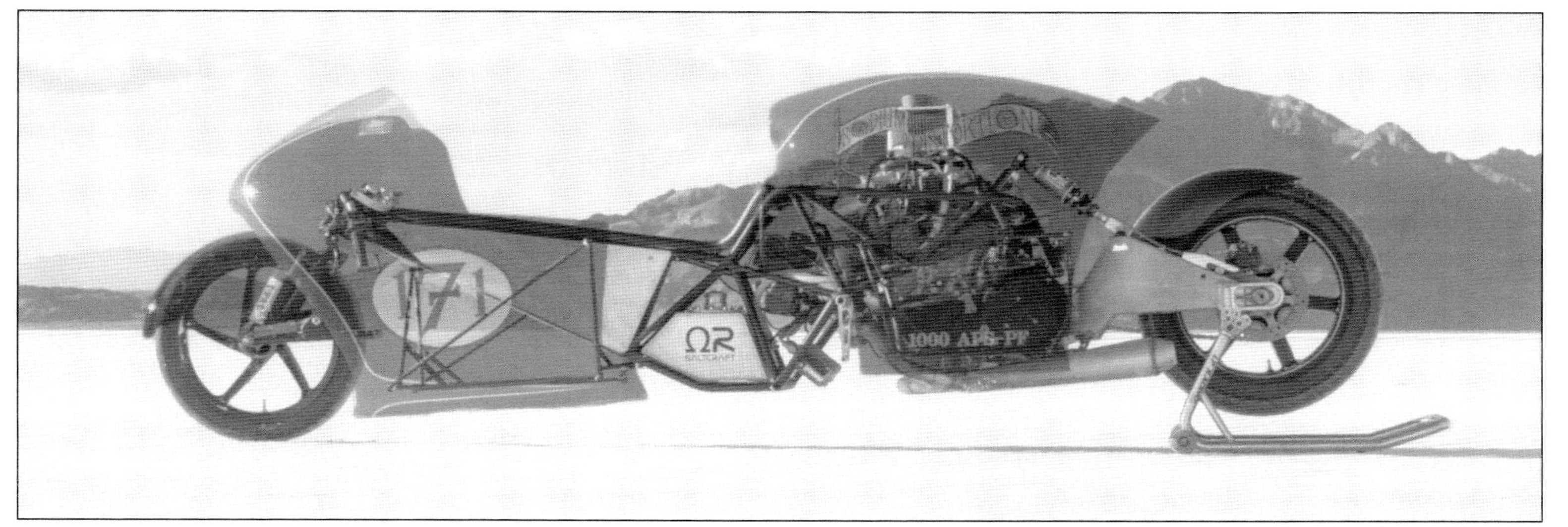

Racing since 2006, the father-and-son team of Lee Omer and Jason Omer not only put their spirit and talents into the "Sodium Distortion" streamliner pictured here, but they also help anyone who asks. Anyone. They have let their machine languish in order to help strangers, and this esprit de corps fills racers from all parts of the country who enhance the team's personal commitment to make Bonneville a memorable experience for as many as they can. (Courtesy of LandSpeed Louise.)

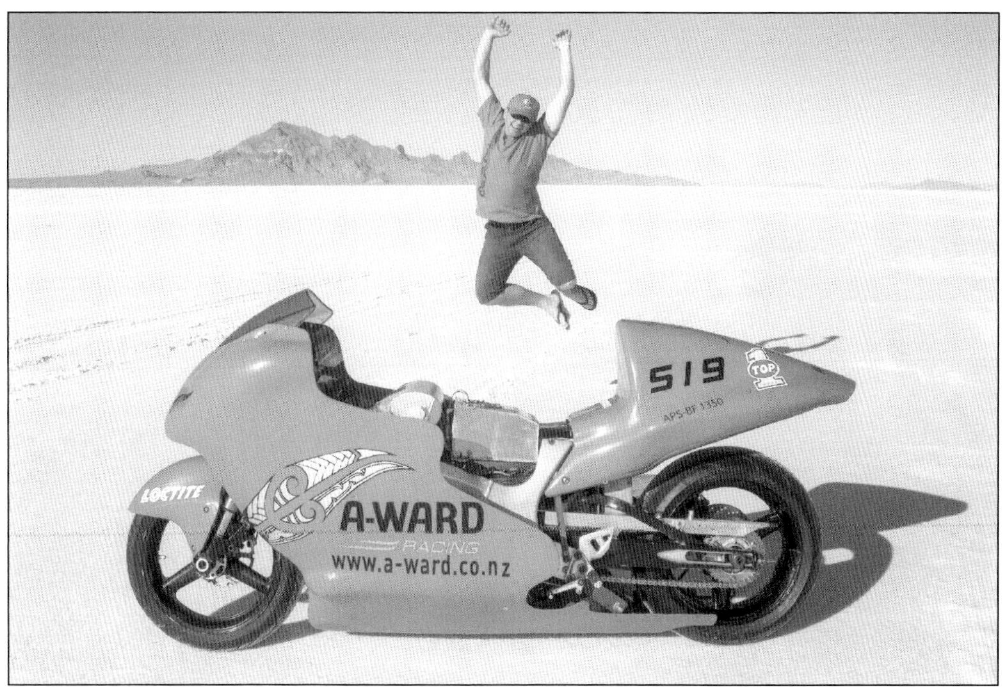

Richard Assen wants all to know that behind every vehicle are so many dreams, skinned knuckles, empty wallets, good mates, and hard unpaid labor—things that define the sport. Here, the Australian, with New Zealand sponsors, is jumping like kid on Christmas morning in celebration of his new world record—261 miles per hour—riding his Suzuki Hayabusa 1,300cc motorcycle. This is a man who laid awake at night replaying every detail in order to get the right jump for joy. (Courtesy of LandSpeed Louise.)

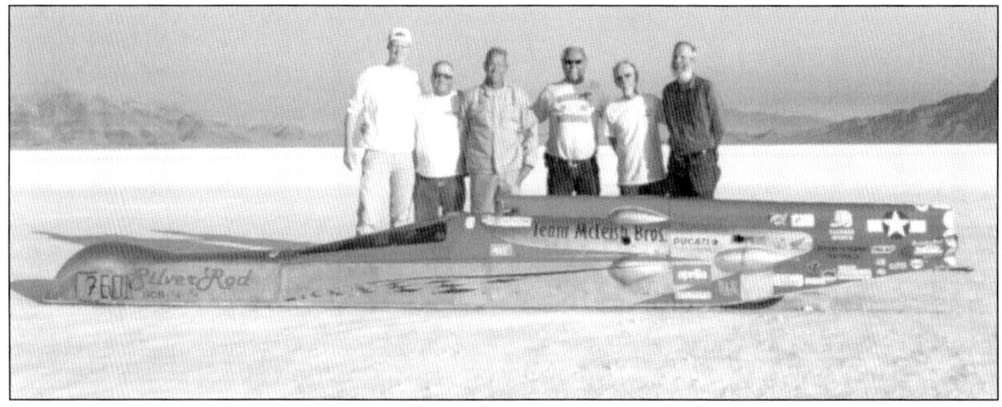

Meet Team McLeish Bros. They are, from left to right, Matt Jacobs, Doug McLeish, Derek McLeish, Jack Miller, Ralph LeClercq, and Ken Brandt, a team of cheerful guys who have had an astonishingly good time setting more than dozens of records. Pictured here is the "convertible" "SilverRod" streamliner that can be set up to run as a motorcycle streamliner, a motorcycle sidecar streamliner, or a lakester. In 2011, the "bros" had the fastest motorcycle at Bonneville Speed Week with an exit speed of 234.886 miles per hour. (Courtesy of Robert McLeish.)

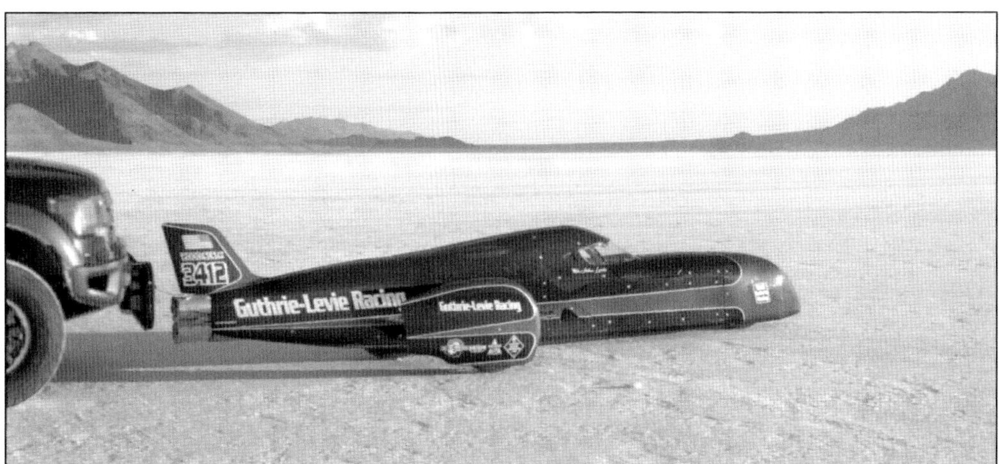

John Levie of Elko, Nevada, in the Guthrie-Levie Racing sidecar motorcycle, leaves the starting line before attaining an incredible top speed of 320 miles per hour in this unique blue and black vehicle. His dad, John Allen, and third-generation motorcycle racer Jacie, John's daughter, may soon be asking dad to vacate the rider's seat in the sidecar. The Levies were invited by the sport's advocacy group Save the Salt to be part of the 2018 booth display during the SEMA Show, an automotive trade show that consumes every inch of exhibit space in Las Vegas. (Courtesy of LandSpeed Louise.)

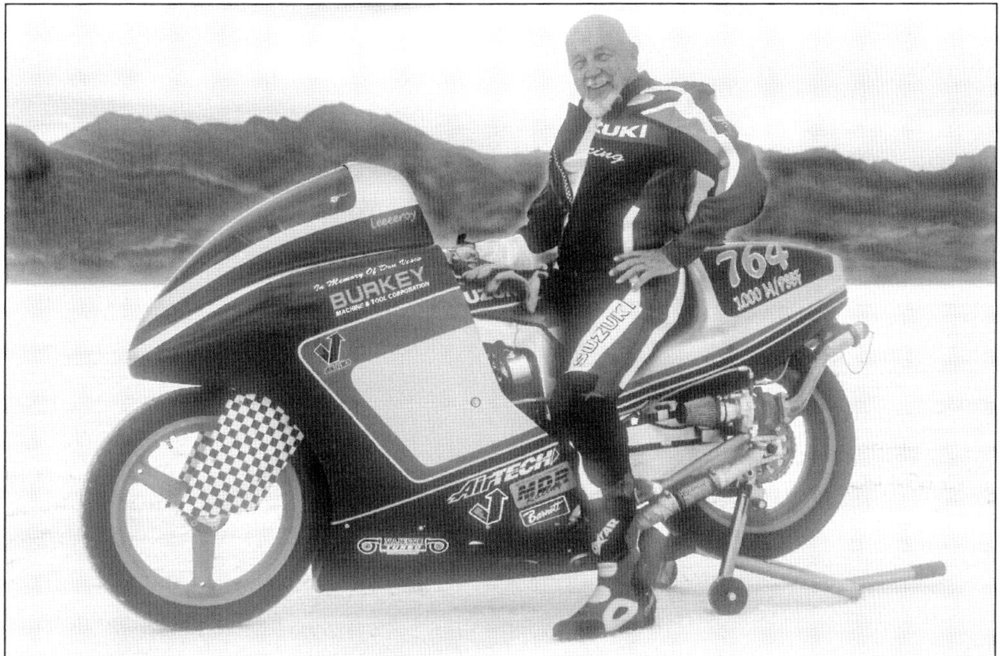

Lee Carl Burkey was 83 years old when he died on the starting line at Bonneville. Sad as his passing was, all with him were very happy the racer expired when and where he did—September 15, 2011, enjoying an exceptionally beautiful morning with his three sons with enthusiasm on yet another mechanical journey. Burkey was a valued crewman with TEAMVesco's "Turbinator," for which he designed major components, and was pals with driver Don Vesco. Burkey humbled blabbermouths simply with his actions, like the notable record he set at 200-plus miles per hour on the bike pictured. (Courtesy of LandSpeed Louise.)

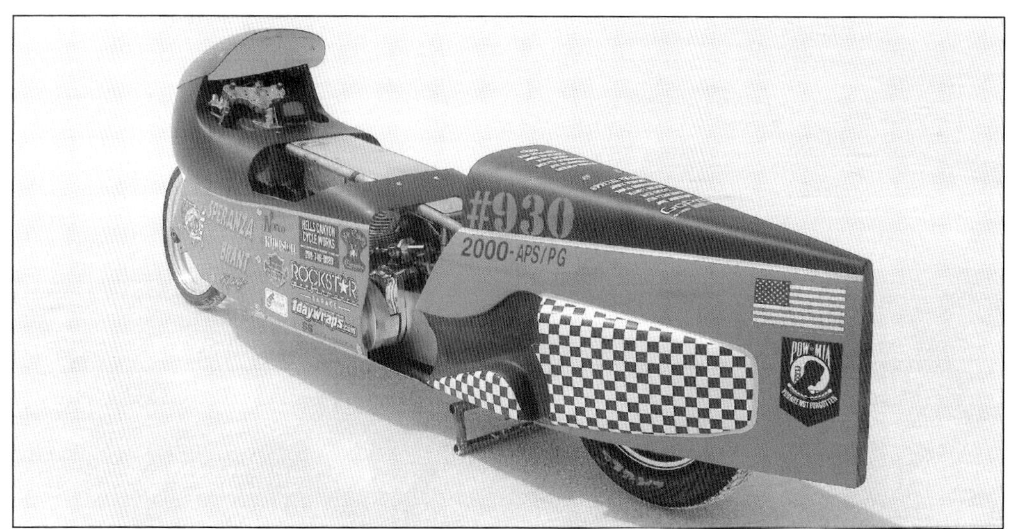

For Randy Speranza, every land speed record he sets is a gift from God. Pictured here in 2012, his Harley-Davidson–powered motorcycle, designed and built by Dave Brant, measures 123 inches long overall and is a bit less than 2 feet wide. Built to use three different engines eligible to race in 36 classes, he and wife DeEtte are busy bikers. On a path to set a 200-plus-mile-per-hour record, having added a sidecar in 2013, they are closing in the mark. At the close of the 2019 season, the bike had a top speed of 195 miles per hour. (Courtesy of LandSpeed Louise.)

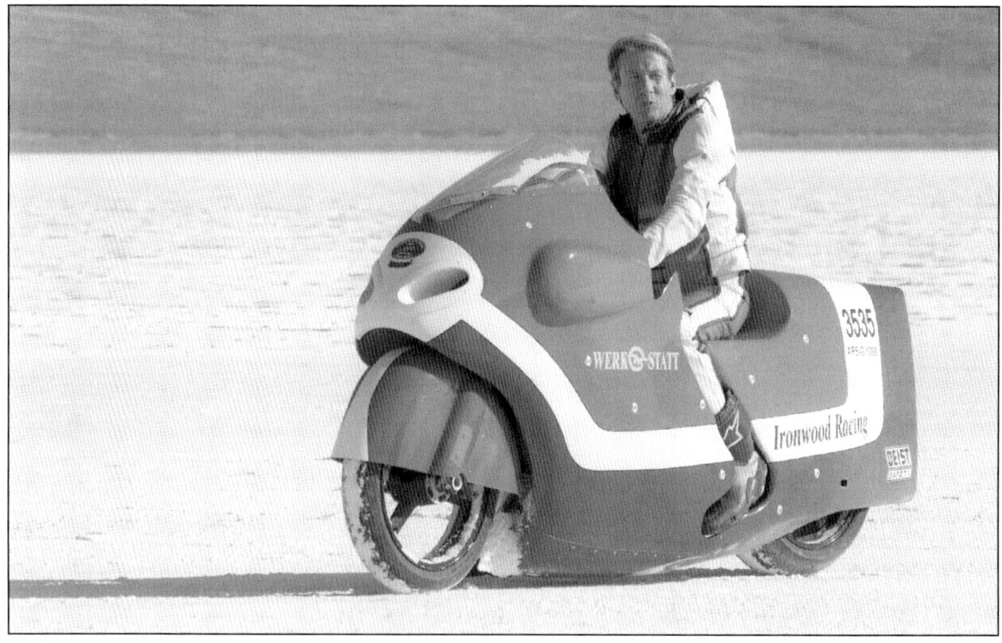

Ralph Hudson was 58 in 2009 when he realized a life-long goal of setting his first 200-plus-mile-per-hour record at 210 miles per hour riding his Class A PS-G (partially streamlined running gasoline). A bit green about understanding what high-speed runs demanded, he learned a hard lesson that air will go wherever it wants to whenever it wants to, even if it means flicking the rider's legs out into passing air. Smart riders learn such lessons only once. Hudson fixed his problem by fabricating a custom front fairing that closed off some of the airflow, and his legs have stayed put ever since. (Courtesy of LandSpeed Louise.)

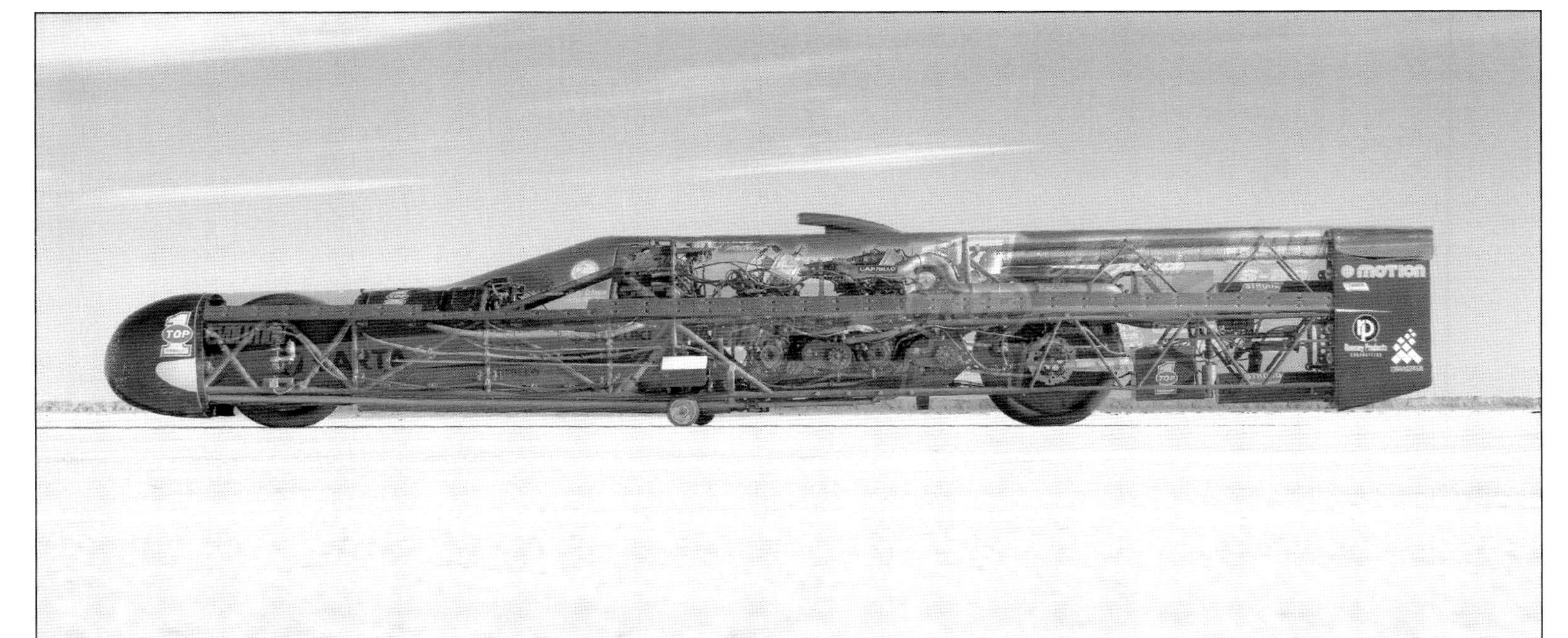

"Ack Attack" is the world's fastest motorcycle, earning its title under the control of Rocky Robinson, who extricated an average two-way speed of 376 miles per hour in 2010 with help from a stubborn Mike Akatiff and his team. This x-ray shows the 20.5-foot bike that is a mere 32 inches high but weighs 2,000 pounds. A pair of thirsty six-speed Suzuki Hayabusa engines drains its 4.7-gallon fuel tank. The center hub steering swings 24 degrees lock to lock, and if the water-cooled disc brakes fail, the parachutes are ready to extract "whoaness." (Courtesy of LandSpeed Louise.)

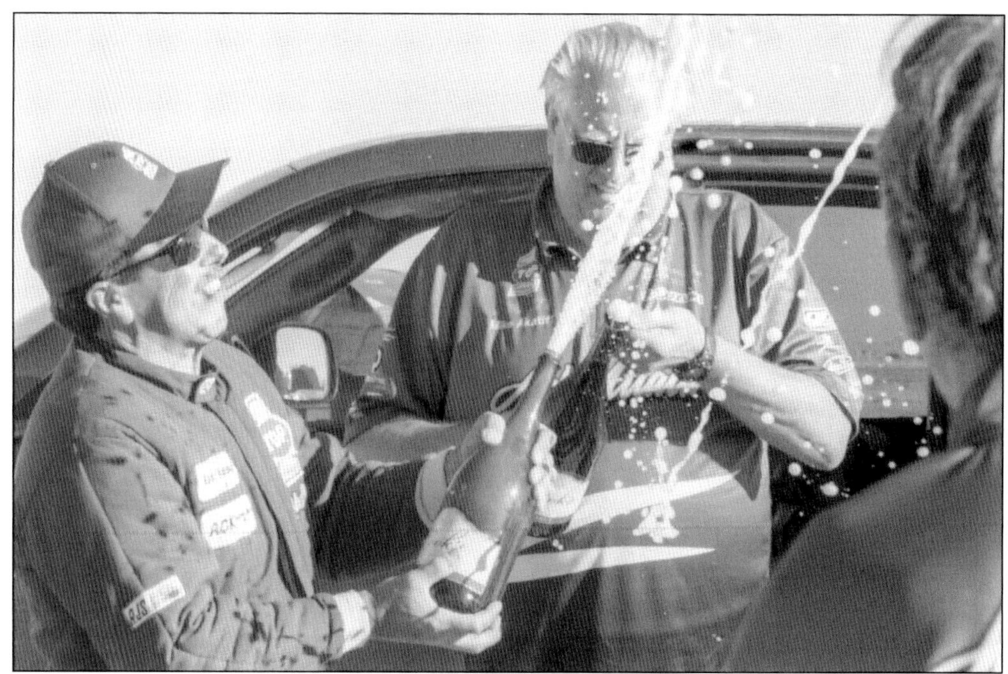

When racing concluded in 2010, ecstatic and relieved "Ack Attack" rider Rocky Robinson, 49, congratulates bike owner Mike Akatiff with a shower of champagne over the team's new motorcycle world land speed record of 376 miles per hour. Not satisfied with their certified world mark for long, the team is now stalking numbers in excess of 400 miles per hour. The biggest problem? Finding a safe racing surface, as conditions on the Bonneville Salt Flats no longer give such speed attempts the cushion of comfort racers long enjoyed. (Courtesy of Tricia Robinson.)

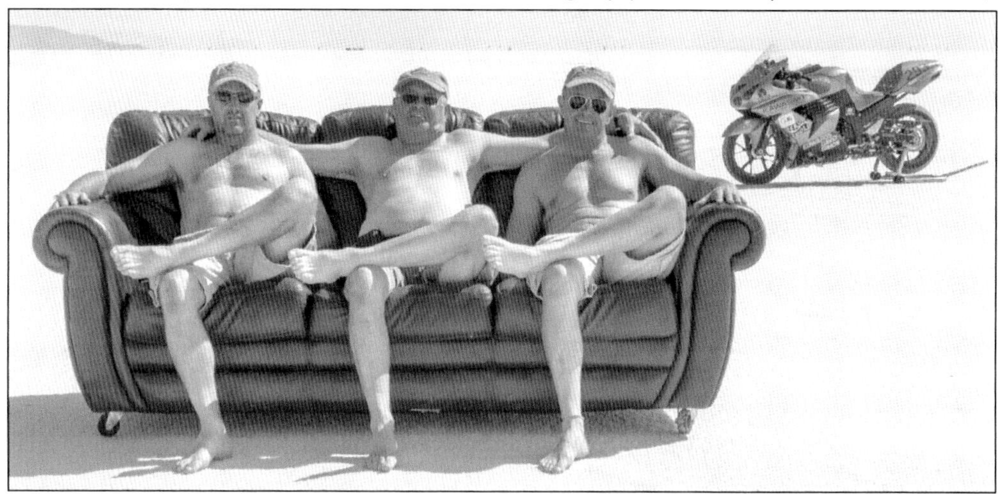

The Edwards family became the envy of the salt when they rolled out a plush leather sofa to watch the sunrise. Pictured here are, from left to right, David, Edward, and Simon Edwards, who arrived with neon-green pedicures to match their Kawasaki racing bike. Simon, a former US Army Special Forces medic, confessed he only found solace and peace from war horrors on the salt. "Unless you come here, you can't explain why you should, you just can't," he said. "Land speed racing is the personification of sportsmanship that brought me back emotionally and mentally." (Courtesy of LandSpeed Louise.)

Nine

Have Power, Need Salt 1998

The Shrinking Speedway

What had been exquisitely formed by nature spanning thousands of years had taken man less than a century to cripple. In 1975, the Bonneville Salt Flats International Raceway was added to the National Register of Historic Places.

Federal officials in 1985 had designated it as an "Area of Critical Environmental Concern" but took no protective action, and the best amateur mechanical extravaganza on the planet slowed down. Those capable of reaching beyond 400 miles per hour became fewer. Seekers of world records, pressured by safety concerns, begrudgingly abandoned Bonneville. By the late 1990s, the once-thick salt measured in feet had thinned to less than an inch in some areas, and the immense saltpan had visibly shrunk, being reclaimed by ubiquitous sagebrush.

For years, the racers had unwittingly blamed the damage on the potash mining companies as the salt surface degraded. Bitterness percolated until Save the Salt (STS), a volunteer organization formed by the racing community, uncovered the ugly truth written into the 10 federal leases by the very people charged with its care—the Bureau of Land Management (BLM).

The original 1964 lease language, which remained significantly unchanged in 2020, told the tale plainly: the BLM demanded as much mineral be extracted with as much possible haste and that no restoration was required until everything had been depleted. In other words, federally planned destruction of the fragile salt crust.

Land speed racers, through STS, became storming mad environmentalists and took to task the federal government with the benevolent help of other motorsports segments and professional automotive associations. In 2019, this multi-decade effort resulted in securing the support and financial assistance at local, state, and federal levels to restore the Bonneville Salt Flats to safe racing conditions for amateur motorsports.

Moving forward, it is still uncertain if federal regulators will follow through with earnest repairs. Bonneville, for the present, remains a sacred speed laboratory fortified for decades by spirit, ingenuity, and potent American perseverance. How long it will remain a place of wonder and hope for the mechanically minded to dream at wide-open throttle is unclear, if at all.

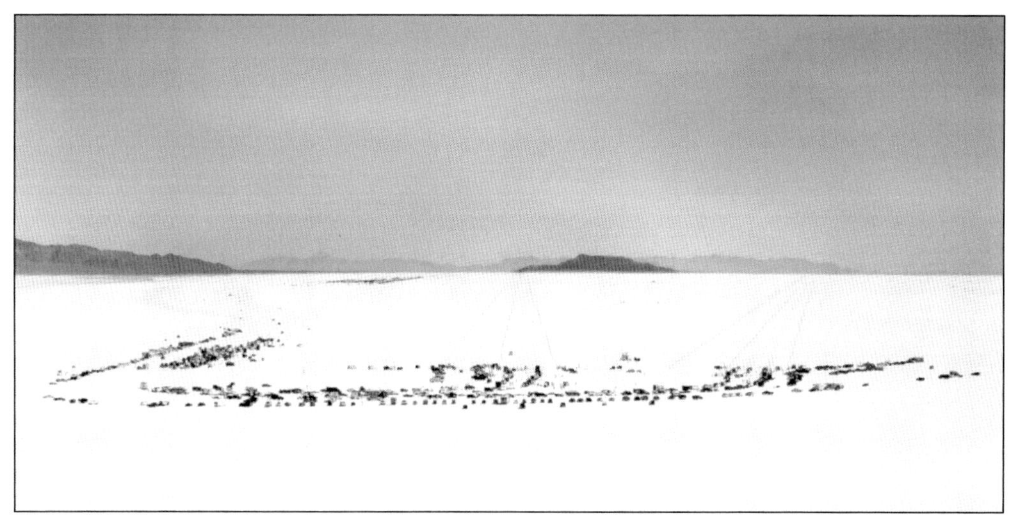

From the pits in the left distance is how racers transit to the starting line via the staging lanes. Looking down the long course used by vehicles capable of 175 miles per hour or more, four lanes are visible, with only one on each side of the *V* layout in use at any one time. Between the *V* is the road used by course workers traveling to and from the timing tower seen in the distance just across from the pit area at left. Spectators' cars are parked along the outside perimeter of the staging lanes. (Courtesy of LandSpeed Louise.)

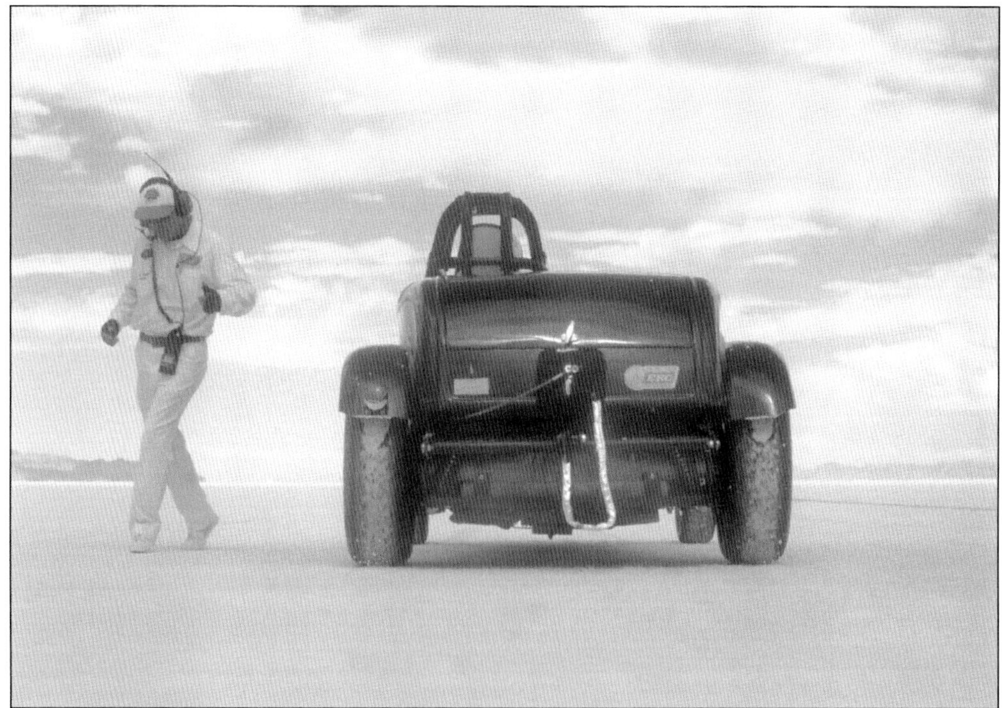

Starter Bill Taylor is not dancing but simply releasing a roadster racer onto the speedway, as evidenced by his left hand gesturing a thumbs up and his head down trying to hear the FM channel course communications. While the starting line sits in full shadow, the white-hot line on the horizon promises the driver will finish this speed run in brilliant sunlight a few miles down the course. (Courtesy of LandSpeed Louise.)

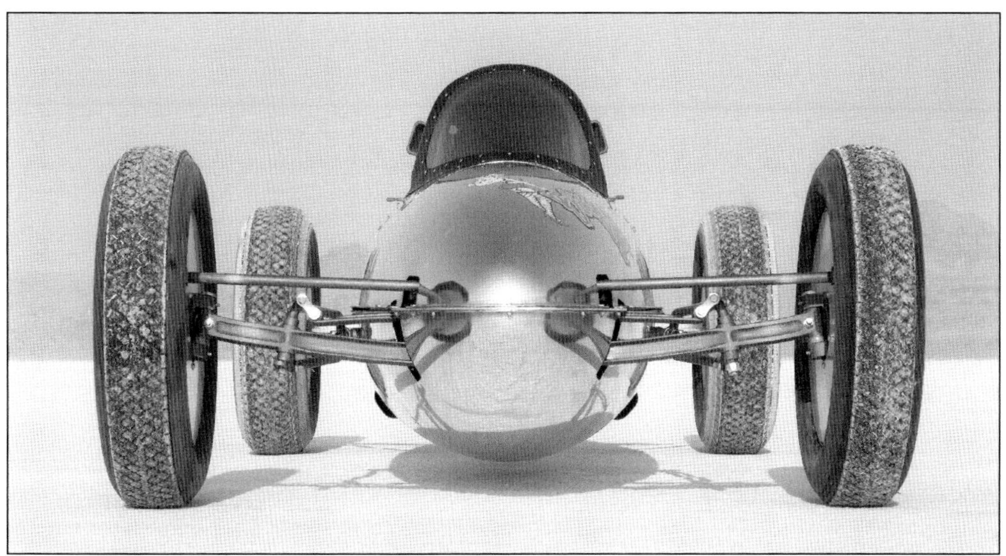

This is a belly tank lakester, a vehicle that emerged from hot rodders using discarded but beautifully aero-shaped World War II aircraft fuel tanks. This speed machine is only found in land speed racing and is without question the foundation upon which the sport's thunderous streamliners were built when all the wheels were enclosed. The 13-foot-long, 30-inch-wide nostalgic beauty was built by Kim and Andy Welker from Berrysburg, Pennsylvania. It is powered by a vintage Ford flathead V8 engine, and when the skin is off, the tank lures the eye for a closer look at artistic, modern mechanical craftsmanship. (Courtesy of LandSpeed Louise.)

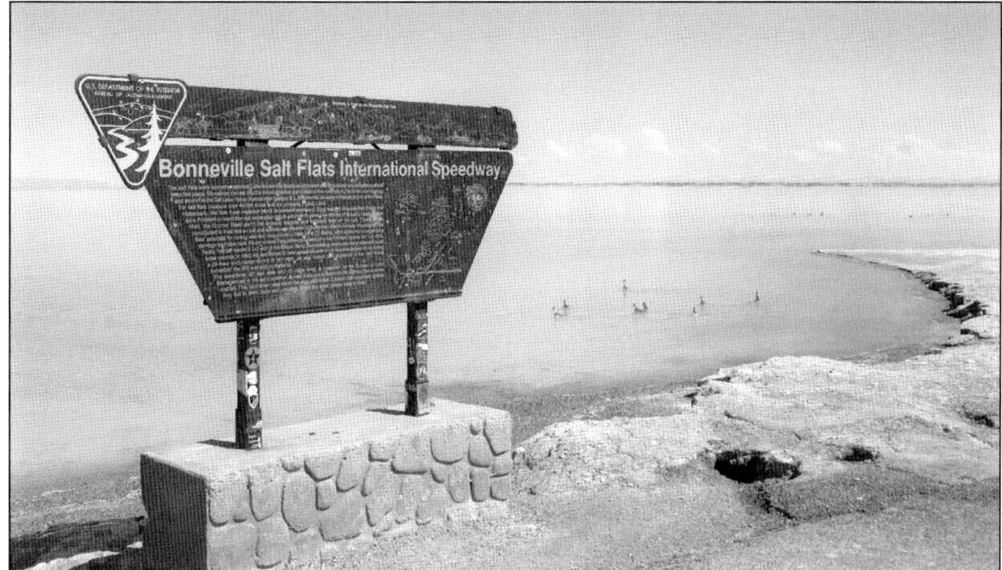

Torrential rains prevented the normal evaporation and salt desiccation cycles in 2016, so the only racing on Bonneville was a feathered flotilla. Although covered with water much of the year, the summer temperatures combine with gusty winds to evaporate the saline pond for a few months each year, revealing the iconic natural speedway. This familiar interpretive sign at the end of the access was unceremoniously hacked down by the Bureau of Land Management in 2019 and taken away by one of the California racers. No word on whether or not taxpayers were reimbursed for the loss. (Courtesy of LandSpeed Louise.)

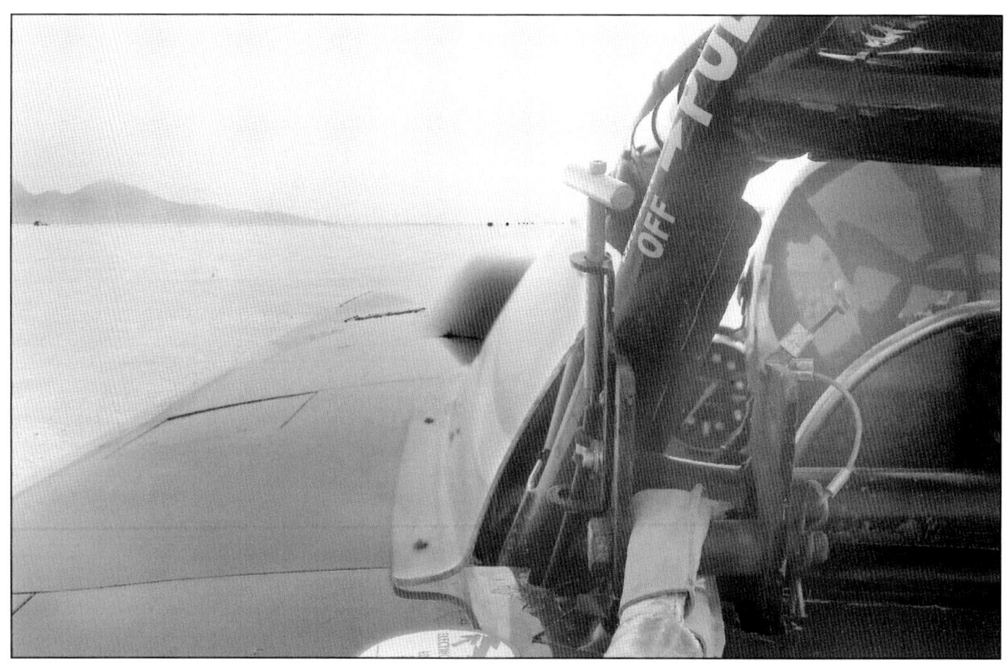

When University of Arizona professor of chemistry and geoscience Bonner Denton peels off the lab coat, he opts for a helmet to climb into "Bonner's Bad Berkeley," a 1957 British sports car he transmuted into hurtling hot rod. In 2008, he set a 298-mile-per-hour class record and posted a top speed of 310 miles per hour. The record remains his as of this writing. In the early 1990s, he had built a bestial 2,000-horsepower aluminum engine dropped into a 1958 Bocar XP4 until the class rules got too silly and the sedate Berkeley was conscripted for speed duty. (Courtesy of LandSpeed Louise.)

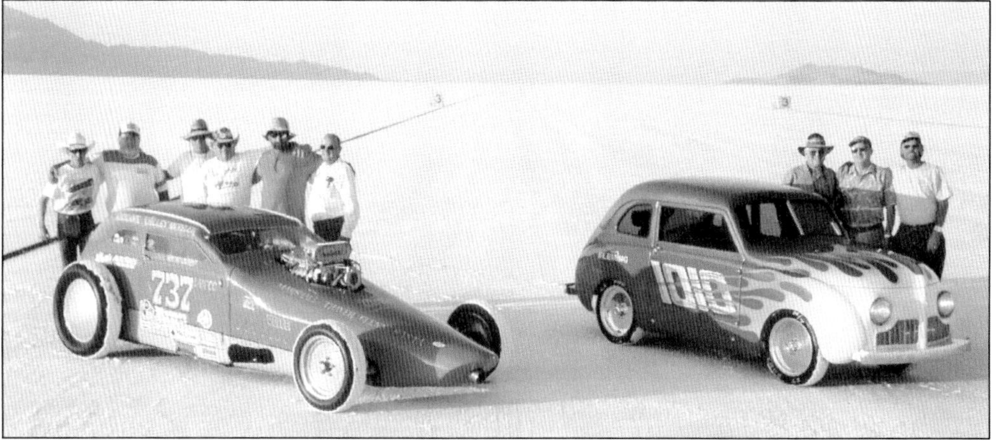

This one photograph visually explains the extreme diversity of Bonneville racers. At right is a stock-body Crosley painted with the hot flames of Hades but campaigned by Gerald Davenport as "The Witness," extolling the Biblical scripture Romans 10:10. On the left is the same car after hot rodders applied their go-fast ideas—the Marshall, Thayer, Glenn, and Banta competition coupe that remained competitive for decades and logged 2,500 racing miles on the salt! One is faster, but neither is better, and both required friendship and dedication to make speed dreams come true. Verlin Marshall, far right, and Gary Banta, third from right, are co-owners. (Courtesy of LandSpeed Louise.)

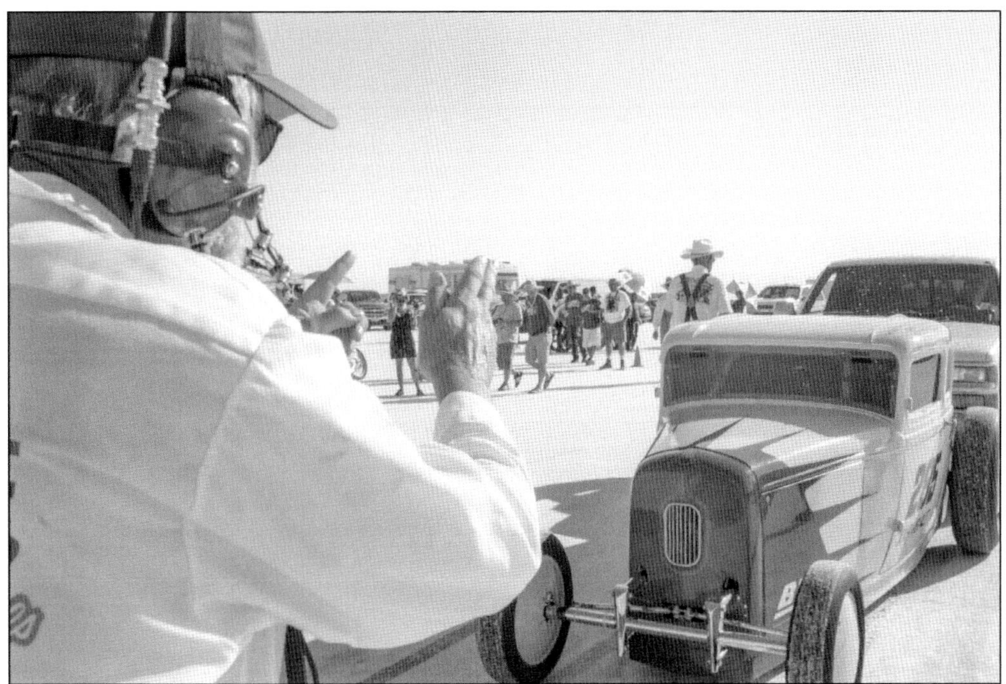

Starter Ron Joliffe is about to signal the driver of the BMR coupe that he can leave the starting line for his trip down the speedway's long course. The man wearing the cowboy hat will join the pickup driver just behind, and together they will push start the race car. Many land speed vehicles start this way because of special gearing to maximize speed in the timing section of the course. At times, they can push the vehicle up to 75 miles per hour before it pulls away on its own. (Courtesy of LandSpeed Louise.)

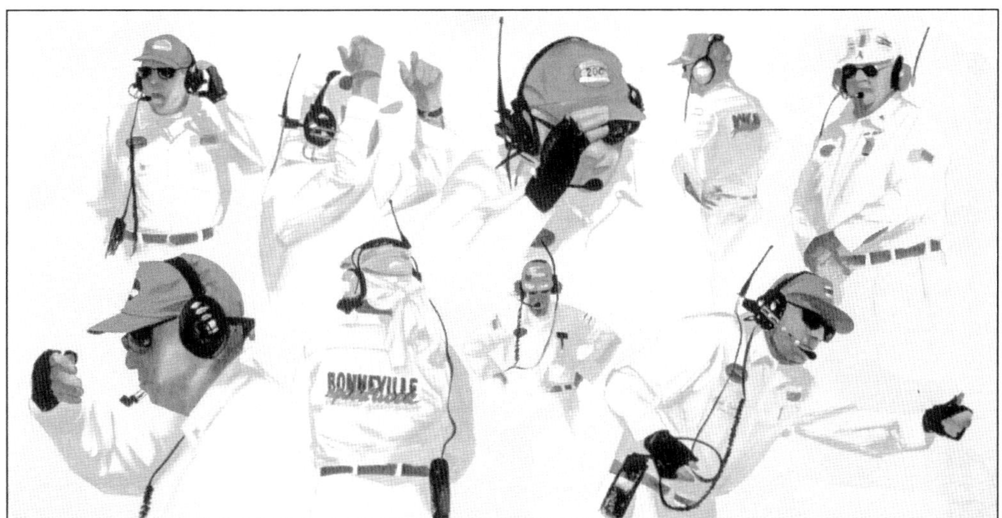

For renowned western, scenic, and wildlife artist Robert Seabeck, it was shiny surfaces, not bellowing engine sound, that lured his paintbrush to Bonneville. Here, he captures three starting line officials: Bill Taylor (black gloves); Jim Jensen (hands up, hands in front, and his back); and Bob Higbee (hands on hips), the most revered of all for his half-century of service. It is reasonable to say all this pictured is occurring simultaneously across the busy racetracks! (Courtesy of Robert Seabeck.)

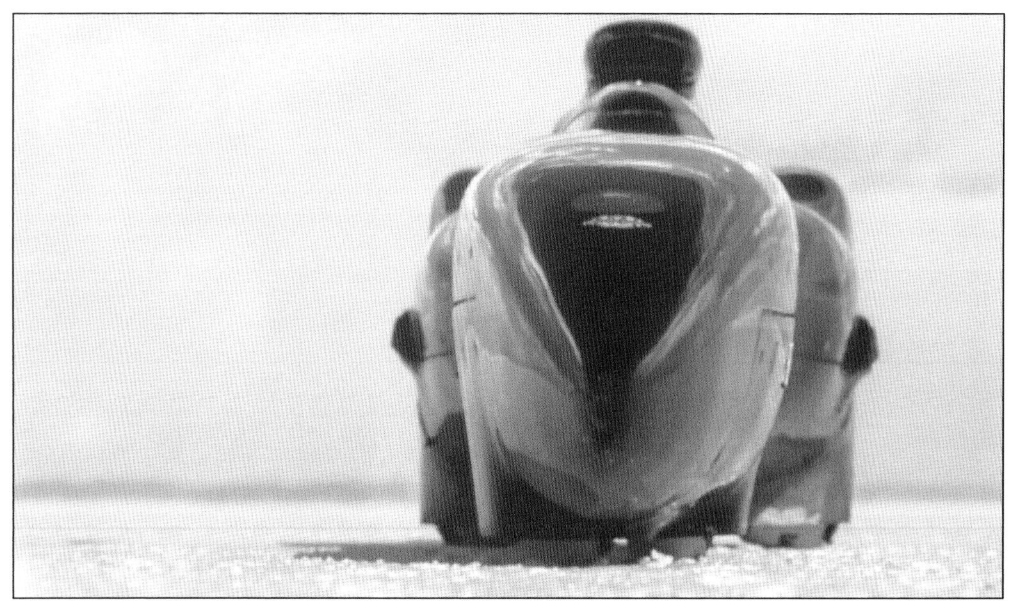

Few would ever view Al Teague's "Spirit of 76" blue-black streamliner from this extreme low front angle, but it provides a fabulous point of view about why such cars are capable of speeds in excess of 400 miles per hour. Teague clocked a 409-mile-per-hour world record in 1992 and hit a top speed of 423 miles per hour during later runs. It is noteworthy to see the clearance, as the car is some two inches off the ground. He spent so much time with this car he nicknamed it "Betsy." (Courtesy of LandSpeed Louise.)

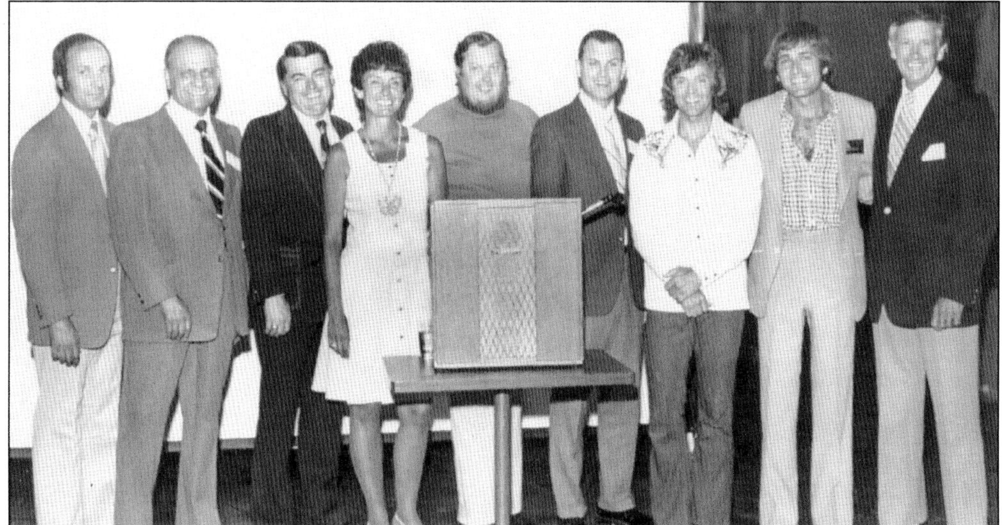

Pictured are, from left to right, USAC steward Dave Petrali; Dr. Nathan Ostitch, first to drive a jet-powered car at 350 miles per hour on the salt; Mickey Thompson, holder of more than 400 speed records; Paula Murphy, twice holder of the women's world land speed record up to 226 miles per hour; Bill Summers, "Goldenrod" co-owner/builder; Bob Summers, "Goldenrod" driver (409 miles per hour); Craig Breedlove, multiple world records, top speed at 600 miles per hour; Gary Gabelich, "The Blue Flame" rocket car driver and world land speed record (630 miles per hour); and Wally Parks, founder and president of the National Hot Rod Association (NHRA) and founding member of the SCTA Bonneville Nationals Speed Trials. (Courtesy of Paula Murphy.)

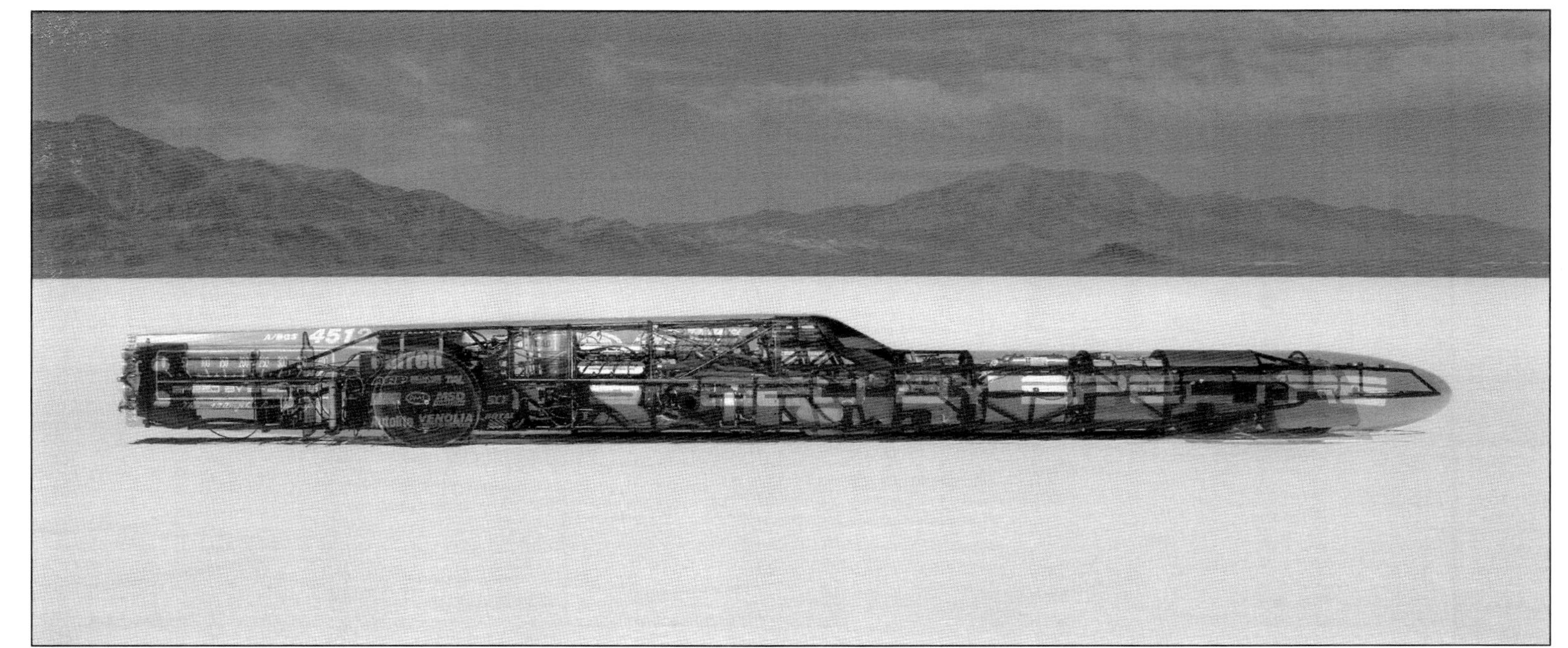

This photograph illustration is a meld of two images shot in the exact same spot, one with the bodywork on and the other with the hand-formed aluminum body panels removed. It takes a long time for the team to do this, but as one can see from the result, it is time well spent. Amir Rosenbaum campaigned the 4,700-pound, ready-to-race Spectre streamliner nicknamed "Infidel," sharing the driver's seat with Kenny Hoover. Measuring 37 feet long by 29 inches wide, it had five engines, one for each class—all 1960s-era turbocharged Cadillacs. (Courtesy of LandSpeed Louise.)

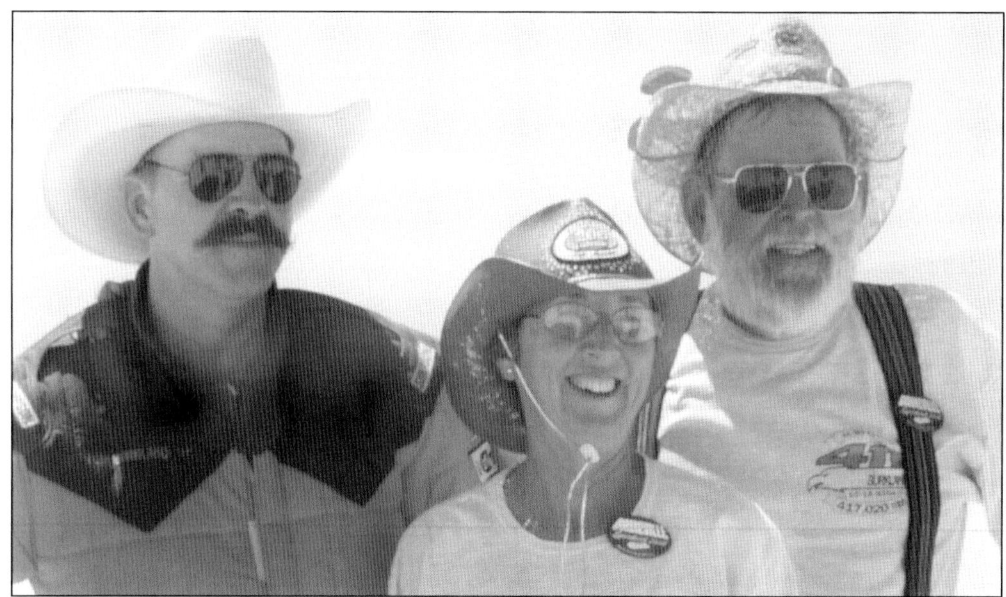

Tom Burkland is with his mom and dad, Betty and Gene, who have not only raced a variety of cars out on the salt flats for decades but have also simultaneously volunteered repeatedly to assist at time trials in almost every job description and performed high-speed tire testing to keep everyone safe. Starting with a Hemi-powered 1953 Studebaker, followed by Hemi-powered Datsun B210, the trio then put two Hemis in the family 411 creamsicle-orange streamliner, which posted a top speed of 450 miles per hour with a world record of 415 miles per hour. (Courtesy of LandSpeed Louise.)

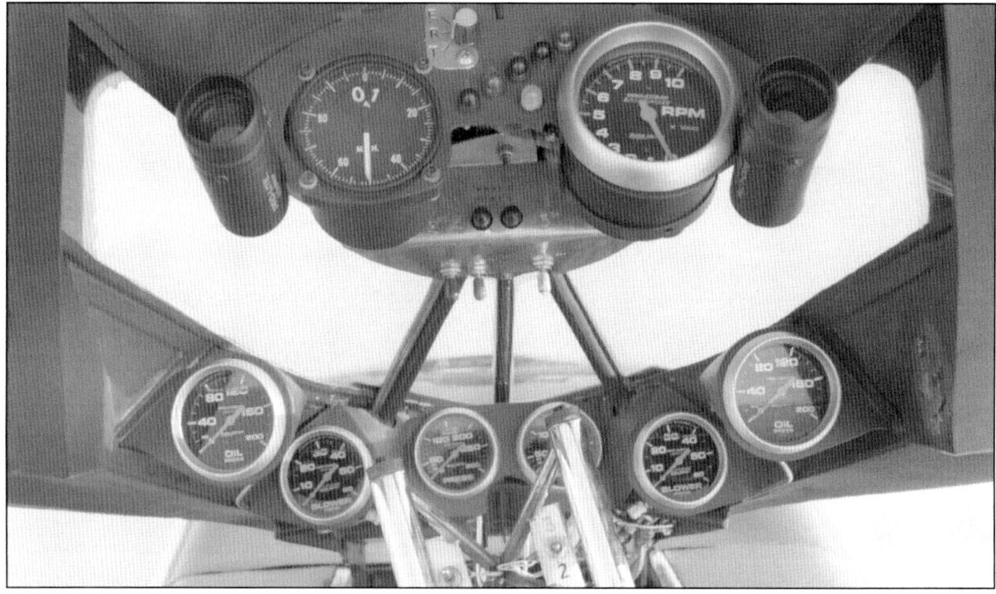

It is not a fighter jet, but this is how driver Tom Burkland set up his instrument panel in his double-engine 411 streamliner. The six gauges on the bottom report oil, blower, and fuel pressures of each engine, and because the two V8s are mechanically connected, only one tachometer in the upper right is used for the V16 rpms. The toggle switches in the middle of the steering wheel are for the parachutes. It is hard to see, but on the far right is a medallion from Burkland's daughter Carly that reads, "Don't go faster than your guardian angel can fly." (Courtesy of LandSpeed Louise.)

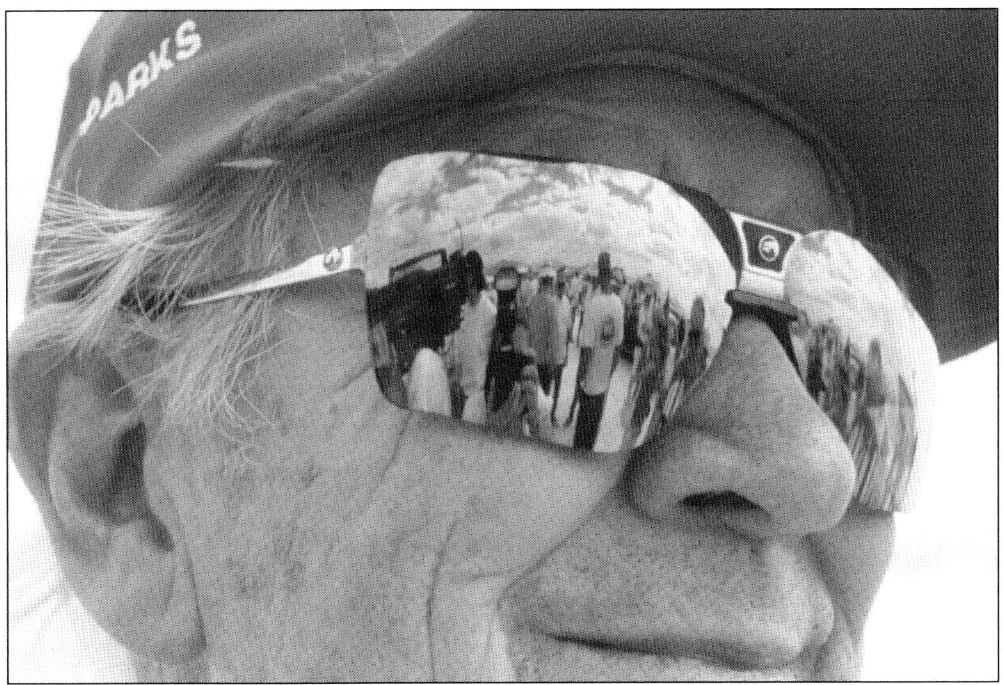

This is not just a close-up of an old man in sunglasses. Meet Wally Parks, a founding father of both the Southern California Timing Association land speed racing and drag racing's National Hot Rod Association (NHRA). Parks's satisfied smile comes from a reflection in 1998 as the "49ers" gathered to commemorate the 50th anniversary of Speed Week. Aside from the photographers, every person in Parks's field of view had helped plan, staff, and conduct the 1949 event. It is akin to having Wilber and Orville Wright attend the first Mercury 7 space launch. If only. (Courtesy of LandSpeed Louise.)

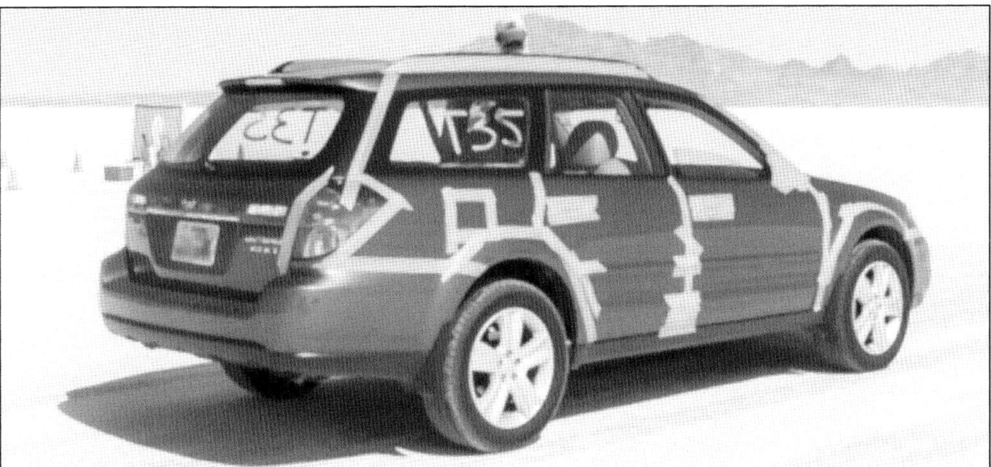

Before this Subaru Outback 2.5 XT with 30,000 miles arrived on the 2011 World of Speed starting line as a 130 MPH Club participant, Jodi and John Griffin dropped off the kids at school 120 miles away in Salt Lake City. The 130 class allows street-driven vehicles to tickle the clocks and go home with certified time slips. Securing every gap with lime green tape to maximize the wagon's aerodynamics properties, John crawled in through an open window and managed 129 miles per hour on his fifth attempt before the couple left to pick up the kids from school. (Courtesy of LandSpeed Louise.)

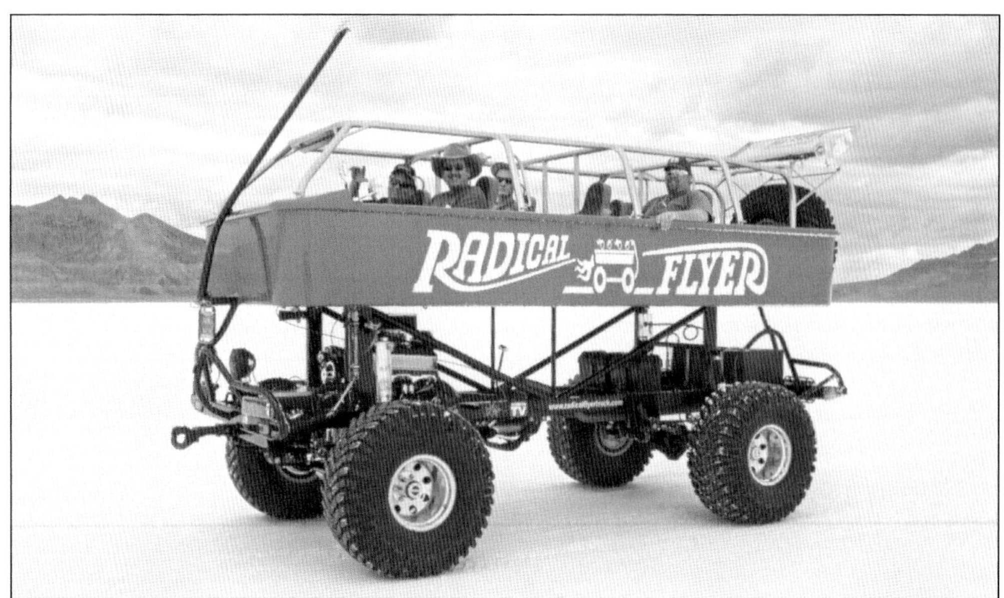

The four-wheel-drive "Radical Flyer" was dreamed into life by Colorado resident Wes Messick (second from left) as a 15-month family project with his wife, kids, and grandkids all chipping in. The hand-formed sheet metal body has six racing seats and a rear bench seat. A Chevy V8 engine powers the 14-foot, 10-foot-tall, 6-foot-wide machine pictured here in August 2009; it ran 70 miles per hour on the salt. A month later, mechanical engineering cadets at the US Air Force Academy got a close look when Messick drove it onto the quad in the middle of the campus. (Courtesy of LandSpeed Louise.)

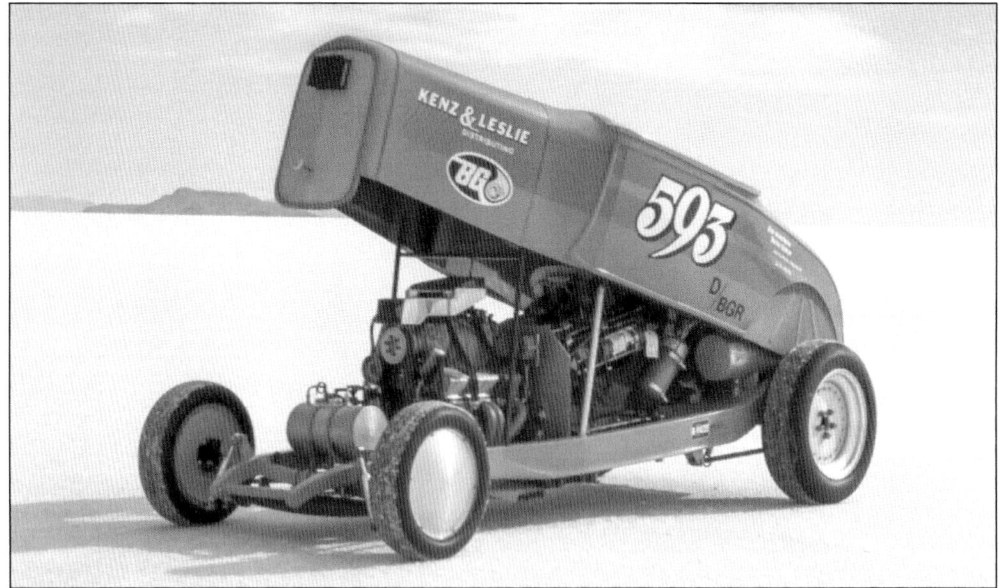

This "flip-top" highway-orange car from Denver, Colorado, is a 1928 Ford Roadster body bolted to a 1932 Ford chassis and is powered by a supercharged Chevy engine that pals and partners Bob Marchese, John Ferrero, and driver Butch Salter campaigned from 1994 to 2002. The trio inked four class records, the highest at 198 miles per hour with a one-way top speed of 202 miles per hour. (Courtesy of Butch Salter.)

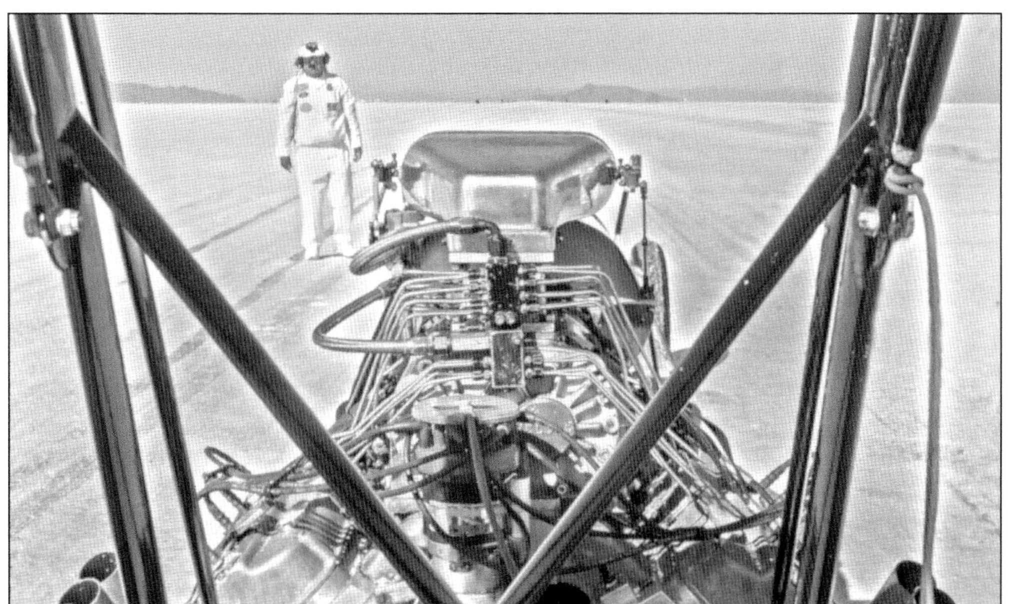

Only one vehicle is on the track at any one time, so long course starter Buddy James is simultaneously in eye contact with the driver and listening on his headset for an "all clear" from the timing tower three miles down course so he can release the next vehicle. A two-mile run-up to the first set of timing lights is followed by three timed miles with additional miles for shut down, parachute deployment, and safe left turn out to the return road. Anyone turning right alerts observers to trouble and instantly scrambles safety and rescue teams to the driver's aid. (Courtesy of LandSpeed Louise.)

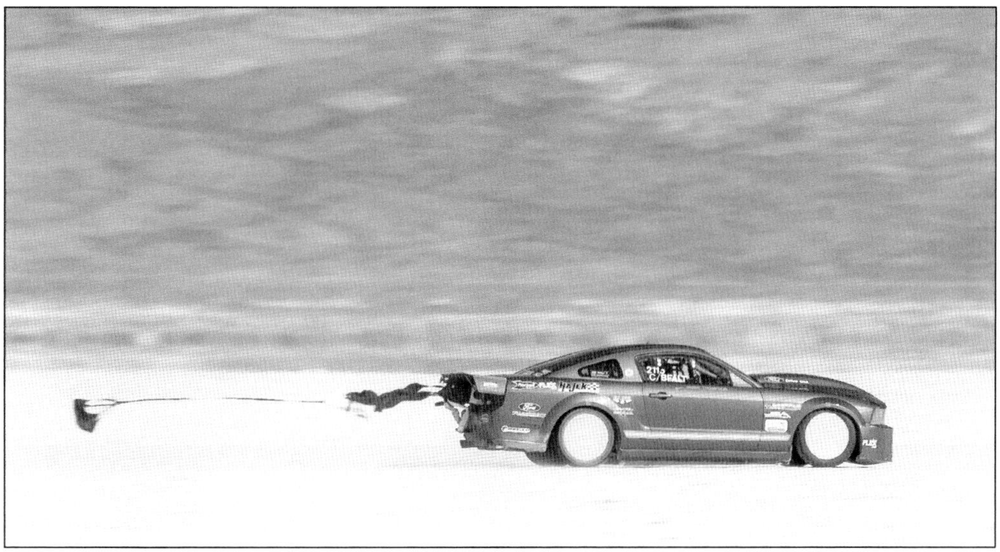

It is as important to "whoa" as it is to "go," as Danny Thompson demonstrates releasing the parachute out of the pack mounted on the rear of the Mustang drinking E85 fuel. Farmer and race enthusiast Brent Heyek wed the modern machine with history asking Mickey Thompson's son Danny to update the family speed deeds in 2003. Traveling 250 miles per hour, the "pop chute" is now fully deployed and pulling out the canopy that will soon "flower," yanking the car's speed down dramatically in few seconds by at least 100 miles per hour so the foot brakes can be used. (Courtesy of LandSpeed Louise.)

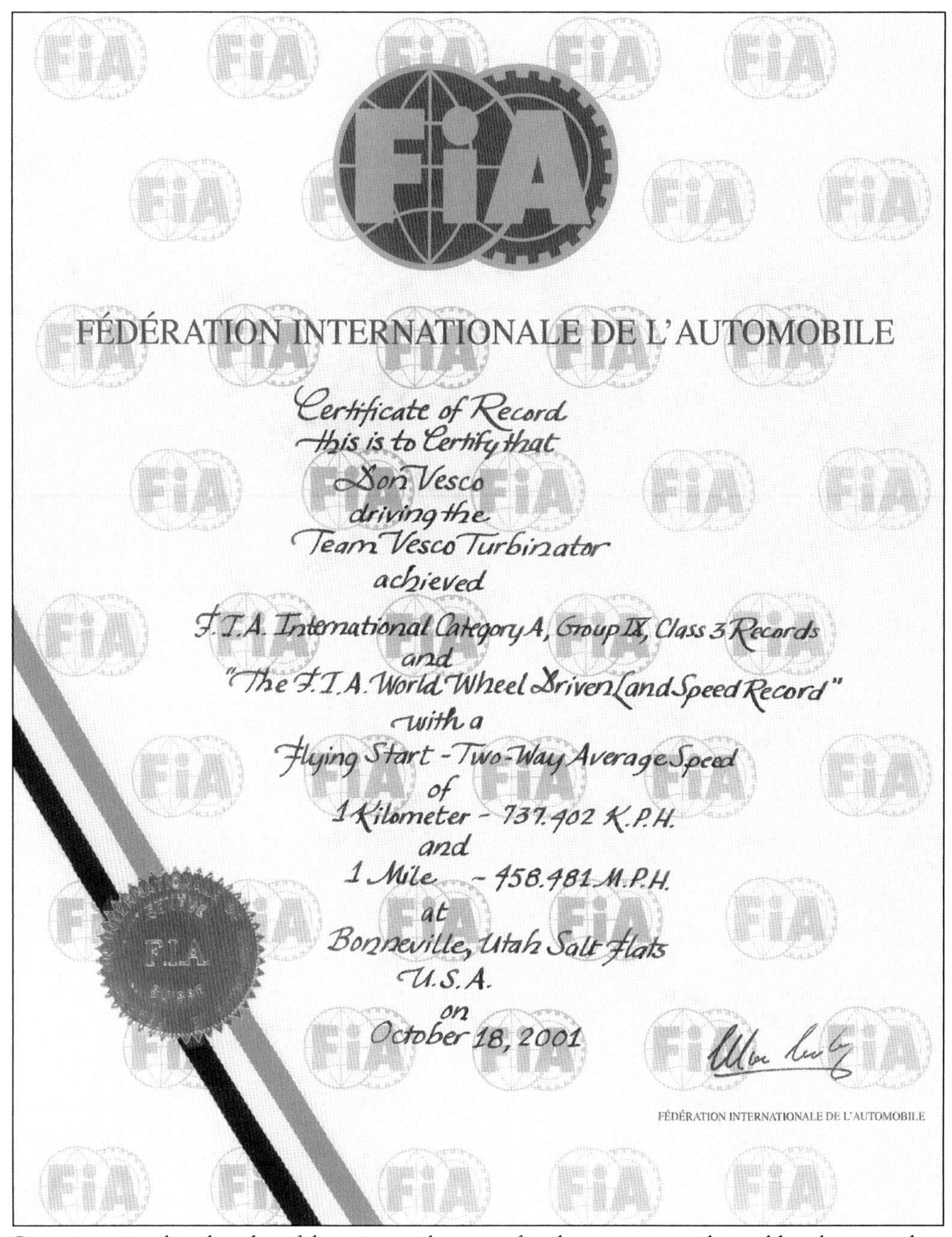

FÉDÉRATION INTERNATIONALE DE L'AUTOMOBILE

Certificate of Record
this is to Certify that
Don Vesco
driving the
Team Vesco Turbinator
achieved
F.I.A. International Category A, Group IX, Class 3 Records
and
"The F.I.A. World Wheel Driven Land Speed Record"
with a
Flying Start - Two-Way Average Speed
of
1 Kilometer - 737.402 K.P.H.
and
1 Mile - 458.481 M.P.H.
at
Bonneville, Utah Salt Flats
U.S.A.
on
October 18, 2001

FÉDÉRATION INTERNATIONALE DE L'AUTOMOBILE

Sometimes it takes decades of devotion and crates of cash racers never dare add up because they might realize how much was spent to earn this piece of parchment. Only driver Don Vesco's name appears—it was his life in the balance after all to deliver the two-way average speed—but without 21 other dedicated people who spent five years working on it, this caption would not have been written. The original FIA World Record Certificate pictured here belongs to LandSpeed Louise, given in appreciation by the Vesco family to each team member. (Courtesy of LandSpeed Louise.)

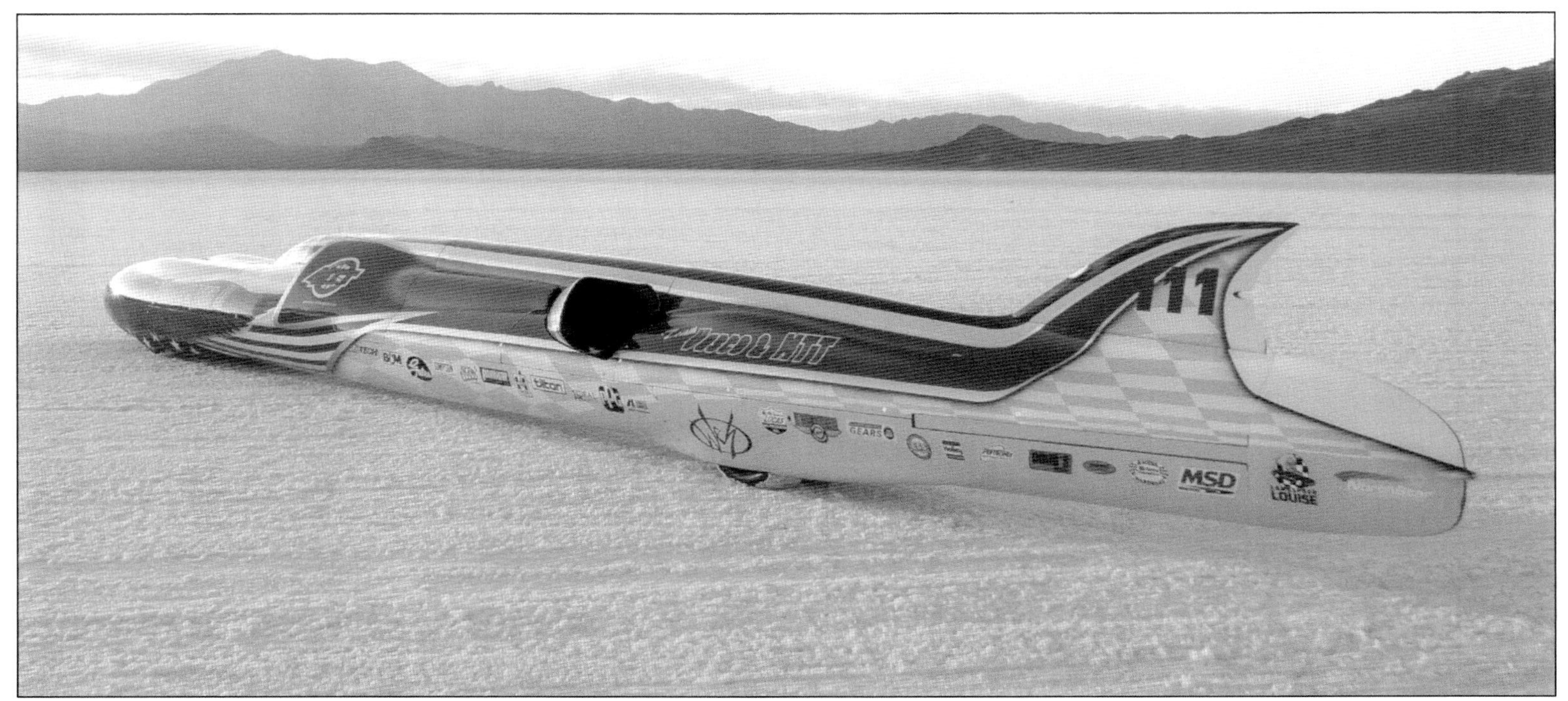

In 2018, TEAMVesco's "Turbinator II" first set the fastest national speed record in history at 482 miles per hour in August before cranking up the number in the flying mile to 493 miles per hour. The season highlight came when driver Dave Spangler laid down a jaw-dropping top speed of 503 miles per hour a day before the rains came and halted everything. Inducted into Dry Lakes Racing Hall of Fame in 2019, the T55-GA-714A shaft gas turbine generates 5,000 horsepower that propels the 36-foot-long, 36-inch-wide, 4,950-pound "slenderella." (Courtesy of LandSpeed Louise.)

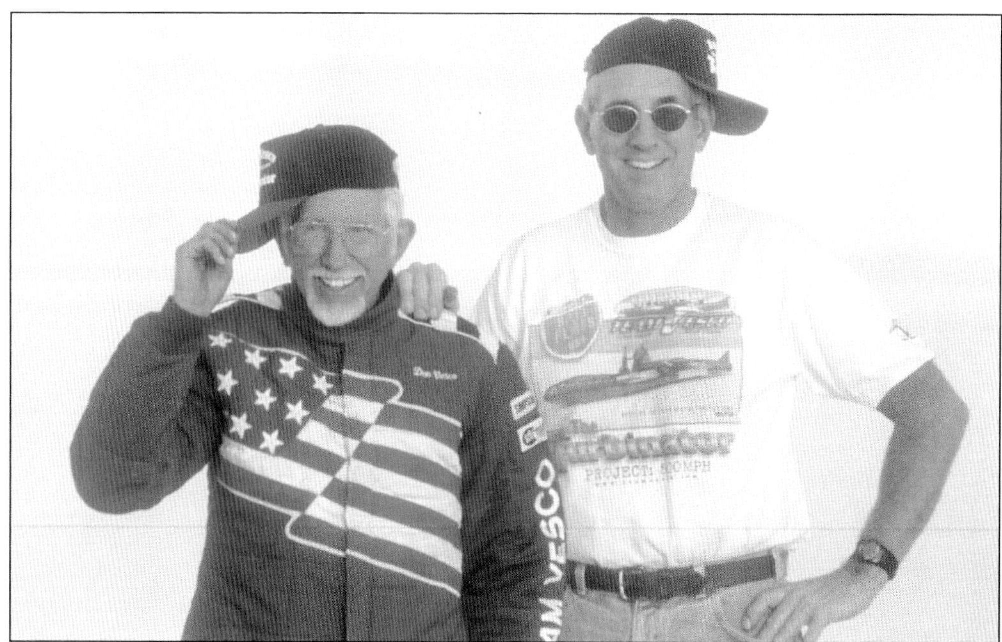

Here are the two main reasons the previous two pages exist. Driver Don Vesco, left, and his brother Rick, right, enjoy a silly moment in October 2001. They designed and built the "Turbinator" together with TEAMVesco and set a new world wheel-driven land speed record of 458 miles per hour, recapturing the FIA class record for the United States from Britain's late Donald Campbell, who had held it since 1964 at 403 miles per hour. (Courtesy of LandSpeed Louise.)

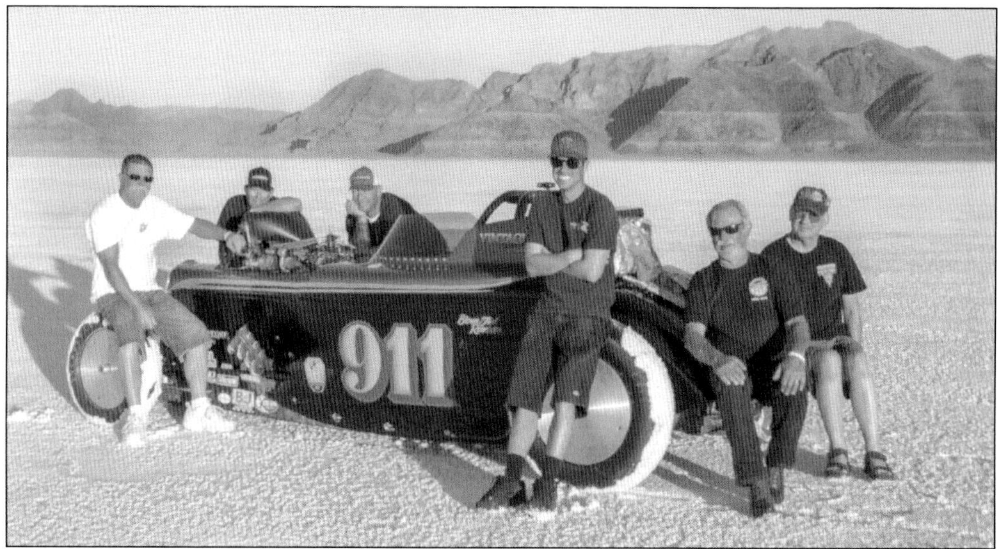

The touchstone for land speed racing began with highboy roadsters, like the one seen here. This iconic racer was created by speed-hungry men during the 1930s by stripping off fenders, running boards, and hoods of early passenger cars, then making magic happen to the engine. When a 1934 car posted its 304-mile-per-hour record using 4,000 horsepower, it was akin to telling Abe Lincoln the United States would land a man on the moon. These boys did just that. Pictured are, from left to right, John Beck, Paul Bowman, Brent Everitt, Donny Cummins, Dave Davidson, and "Motorbike" Tom. (Courtesy of LandSpeed Louise.)

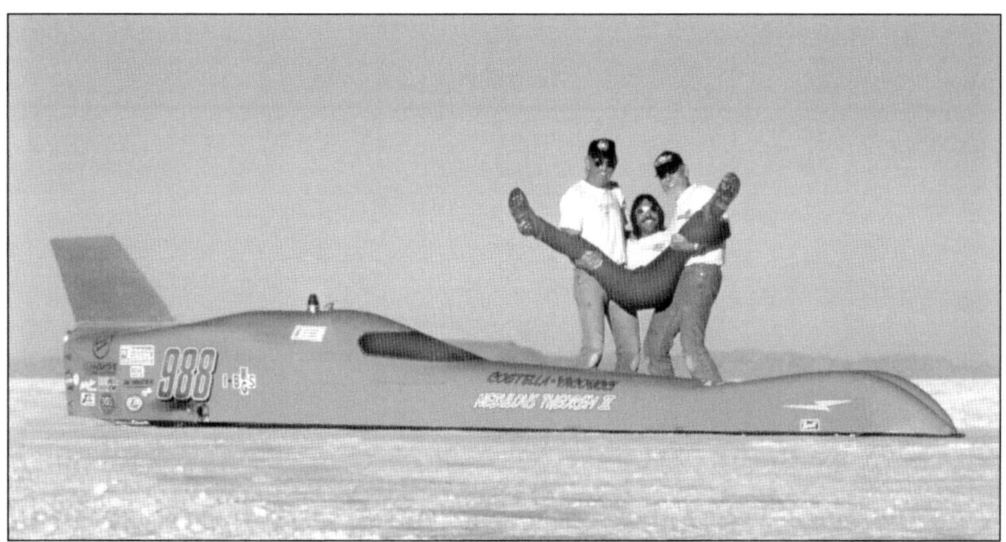

When Rick Yacoucci stuffed one of his hotted-up motorcycle engines into one of Jack Costella's 24-inch-wide, 24-foot-long Nebulous Theorum bodies, the sport braced for speed. Here, crewmen Bill Daniels (left) and Steve Smashey (right) try hoisting Yacoucci, with limited success, in celebration of his 315-mile-per-hour record in October 2003. Many questioned Costella's methods, but with more than 105 land speed records inked using his low-slung design, there was no mistaking the man with a shoestring budget had the speed touch. (Courtesy of LandSpeed Louise.)

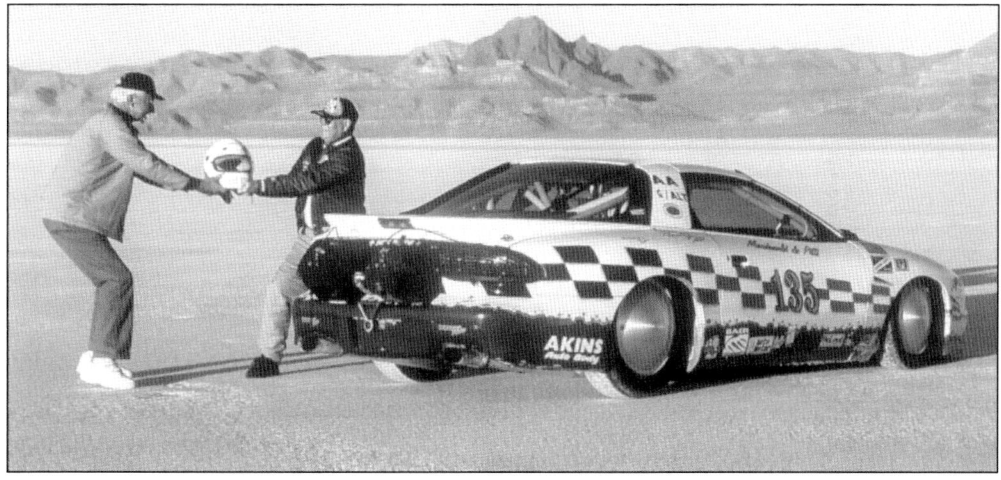

The boys and their toys—the things they do to make noise. With only one fire suit between them, partners Dave Macdonald and Lionel Pitts resolved the problem easily: Lionel would only set records using gasoline, and Dave would go after the higher-octane fuel marks. Throughout their decades of racing together, never once did they have an argument. This photograph is a total gag, because anyone who knew them also knew the duo enjoyed pulling pranks. Lionel's best gas record was 274 miles per hour in 2008, and Dave's best fuel record, posted the same year, was 308 miles per hour. (Courtesy of LandSpeed Louise.)

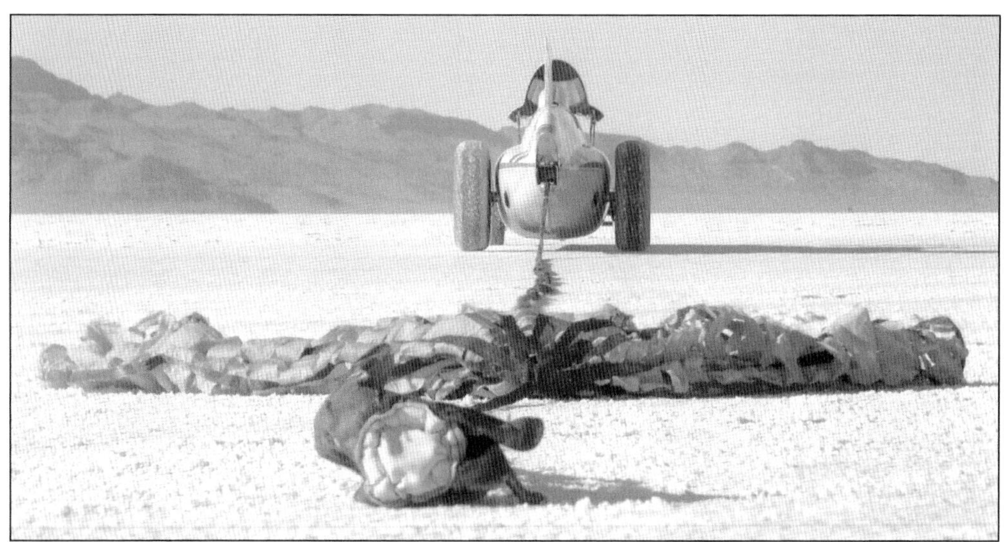

Although done with her run and having already lifted off the driver's compartment canopy, Tegan Hammond is still sitting in daddy's lakester, probably savoring the silence. The snarling engine is shut down, and the chase crew has yet to arrive. This is what the Hawaiian Island resident and professional stunt driver does on her days off: sets a 302-mile-per-hour land speed record, just like her momma, Tanis, did and her daddy, Seth, did, as well as brother Channing, who also designed the car. (Courtesy of LandSpeed Louise.)

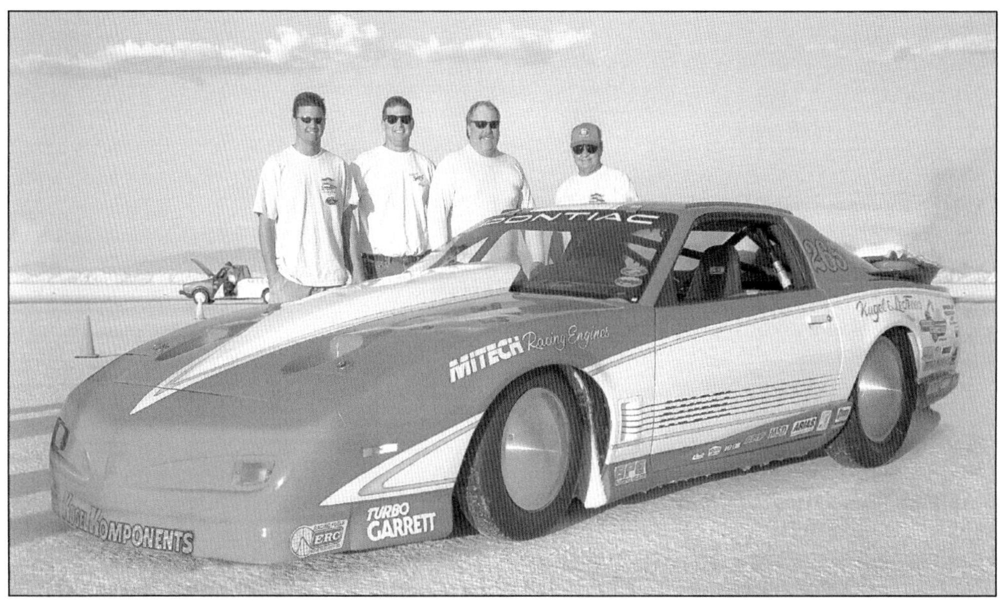

Performance patriarch Jerry Kugel, 60, far right, started racing at Bonneville in 1962 and continues to campaign cars to the present day, with the 1992 Pontiac Trans Am seen here in 1999 being the fastest. Sons Joe, 29 (far left), and Jeff, 27 (second from left), helped dear old dad along with engine builder Mike LeFevers (second from right), and together, the quartet took what was once a street-driven Pontiac Firebird and reworked it into the first stock-bodied car to post a 300.788-mile-per-hour record. All have driven the car, which exceeded 300 miles per hour on at least six other runs. (Courtesy of Butch Salter.)

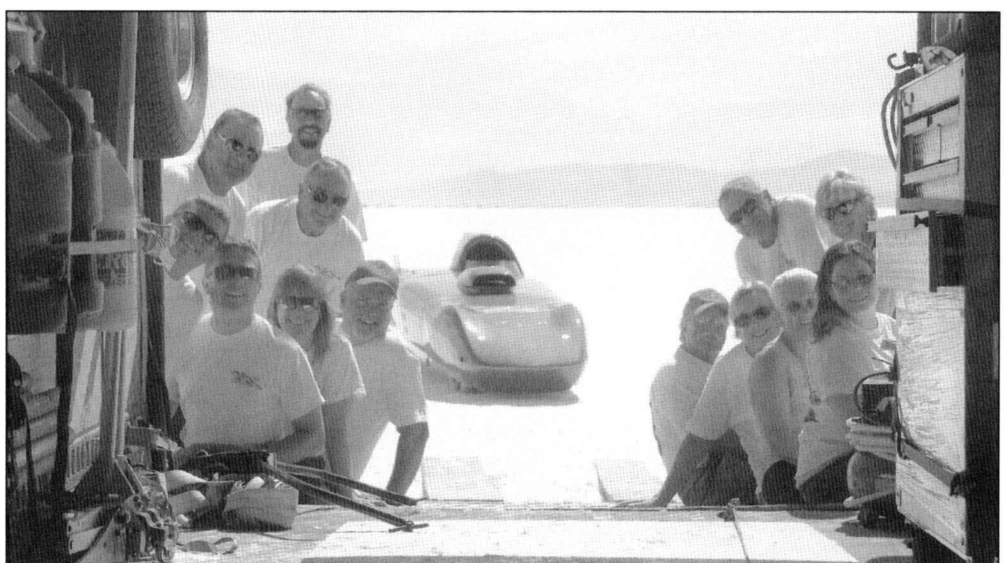

John Staiger, guided by Gary Hensley, began his hunt for salt speed in 2010 with a "racified" meld of a dainty British Berkeley and an Opel GT entered as "Spirit of the Lakes" in the modified sports class that extracted its "go fast" from the alcohol-burning Aurora Indy car engine. Each of the 13 people seen here all helped in some way—even if it was simply to allow their spouse to be part of Staiger's speed dream that netted a 244-mile-per-hour class record in 2011. (Courtesy of LandSpeed Louise.)

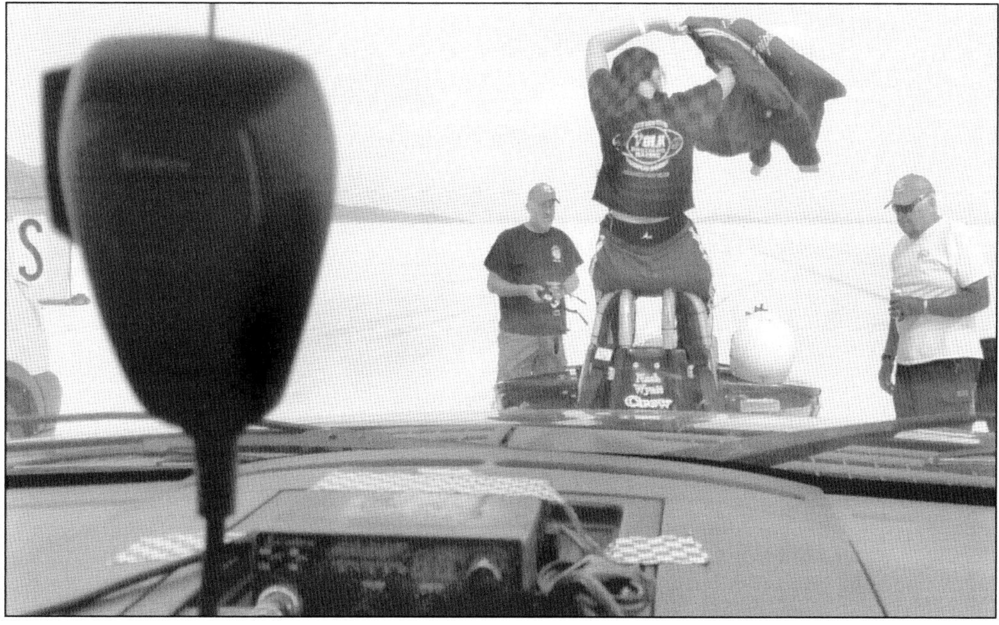

Pictured here are three generations of the Volk family. Driver Megan Volk, 22, dons her 78-year-old grandfather Larry's (in white shirt) five-layer Nomex fire suit as her father, Dallas Volk, 51, prepares to start the car. Racing runs in this family, and all members have a chance to drive fast. "As long as you have Volk blood, that's all that matters," remarked Megan. "As soon as you put the helmet on, no one can see who you are they just notice how well you can drive." Racing in the Volk family has been going on for more than 50 years. (Courtesy of LandSpeed Louise.)

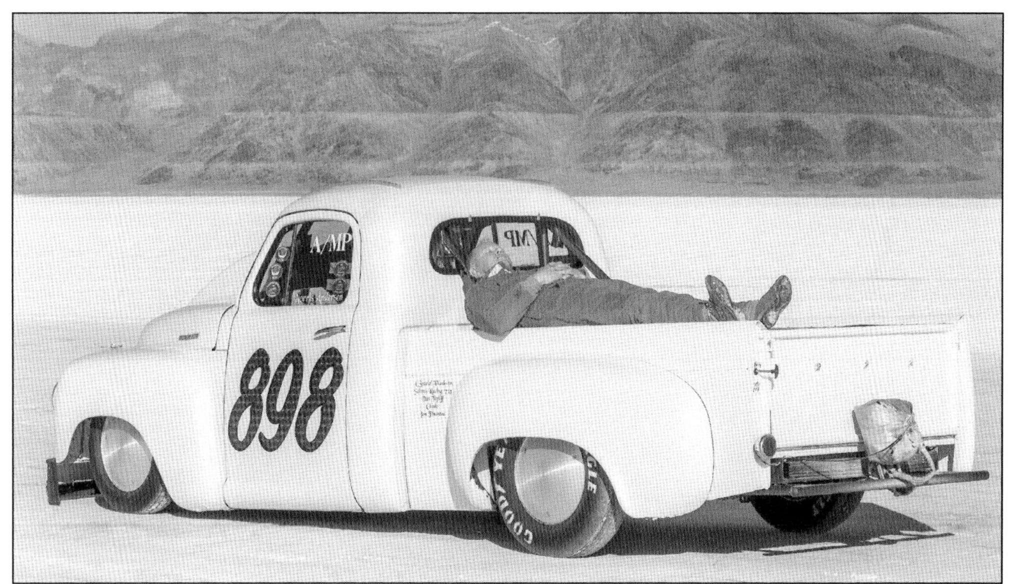

Bonneville high-speed racing is often a "hurry up and wait" program. Racers hasten to get into the staging lanes for what become hours of waiting before they inch up to the starting line. Here, in 2010, Norris Anderson, 64, a retired SR-71 US Air Force mechanic from Jamestown, Kansas, grabs a speed snooze on the bed of his 1949 Studebaker pickup truck. He made good on his motto, "Safe Trucks Travel Fast," when he woke up and ran back-to-back runs in excess of 200 miles per hour to set a 219-mile-per-hour class record. (Courtesy of LandSpeed Louise.)

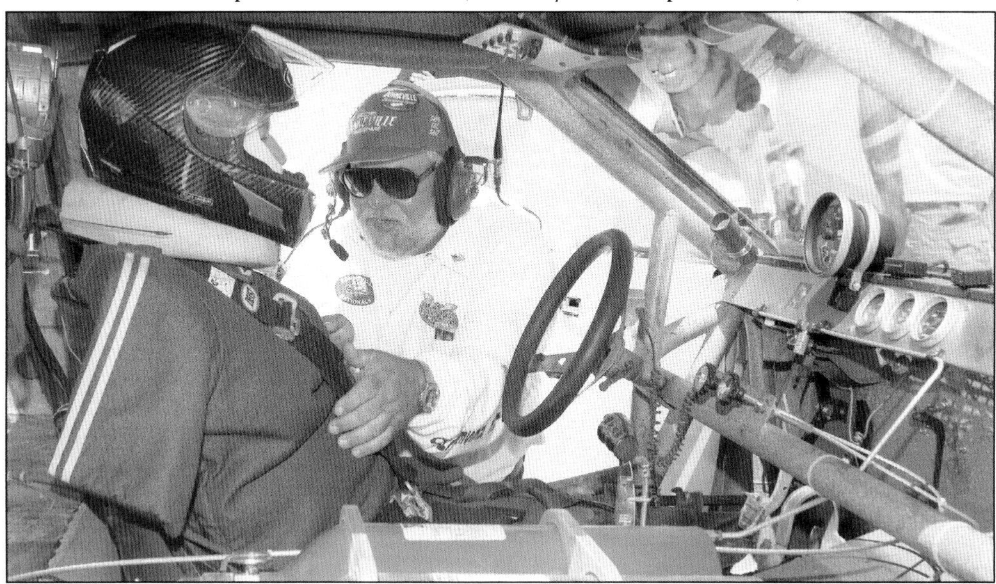
Starter Wes Hutchins checks the safety belt tightness of driver George Vose in his 1975 Chevy Monza, entered as Hairball Racing Team. Team mascot Garfield the cat watches from his windshield seat. Vose began setting land speed records as a teenager in the 1960s and continued until his death in 2018. Little daunted him, or his humor, even after his right arm was amputated; George adapted accordingly and kept driving along with his friends Howard Hoffman, Martin Hansen, and Chris Blue. And the motorized bar stool he built? The one-armed wonder drove it proud and fast grinning all the while. (Courtesy of LandSpeed Louise.)

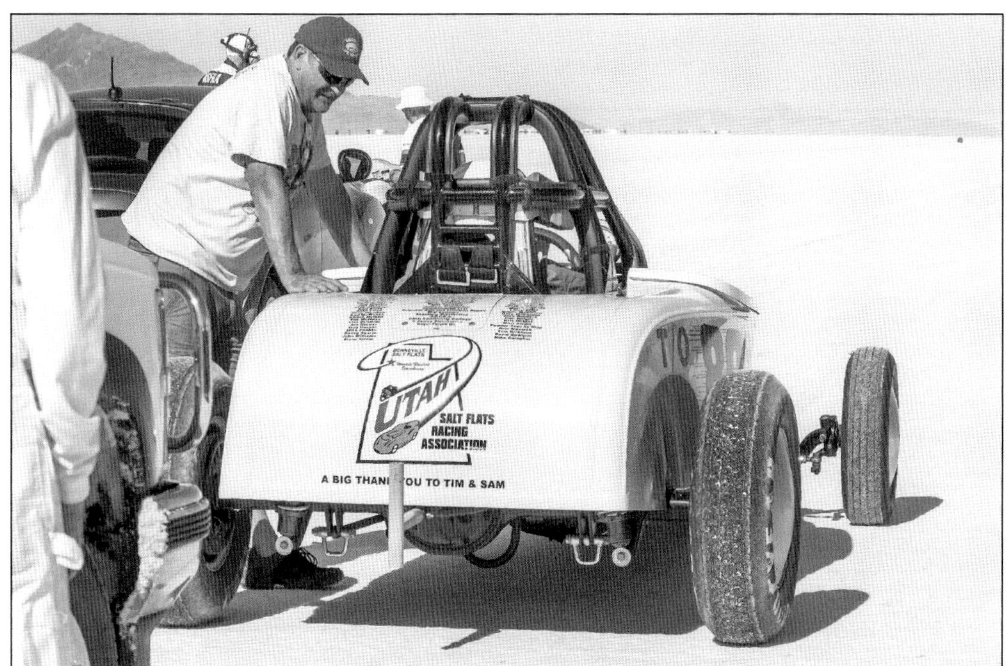

Pictured here in 2018, driver Melanie Nish, in the Utah Salt Flats Racing Association club car, is being encouraged by her 300-mile-per-hour husband, Jeff Nish. The club car is a 1929 Ford roadster built to give event volunteers aged 18 to 80 who do not have a speed machine of their own a chance to experience the thrill of running without limit down the fabled raceway. Every driver with enough courage in his or her throttle foot can trip the timing lights up to 160 miles per hour—plenty fast in a car without a windshield and only four inches of windscreen. (Courtesy of LandSpeed Louise.)

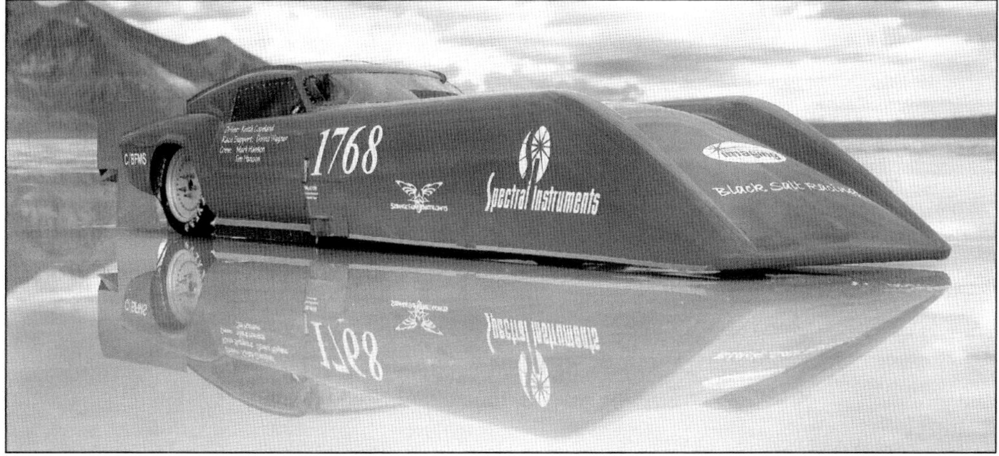

Keith Copeland, owner, driver, and speed engineer of his Black Salt Racing Team (BSRT), took a tiny Triumph GT-6 and built this modified sports car behemoth, eyeing 400 miles per hour. After a 225-mile-per-hour learning experience crash, he returned with this car, posting a remarkable 364-mile-per-hour record in 2012. It takes a lot to get ready and keep things rolling at the track. Without Donna Wagner handling all the race support, the team would always get a lot less done. Mario Rigoli and Mark Hansen have also contributed to BSRT's pillar of power. (Courtesy of Cody Hanson.)

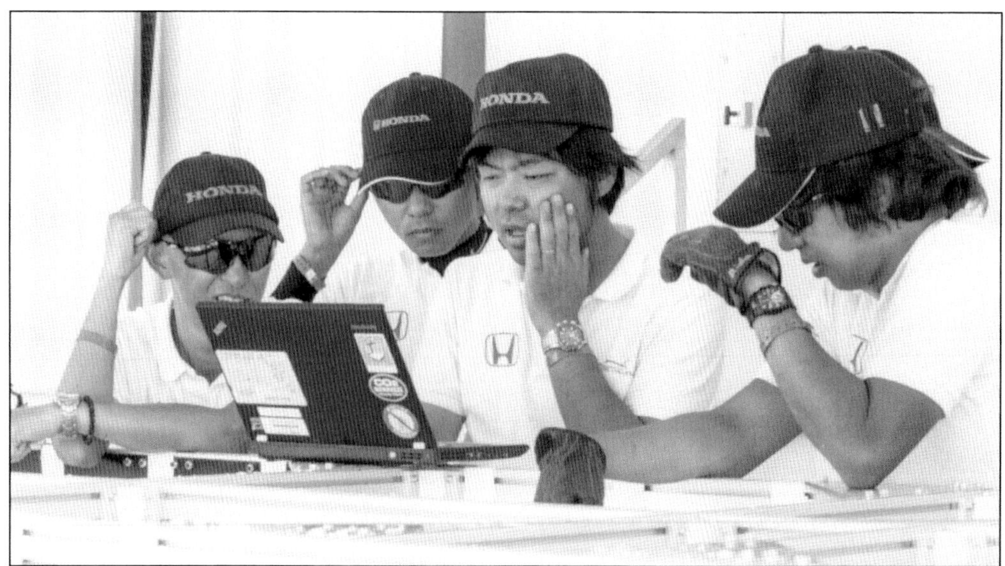

When a Japanese research and development department asked for volunteers to staff its "Bonneville Speed Challenge," 100 hands shot up. The 2016 project goal was to secure a world speed record with a 660cc engine, and 16 were chosen to build and race a Honda S-Dream streamliner. Here, the salt rookies' expressions show why world records are tough stuff to get, as each run was another unexpected education in speed. They went home victorious with a 261-mile-per-hour record with driver Hikaru Miyagi at the controls and also managed to trash the BAR Honda Formula One record set years earlier. Break out the cold sake! (Courtesy of LandSpeed Louise.)

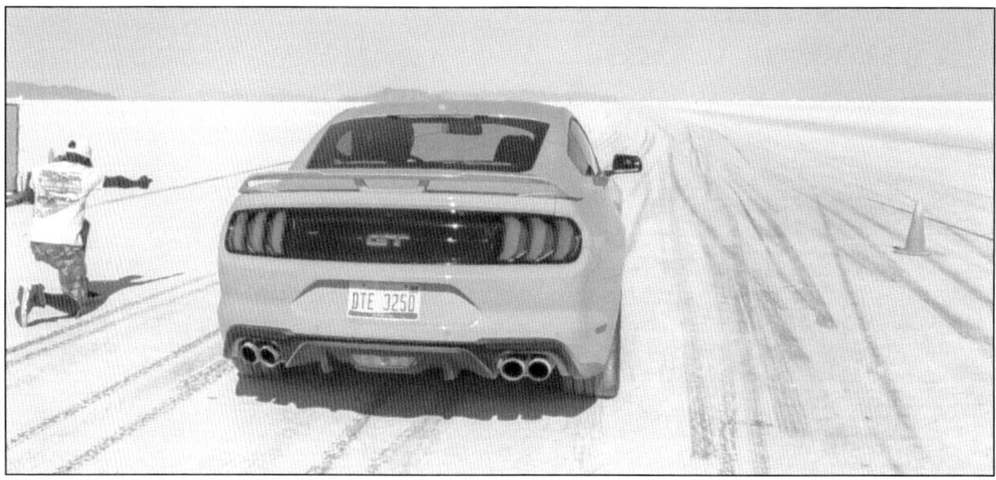

On his days off at Hill Air Force Base, Lt. Sam Sentongo, chief of aircraft battle damage repair engineering, is in charge of the Rookie Race Course for the Utah Salt Flats Racing Association. Here, he uses his best aircraft carrier release method to send Utah governor Gary Herbert's deputy chief of staff, Mike Mower, on his salt virgin voyage as a land speed racer. The Ford Motor Company graciously lent the Mustang GT to provide government leaders and elected officials a chance to live the speed dream and not just watch from the sidelines. (Courtesy of LandSpeed Louise.)

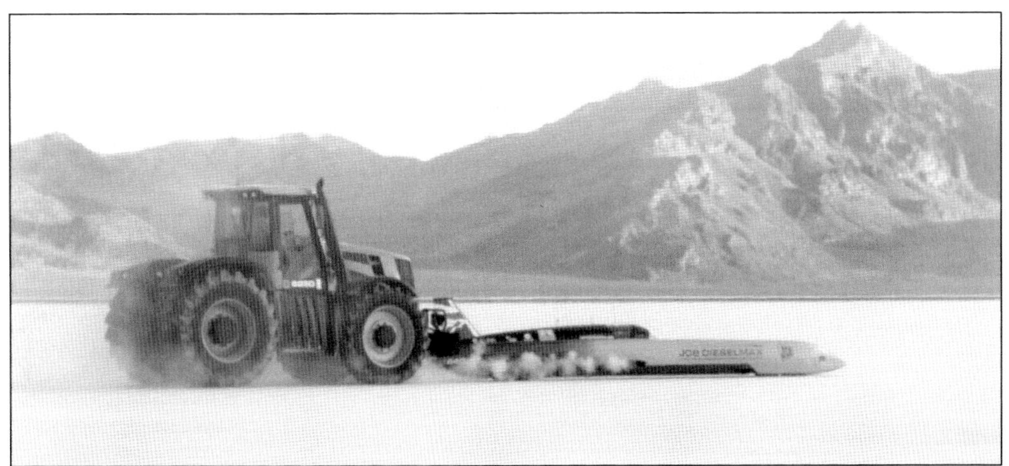

In 2006, a gang of ditch-digger builders showed up on the salt with a brand new diesel engine looking to calm customers' fears that the new JCB version for backhoe loaders would be reliable. CEO Anthony Bamford had been mesmerized by salt records since childhood and threw corporate coin at the idea that a world land speed record would be the ultimate marketing scheme. That was a good call. Here, push start driver Colin Bond sends driver Andy Green onto the course, and in minutes, the Brits waltzed off with a 350-mile-per-hour world record that remains intact today. (Courtesy of LandSpeed Louise.)

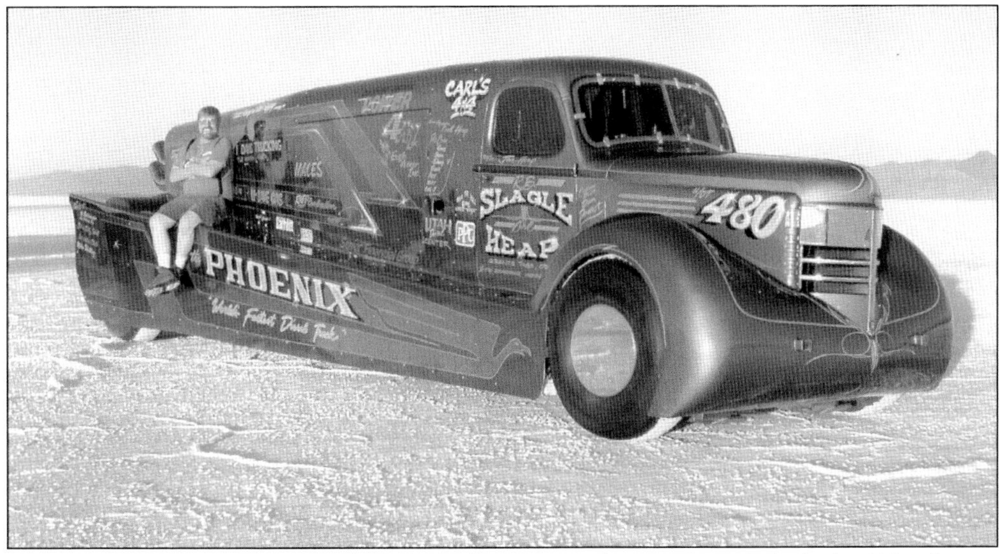

Longtime logging trucker R.B. Slagle built this race truck in 1992 and clocked a 212-mile-per-hour record before he died in 1998. Always affable Carl Heap sits on the massive fender of "The Phoenix," which he took over, and chiseled the still-current 272-mile-per-hour record in the history books by 2003. Behind Heap is the hulking Detroit V16, 1,472-cubic-inch diesel engine fitted with four turbochargers and two superchargers that generated an estimated 4,000 horsepower. The front tires are 16-ply monsters built for a Boeing 707's nose wheel, while the 32-ply rear tires are used by 747s. (Courtesy of LandSpeed Louise.)

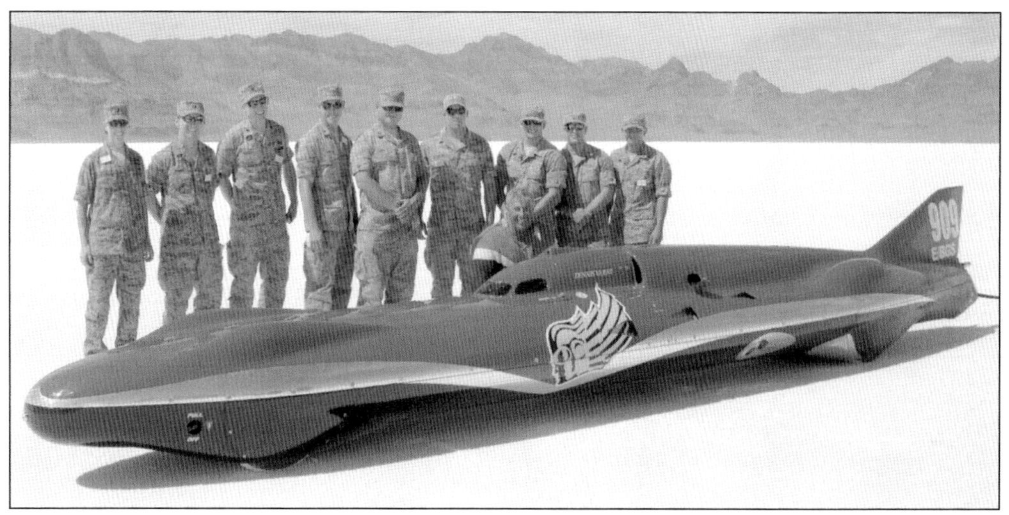

"Speed Nymph" streamliner 300-mile-per-hour driver Dennis Varni is lost against a backdrop of camouflage worn by mechanical engineering cadets and instructors from the US Air Force Academy. They were touring the race pits as part of the Creative Research and Development Program with Landspeed Productions, which matches racers with students to solve speed issues and earn credit toward graduation. Take note of former cadet Capt. Kate Hellerberg, far left, who went on to fly B-1s so well she got tapped to teach other deft fliers how to handle drones, in combat no less. (Courtesy of LandSpeed Louise.)

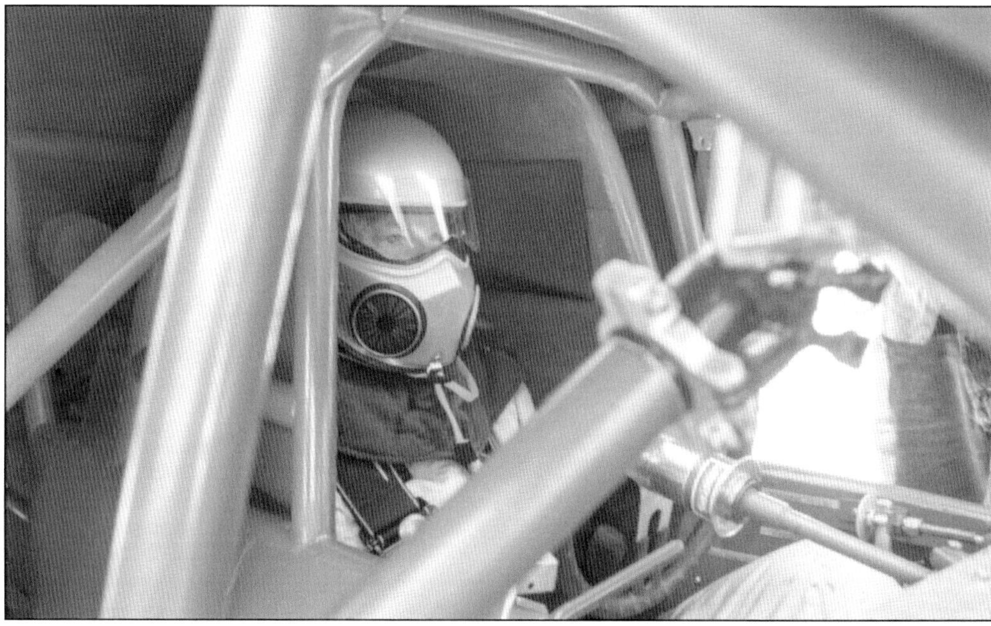

Dwelling on this point of view proves that land speed racers do not have a "death wish." Cocooned into an exceptional safety platform, 300-mile-per-hour driver Rex Svoboda is strapped in to what might be the world's fastest, highly modified Saab with limousine rocket ship styling cues. "Land speed racing is a representation of all that is good about America," sagely observed Svoboda, course director for Bonneville Motorcycle Speed Trials, who choreographs 800-pound missiles that travel at 200-plus-mile-per-hour speeds in very close proximity to each other. "It's ingenuity, it's you and your machine challenging the record." (Courtesy of LandSpeed Louise.)

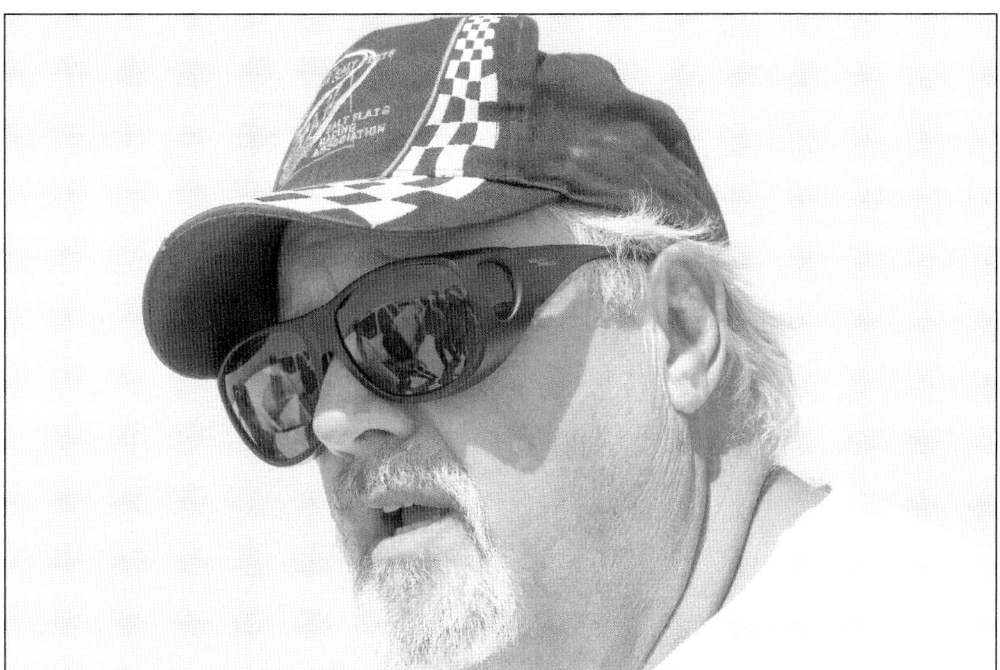

Utah Salt Flats Racing Association president Dennis Sullivan, 73, from Layton, Utah, leads an all-volunteer group of 50 people who plan, prepare, and operate the group's premier racing event, World of Speed, held annually since 1976. Upwards of a dozen of his volunteers also race their own speed machines in between their assigned duties. "Our September event attracts between 175 and 200 cars, trucks, and motorcycles," Sullivan noted. "It's nearly 20 degrees cooler, Wendover lodging is cheaper and the food lines much shorter. Besides, we're nicer and better looking than the other group." (Courtesy of LandSpeed Louise.)

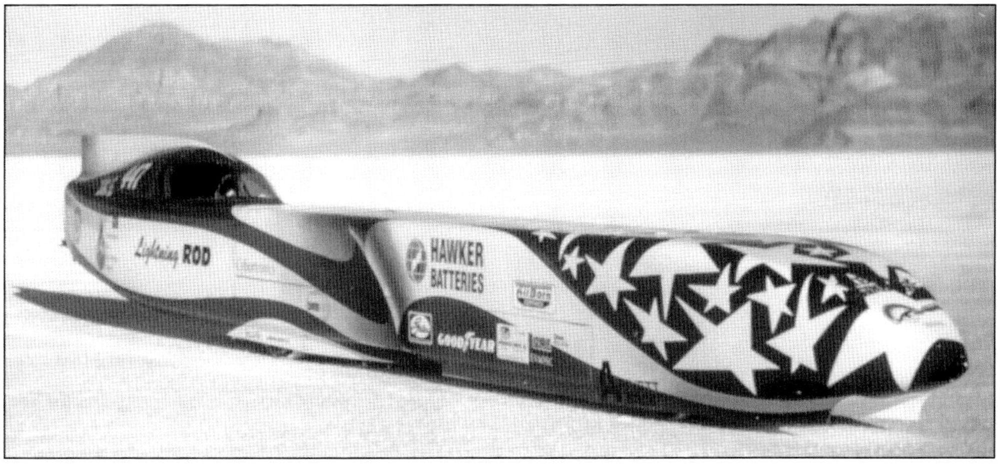

Ed Rannberg built and brought "Kawashocki," an electric motorcycle, to Bonneville in 1988 and returned with the "Lightning Rod" streamliner in 1996. At 64, he became the first to post an electric-powered top speed in excess of 200 miles per hour. One of his electric motors failed, and he was unable to complete the record run requirements. Rannberg's sudden death in April 1997 prompted his son Randy and Eric Luebben to return to the salt in October 1997 to set a 212-mile-per-hour national record and a 215-mile-per-hour FIA world record. Ed is credited with helping fabricate more than 25 electric vehicles. (Courtesy of LandSpeed Louise.)

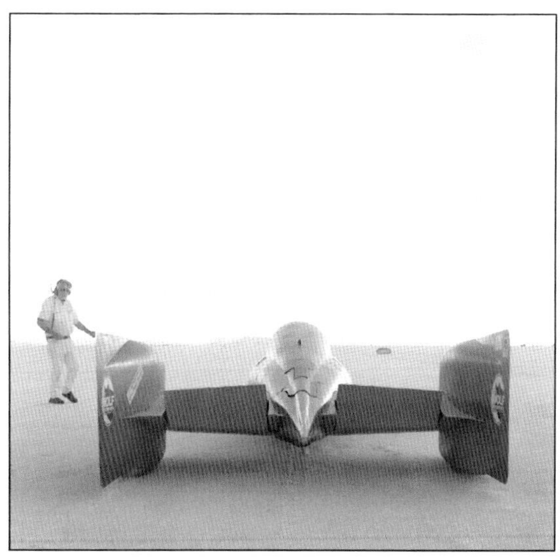

The hand signal from starter Ron Joliffe tells Pennsylvanian driver Rob Freyvogel in his No. 496 "Carbiliner" streamliner to hold up from starting his speed run. Joliffe is in radio contact with the timing tower several miles down course, which ensures the course is clear for each person making a speed attempt. It is no surprise that the evocative, metallic, interstellar-styled car turns heads; it was built to crack the 500-mile-per-hour barrier for wheel-driven cars. Freyvogel's personal best top speed is a respectable 420 miles per hour, but he would be quick to note that is not fast enough and poor surface conditions have frustrated his many attempts. (Courtesy of LandSpeed Louise.)

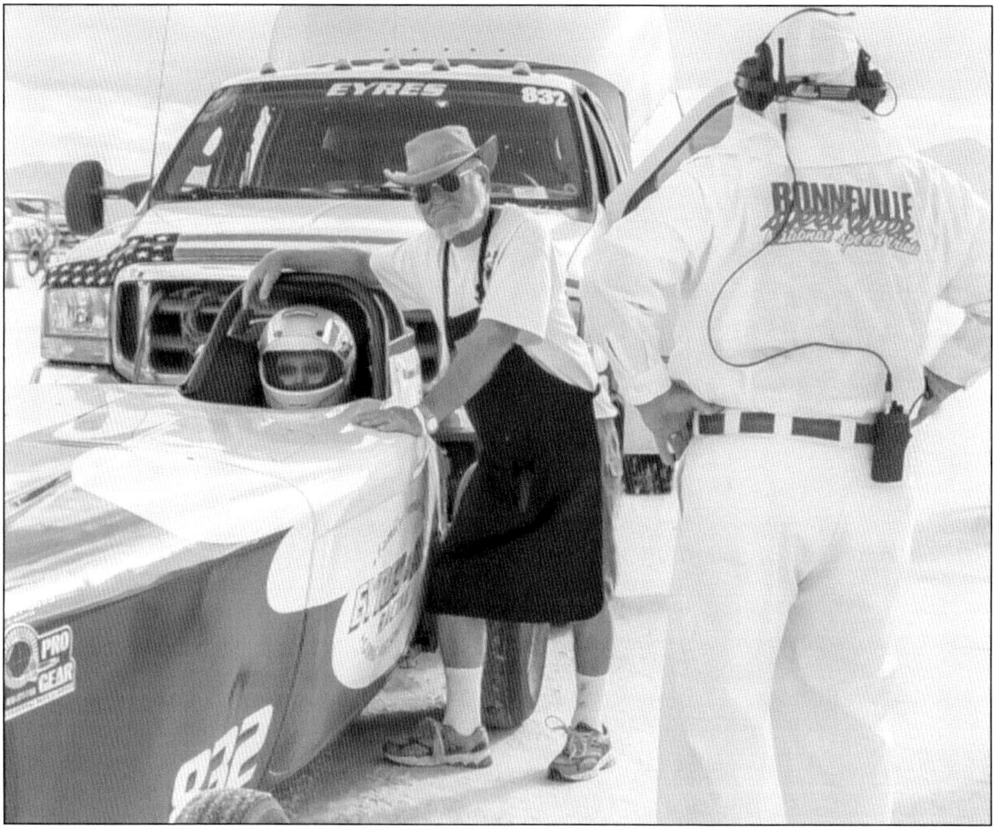

San Diegoian Russ Eyres began salt racing in 1956. Joined in the early 1980s by his 15-year-old son Eric, together they this built this 1929 Ford roadster body with a Chevy engine. A family friend, Terry Simonis, helped with the build. Pictured here in 2009, driver Eric, 43, waits with dad Russ, 73, on the starting line. Russ and his son shared driving duties and have posted times and records in excess of 200 miles per hour. In 2020, Eric's son Logan, 19, joined the team and may be its next driver. (Courtesy of LandSpeed Louise.)

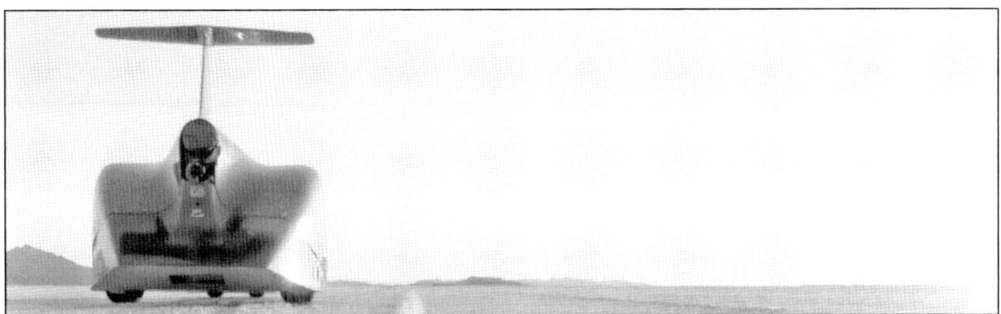

The mountain on the horizon line is nearly 30 miles away. Dave Brant, Randy Speranza, and John Wright are the modern-day embodiment of Mark Twain adventure stories with help from Doug Robinson. Together, in 1994, they began BWS Racing, which in seven months conceived and built the "Dreamliner," a 17-foot, 726-pound streamlined race car that set nearly a dozen certified land speed records and won the 1998 SCTA points championship. It was, at one time, the world's fastest 500cc one-cylinder vehicle. The top speed to date is 226 miles per hour with a four-cylinder motorcycle engine. Judy Brant is the team photographer and hydration monitor. (Courtesy of LandSpeed Louise.)

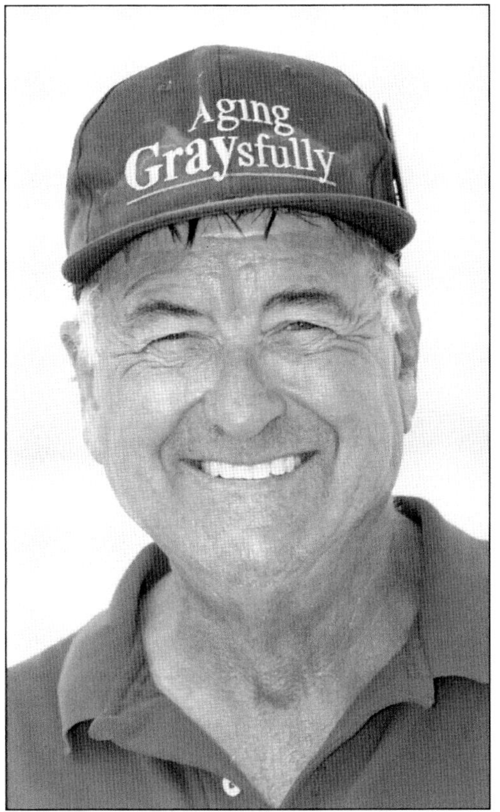

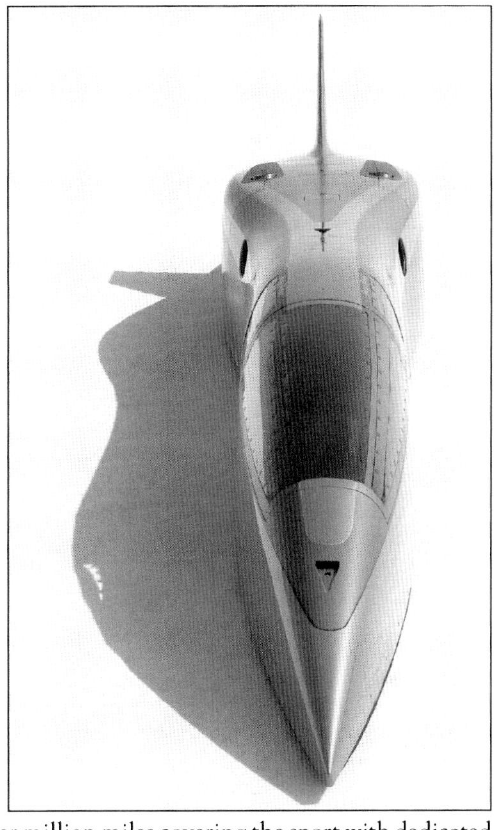

Hot Rod Magazine's Gray Baskerville drove a quarter-million miles covering the sport with dedicated insight and colorful observation, maintaining "real hot rods were race cars first, everything else is silliness." Baskerville is responsible for sticking the author with her nickname. At right is the 2016 "Speed Demon" streamliner, which has repeatedly earned the *Hot Rod Magazine* Top Time trophy by posting the highest one-way speed during Speed Week. Owner and driver George Poteet, 71, a Mississippi native, has taken a staggering number of rides in excess of 400 miles per hour. (Left, courtesy of Bill Taylor; right, courtesy of LandSpeed Louise.)

Bibliography

Arneson, Erik. *Mickey Thompson: The Fast Life and Tragic Death of a Racing Legend*. St. Paul, MN: MBI Publishing Company, 2008.

Baechtel, John. *Goldenrod: The Resurrection of America's Speed King*. Landspeed Media Group, 2018.

Batchelor, Dean. *The American Hot Rod*. St. Paul, MN: MBI Publishing Company, 1995.

Boys of Bonneville: Racing on a Ribbon of Salt. Directed by Curt Wallin. Salt Lake City, UT: Curt Wallin Media Arts, 2012.

Eyston, George, and W.F. Bradley. *Speed on Salt: A History of the Bonneville Salt Flats, Utah, U.S.A.* London, England: B.T. Batsford, Ltd., 1936.

Jenkins, Ab, and Wendell Ashton. *The Salt of the Earth*. Salt Lake City, UT: Deseret News Press, 1939.

Kasprowicz, Sarah. *The Reluctant Rocketman: A Curious Journey in World Record Breaking*. Waukesha, WI: GreenBean Creative Solutions LLC, 2013.

Noble, Richard. *Take Risk! The Amazing Story of the People Who Made Richard Noble's Extreme Projects Possible on Land, at Sea, and in the Air*. Holwell, England: Evro Publishing, 2020.

Noeth, Louise Ann. *Bonneville Salt Flats*. St. Paul, MN: MBI Publishing Company, 1999.

Robinson, Rocky. *Flat Out: The Race for the Motorcycle World Land Speed Record*. St. Paul, MN: MBI Publishing Company, 2007.

Rosler, Horst. *Bonneville: World's Fastest Motorcycles*. Stillwater, MN: Wolfgang Publications, Inc., 2007.

White, Gordon Eliot. *Ab & Marvin Jenkins: The Studebaker Connection and the Mormon Meteors*. Pepin, WI: Enthusiast Books, 2006.

About the Organizations

The J. Willard Marriott Library Special Collections Division serves the University of Utah community, the citizens of Utah, and scholars around the world through the stewardship of original and scarce resources. Part of its mission includes the development of a repository of knowledge on land speed racing at the Bonneville Salt Flats. Its curatorial and archival staff collects, preserves, and provides access to materials that extend across a broad range of topics and formats.

Rare books, maps, and ephemera document the record of human communication and provide diverse perspectives on local and global history. Unpublished archival manuscripts, photographs, posters, and video and audio recordings document the past and current history of Utah and the Intermountain West through different experiences of Western life. Extensive secondary publications support these collecting areas, while a fully developed preservation program ensures that these unique materials will be available for future generations.

Rampton Art & Design owner Robert Rampton of Taylorsville, Utah, is an accomplished freelance automotive artist, graphic designer, and illustrator. Rare is the designer that researches his subject matter in such excruciating detail, making repeated revisions as new historical information surfaces and thereby fortifying the work with visual authenticity. Specializing in pre–World War I American auto racing history and vehicles and land speed racing history, especially Bonneville Salt Flats, he is a noted 1908 New York–Paris auto race subject matter expert. Rampton also has a soft spot for vintage motorcycles, hot rods, and just about anything old with wheels. His illustrations in chapter one are a significant contribution to this book. Here, for the first time, is a collection of every known car and motorcycle that took part in the first time trials ever held on the Bonneville Salt Flats in August 1914. Rampton not only drew the speed machines but also investigated where each was built, its racing heritage, and the fate of each vehicle after its time as a race car came to an end. He did the same for each driver and the key people connected with this historic moment in motorsports. Each illustration is the product of more than 25 years of dogged detail documentation followed by hundreds of corrections to illustrations. Author and photographer Louise Noeth is utterly wowed by Rampton's devotion to this resonating visual touchstone and is forever humbled and grateful that he allows his work to appear in this book.